D1526540

the 22 RULES *of investing*

Earn Consistent Returns in Volatile Markets

Jon "DRJ" and Pete Najarian

The 22 Rules of Investing:
Earn Consistent Returns in Volatile Markets

Investitute, LLC
Attn: Director of Operations
8201 Peters Road, Suite 1000
Plantation, FL 33324
1-888-982-8342
support@investitute.com

Book and Cover Design by
Jeffective Design & Illustration, and Funnychord Creative
Manufacturing by Mid-Western Printing
Printed in the United States of America
First Edition

This book is dedicated to the technology revolution that drove computers to think, opportunities to expand, and traders to imagine the endless possibilities for profits.

TABLE OF CONTENTS

INTRODUCTION

Every profession has a simple piece of advice – a golden rule – that drives decisions and determines success.

When Pete and I played professional football, our coaches reinforced the words of renowned coach Paul Brown: "Football is a game of errors. The team that makes the fewest errors in a game usually wins." The winning team is rarely the one that trains harder or motivates more. It's usually the one that avoids the interception, bad snap, or unfortunate fumble. The same idea has always applied to investing. You must reduce errors. It's the timeless golden rule.

While some rules are timeless, times can change…

Today, information flows faster, and techniques for controlling errors must change too. In the 1800s, market-moving news could take days to reach the stock exchanges. The guy with the fastest horse had the advantage. Now information moves in microseconds – one millionth of a second. High-frequency computers can trade a mind-boggling 10,000 times per second. Today, the machines with the most megahertz have the advantage. By the time the opening bell on the New York Stock Exchange has finished ringing, 30,000 orders have been filled. And by the time we're done writing this book that speed will likely double – making a lightning bolt move like a hobbled horse.

Exchanges are already preparing. As we're writing this book, a news headline just scrolled across the television that the New York Stock Exchange and Nasdaq are going to eliminate stop orders and good-til-canceled (GTC) orders beginning early 2016. Their reasons are to reduce the daily volatility and investor regrets that have come from the unavoidable market whipsaws. If the exchanges are making historic changes, you must change too.

There is no time for mistakes. Risks must be controlled at the time of the trade – and managed as information changes. The way information flows has changed, and you must change the way you invest. In our last book, we showed you how we trade options. Now we'll show you how to control risks and reduce errors in today's microsecond market.

We'll show you the new rules of investing.

RULE 1

New Exchanges, New Needs, New Rules

It's no longer man versus markets. It's man versus machine.

As long as stock exchanges have been around, people have loved to invest, predict, and marvel over the stock market. It's the only market where all prices effectively filtered through one channel and broadcast to everyone, and in the process, create a market with a life of its own. It's the closest thing we have to a perfectly competitive market.

The basic idea of the market is to create a forum where publicly traded stocks, bonds, and other assets can trade. That way, people who buy bonds from the government or shares of stock during an IPO, for example, can have an easy way to sell if they decide. By having a place to easily sell, it creates market liquidity, and investors with higher confidence that are more willing to buy stocks and bonds to provide capital for economic growth.

The stock market is really a "used" market for securities. In the process of all the bidding, investors discover the price at which buyers and sellers believe to be fair, and a trade is made. No person is going to pay more than he thinks it's worth, and no seller is going to sell for less than he thinks it's worth. The last trade represents the market's best guess as to the securities value. That's one of the great mysteries of the market – every second that valuation is changing. We're never quite sure why someone traded at that price; all we know is that they did. The stock market also provides another important function – price discovery. If you want to know what a share of stock is worth, today's market price shows the collective opinion of all investors.

The market is made up of two basic groups – investors and traders. Investors are those who buy and sell stocks and bonds for long-term investments. They're providing capital to the market. Traders are those who try to capitalize from pricing discrepancies. If shares of IBM are priced at $135 and traders think it's worth closer to $140, they will buy in anticipation of the price rising. As they buy, they push the price toward that $140 expected future price. So again, the market price reflects the collective opinion of everyone.

The stock market has a life of its own as investors compete for publicly-traded securities with profits going to those who can identify the good opportunities – and tax write-offs to those who don't.

If you understand the recent changes in the stock market, you'll immediately see why there are new rules to follow. It's not just about competing against other investors and traders anymore.

Stock exchanges are nothing new. The Venetians used primitive forms as early as the 1300s to buy and sell government securities and merchant debts. They filled important needs as they tried to find the lenders who were most suited to hold that debt. While the benefits were obvious, it wasn't until 1773 when London opened the first official stock exchange. The U.S. followed in 1790 with the Philadelphia Stock Exchange, and then the New York Stock Exchange (NYSE) in 1817.

We've had many regional and specialized exchanges as well, including the Boston Stock Exchange, CBOE Exchange, Chicago

Exchange, Chicago Mercantile Exchange (CME), National Stock Exchange, and Pacific Stock Exchange.

In 1971, Nasdaq was formed, which was our first electronic exchange. It's not really an exchange like the NYSE but, instead, a series of dealers linked through computers.

It's been a race for the largest market share, and recently, buyouts and mergers have been as common for the exchanges as they are for publicly traded companies. The NYSE acquired the Pacific Stock Exchange in 2006, and merged with Euronext that same year to become the first trans-Atlantic exchange. That forced Nasdaq to acquire the Boston Exchange and Philadelphia Stock Exchange in 2007. In 2013, the Intercontinental Exchange (ICE) purchased NYSE and now owns 23 different exchanges. The historic NYSE is now owned by another group. Things are changing.

Enter the Machines

Exchanges have always sought to find faster ways to execute orders. The CME introduced Globex in 1992, which was the first global e-platform. Archipelago (Arca) began trading stocks and options electronically two years later in 1994. In 1999, the Pacific Stock Exchange was purchased by Arca, which later merged with the NYSE in 2006. The Boston Stock Exchange formed the Boston Options Exchange, or BOX, in 2002. These were the early pioneers of e-trading, but now it's all heading that way. Trading has become too big and too fast for trades to take place face-to-face on a trading floor.

Today, we have many pure electronic exchanges – and continuing to add more. In 2000, the International Securities Exchange (ISE) was formed. In 2005, we added the Better Alternative Trading System, or BATS. Direct Edge, created in 2010, operates two separate platforms – EDGA and EDGX. The CBOE created C2 in that same year. And in 2012, we had yet another e-platform join the group, the Miami Options Exchange (MIAX), which operates out of – you guessed it – New Jersey.

You probably had no idea that all of these exchanges even existed. Each year, the face-to-face trading is decreasing from the bricks-and-mortar buildings, and the machines are taking over. We're moving from bricks to clicks.

Trading is rarely done by floor traders, it's done by algorithmic robots, or algobots. That doesn't mean things will be better; they'll just be different. In order to compete, the stock exchanges have made changes. Investors must change too.

New Exchanges, New Needs

The NYSE has long argued that it's better to have human intervention in times of high volatility. But when trading gets too fast, it has to take shortcuts. In late 2007, Rule 48 was created by the SEC (Securities and Exchange Commission) to waive certain requirements when markets heat up. The rule is also known as Exemptive Relief – Extreme Market Volatility Condition. Normally, the designated market makers (DMMs) on the trading floor must have the time to disseminate market price information before the opening bell to ensure an orderly market open. Prices have to be approved by floor managers before trading can begin. But if the news is too fast, the exchange can pitch that approval process right out the window by invoking Rule 48. Since 2008, the rule has been used 77 times. But in late August 2015, the exchange invoked it three times in a row, and one more time the following week. The face-to-face format seems to be losing.

Okay, chalk up one point for the machines...

But then in May 2010, we had the mysterious Flash Crash, which lasted for 36 minutes. Most of the major indexes collapsed and rebounded sharply with the Dow plunging nearly 1,000 points, or about 9%, within minutes. The Commodities Futures Trading Commission (CFTC) reported it as one of the most volatile times in the history of financial markets. What's going on? Why can't the computers handle the trading volume?

Well, it's not that they can't handle it. It's just that the new markets have created new incentives and new ways for people to trade. We now have dark pools to try to hide trading activity so that the computers can't see the number of shares or the price for the orders in an attempt to front-run the customers. Computers also engage in "spoofing" where they will flash fake orders in an attempt to trigger another computer to raise bids or lower offers so that it can get more favorable pricing. We have new exchanges, and traders have new needs. Computers aren't going to eliminate market volatility. They're just going to new ways for it to appear. We now have new risks. We have new needs for investing.

BATS in the Belfry

March 23, 2012, should have been a great day for BATS. It is, after all, the Better Alternative Trading System, a fully-electronic exchange. It was formed in 2005 by Wall Street companies looking to break into the two-tiered turf of the NYSE and Nasdaq. That day it would offer shares to the public at $16 in its Initial Public Offering – and even list its own shares. It was an historic moment for the machines. The opening bell rang...

...and things went downhill from there. Just 90 minutes into the session, computer algorithms malfunctioned, different prices were being displayed – some showing as low as two cents on its own shares. The trading also affected shares of Apple Computer, sending them spiraling down more than 9%. While BATS thought it figured out the problem and was debating on whether or not to continue trading, it decided later in the day to withdraw its IPO. Investors were able to cancel their orders, but those who were attempting to sell on the opening bell would have to wait for another day.

BATS later reported that the computer glitch didn't allow open customer orders to be accessed, and it also prevented BATS from soliciting orders on its own stock. It should have been the biggest day in the company's history but, instead, will likely go down as the worst IPO in history.

Take back that point for the machines...

Even though the systems were restored within hours, it has raised serious concerns for investors. Computer systems are just that – systems. They can't think. They can miscommunicate with other computers or software and cause crashes. Anyone who even tries to do simple things like send e-mails or operate a cell phone knows how finicky computers can be. As speeds increase, pushing 10,000 trades per second, the fragmented market is leaving investors wondering just what may happen in the future.

We Have New Rules

When things get volatile, automated orders can trigger extreme price swings. Many of the algorithms don't take price or volume into account. They just execute orders. The market is a complex dynamic, and it's difficult to program all of the "if-then" statements to account for all conditions.

Another problem arises with the fragmented, uncoordinated markets. Having a centralized location was a big advantage of the NYSE – all trades filtered through one location. Today we have many electronic exchanges, so trading is decentralized. If one computer shuts down, it can cause rapid price increases in another. It's as if there's a sudden increase in demand. The reverse can also happen. In fact, one of the great ironies of the Flash Crash wasn't because of computerized trading; it's because computerized trading stopped. Their algorithms sensed it was too risky to be in the market. They all abandoned ship, and it's as if there was instantly no demand for shares. Prices plummeted.

Computers are programmed to sense price changes. They pick up on volatility, and begin putting more buying or selling pressure on the shares. It creates a system where you can get rapid swings – up or down – for no rational reason other than computer glitches.

Computerized trading has proven it's fallible. There's no question it's required to handle today's volumes. But with the way it's currently structured, we're going to see a lot of unnecessary volatility. Anyone can send orders instantly from a computer or cell phone. The exchanges – the computers – can get bombarded with information if a big even strikes the market. The real problem, however, is how the computers will respond to each other.

The technology can get to a point where it's doing more harm than good. And who are the regulators? Are they computer programmers? Are they traders who understand economics, order flows, and markets? No, they're mostly SEC attorneys. The more rules and regulations they put into place to try to solve the problems, the more places they create for future computer problems to hide.

We Have New Opportunities

Problems are just opportunities in disguise. Without question, we're going to see some of the best trading opportunities because of these unprecedented changes. The computerized trading has created a need for speed – information flows quickly, and orders have to be placed quickly. Technology is emotion neutral, and the executions are based on data and analytical algorithms. But people are emotional, and they react to the sound bites of modern media. We're able to instantly enter trades on computers or cell phones. Computers may match the trades, but people are still calling the shots, and that brings emotions back into it. We're still the X-factor. Information will be flowing infinitely fast – and emotions can run just as high. When computers fail, people react, and that's exactly what will create new problems – and new opportunities.

If you're going to go match wits with the machines, you need to have new ways for managing risks. You need new rules.

Investitute Takeaway

The electronic markets haven't really eliminated problems. They've only served to speed up executions – and the chances for errors. With all the speed and instant feedback, markets will face bigger swings. The bigger swings also mean bigger opportunities, but only if you can hedge risks ahead of time. Investors won't have time to react, so you're going to have to make changes to the way you invest. We have new markets. We have new risks. We have new rules.

RULE 2

Know Your Options!

Today's markets create new risks, but that doesn't mean we stop investing. It means we must find new ways for battling those risks. Options are the only tools that allow investors to alter risk-reward profiles. You can get rid of risks you don't want, and you can get paid to accept risks you're willing to take. No matter what type of investor or trader you are, you can absolutely put yourself in a better position by using options. Options are not risky. The risk comes from not knowing how to use them.

For today's investing, you must understand options.

Options are financial assets that trade on regulated exchanges much like shares of stock. The big difference is that options fall into a separate class of assets called *derivatives*, which just means their prices are tied to – or derived from – another asset. If you buy a Microsoft option, that option's price depends on the price of Microsoft.

But why bother with options? You've probably heard they're risky. In 1994, Proctor and Gamble reported a $102 million loss by using derivatives – the largest loss by an industrialized company at that time. That was dwarfed in 1995 when Nick Leeson used derivatives to bring historic Barings Bank to ashes. Derivatives were also blamed for the fall of AIG, Bear Stearns, Lehman Brothers, Fannie Mae, Freddie Mac, and Orange County, California. So how can derivatives not be risky?

The first thing to know – and probably most important – is that options are not risky. They don't know; they don't think. They're just tools that investors can use to alter risks. Yes, you can certainly use them to crank up risks to unbearable levels, and unfortunately, that's how many have chosen to use them. Sometimes it's intentional. Other times it's from not understanding. But the sensational losses you've read about are never from the use of options. They're from the misuse.

Risk can be cranked up, but it can also be shut off. That's right – 100% eliminated. That means you can create an options position that will have a guaranteed profit. But hold on, don't head out the door just yet to go yacht shopping. Guaranteed profit also means the strategy will return the risk-free rate, so it will behave like a bank CD. There won't be much profit in it.

That's just the risk-reward relationship at work. Any time you have a financial asset that has a guaranteed profit, it returns the risk-free rate. Options do not allow you to violate the risk-reward relationship. You can't use options to guarantee 30% per year for taking no risk. Options can, however, allow you to exactly tailor the risks and rewards you're seeking to accomplish your goals. That's something stock traders simply cannot do.

The markets are changing, and investors have to change too. Even billionaire investor Warren Buffett once advocated that derivatives were risky. Today, he's the largest seller of S&P 500 put options – to the tune of about four billion dollars' worth in a single year. Selling puts is considered one of the riskiest of all options strategies. Why did he change? Times have changed, and you must know your options to safely invest.

Still, we encounter investors who think derivatives should be avoided and stand by stock investing. Well, shares of stock are technically derivatives too. Share prices are derived from corporate sales. The only reason shares of stock have value is that they give the holders claims on corporate profits. Options have value because they give owners claims against stock. There's no reason to fear derivatives, but there is a big fear from leaving your portfolio wide open to the rapid flow of today's information. Options are necessary for reducing errors in today's markets. It's a new world of investing, and you must know your options.

What is an Option?

Options are securities. They trade on regulated exchanges, so they're every bit as easy to trade as stock. Just click a button to buy or sell. It's that easy.

Not all stocks have options on them, but those that do are called *optionable* stocks. Nearly all big-name companies you can think of are optionable. The stock is called the *underlying* stock because its value determines or "underlies" the option's price.

Options are legally binding contracts, so they trade in units called contracts rather than shares. If you buy one option contract, it generally controls 100 shares of stock. Exceptions can occur when stocks go through splits, mergers, or other corporate actions. In those cases, the contract size may be adjusted to keep the original contracts fair to the buyer and sellers.

Even the 100-share contract size is changing. Today, we're starting to see the introduction of mini contracts – ones that control 10 shares of stock. They're just offered on a few stocks right now, but will likely be rolled out to nearly all optionable stocks in the near future. But for now, most contracts control 100 shares. If you wanted to control 500 shares of stock, you would buy five option contracts.

Option contracts are standardized, which just means they carry the same terms. That's what makes them interchangeable, or tradable, on the open market. Think of it like money: If you borrow $100 from a friend, you can cancel, or offset, that debt by paying back $100 – even though you didn't pay back the dollars with the identical serial numbers. Money is interchangeable. That's exactly how options trading works. The contract terms are all identical, so traders can buy and sell in the open market to open and close positions. It's every bit as easy as buying and selling shares. Click on "buy" if you want to own it; click on "sell" to get rid of it.

Like most financial assets, options have limited liability. If you buy an option, the most you can lose is the amount you paid. As you'll see, however, that amount will be a very small fraction of the stock's price. It's one of the immediate benefits. You can control shares of stock but at a greatly reduced price. Your small maximum loss is known at the time you place the order.

Options can be traded on many underlying assets. For most investors, that will be shares of stock. But you'll also find options on Exchange Traded Funds (ETFs), indexes such as the S&P 500, currencies, or even commodities such as wheat, gold, or oil. The choices are nearly endless, but they all revolve around just two types of options.

Just Two Types of Options

You may have heard about options strategies and the many colorful names such as the butterfly spread, iron condors, or covered calls. Even though there are many strategies, they're all built on just two types of options – calls and puts. These are the building blocks of every single strategy. However, you can buy or sell calls, and you can buy or sell puts, so there are four combinations of trades:

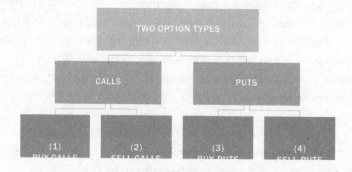

Option buyers have rights. If you buy an option, you've just purchased a right to do something. Option sellers, on the other hand, have some type of obligation. Don't think that obligations are bad; they're just a normal part of buying a selling shares. If you place an order to sell 100 shares of stock, that's an obligation. The difference is that option sellers can get paid for accepting an obligation they were perfectly willing to accept anyway. But for right now, just understand that option buyers have some type of right, and option sellers have some type of obligation. Options are a market between rights and obligations. So what exactly are the rights and obligations?

Call Buying: A Bullish Outlook

Let's start with call buying. If you buy a call option, you have the right, not the obligation, to buy 100 shares of the underlying stock, at a fixed price, over a given time. A big misconception among new options traders is that if they buy a call option they must eventually buy the stock, or they must have the shares in their account. Not true. If you buy a call you're not required to have any shares or do anything in the future. It's simply the right to purchase shares of stock in the future.

However, you don't get an unlimited time to make that decision. All options eventually expire, but you can buy many different expiration dates ranging from one week to nearly three years.

Technically speaking, an option that expires within one year is a standard option. Those with expirations greater than one year are called LEAPS, which stands for Long-term Equity AnticiPation Securities.

In 2012, the Chicago Board Options Exchange (CBOE) added Super LEAPS to the mix, which are options going out five years. However, they're currently only available for the S&P 500 index – not individual stocks. The option's expiration date is usually on the third Friday of the expiration month, but on the previous day for index options. For the weekly options, there's an expiration every Friday. Don't worry about these details as the OptionsHouse platform always shows the expiration date and number of days until expiration.

So how does call buying work? Let's take an example using Apple Computer (AAPL), which is currently trading for $120. Rather than buying the shares, which would cost $12,000 for 100 shares, you could buy an option and have the right to buy the shares. As you'll see, you'll never need to buy the shares of stock. The value of the call will change as Apple's price changes. Instead, you can just sell the call to capture the profit.

All you'd have to do is look at the list of options quotes, which is called the options chain. While there are about 15 different expirations now, you'd select the one that fits your needs. Perhaps you like the January 2016 $120 call, which has 90 days to expiration. Its price, or *premium*, is $5. Because each contract controls 100 shares, however, that price must be multiplied by 100, which means you must pay $500 plus commissions.

All you'd have to do is click on it, and click "buy." It's that easy. By purchasing the call, the most you can lose is the amount paid.

If you buy this call, you have the right, not the obligation, to purchase 100 shares of Apple Computer for $120 per share at any time through the expiration date in January – no matter how high the stock's price may be. You're locked into the $120 price, so you always have the right to buy 100 shares for $120 per share. Call options got their name because the buyer can choose to "call shares away" from another investor – the one who sold the call. It's the call buyer's choice – or option – to decide whether or not to buy the shares.

The fixed $120 price is called the *strike price*, or the *exercise price*. It may help you to remember that the strike price gets its name because that's where the buyer and seller "struck a deal." It's also called the exercise price because if you choose to use this call and buy the shares you must exercise the call. You'll pay the $120 price upon exercising – and receive 100 shares of Apple in exchange.

For any option expiration, you'll find many different strikes. For the January 2016 expiration, there are currently over 70 different strikes, ranging from $64 to $195. If the stock moved outside of this range before expiration, the exchanges would add new strikes to accommodate the new prices.

New traders are often overwhelmed at the many strike choices. As you'll find later in this book, each strike behaves a little differently. Depending on your strategy, one strike may be a better choice than another. Having so many choices is what creates the hundreds of strategies and risk-reward profiles we can create with options. They're strategies stock traders simply cannot do.

If you did wish to buy the shares, you would submit exercise instructions. Exercising a call is easy; it's just a click of a mouse to let the broker know that you've elected to buy the shares. If you choose to exercise this call, you'd pay the $120 strike * 100 shares, or $12,000 plus commissions and you'll own 100 shares of Apple. There's nothing to fear from a call option. You can see, after all, it's just a way to buy shares of stock.

How Do Options Make Money?

Option buyers are never required to exercise an option to capture profits. Instead, they can just sell the contract in the open market.

You're not required to exercise a call to buy the shares in order to capture a profit. In fact, about 90% of all option contracts are never exercised. So how to traders profit without ever buying shares? How do options make money?

Remember, options are derivatives, and their prices are derived from the underlying stock. As the stock's price changes, so does the option's price.

For example, if Apple is trading for $130 at expiration, your $120 call must be worth at least the $10 difference. With the stock at $130, you could exercise the call, pay $120, and immediately sell for $130 to make the $10 cash. But rather than go through those motions, the market automatically prices the call at the $10 difference. That $10 is called the *intrinsic value*. If an option has intrinsic value, it's called an *in-the-money* option. Any time the stock's price is greater than the strike price, it's an in-the-money call.

If you bought the $120 call for $5, you could sell it for $10 to capture your profit. That means you made 100% on your money – even though the stock only rose 8% (from $120 to $130).

One of the biggest options benefits is that they provide leverage, or magnifications in returns. The leverage comes from not being required to ever pay the $120 strike for the shares. Mathematically, you're borrowing that money because you get to float those dollars; however, you'll never pay margin interest like stock traders do who borrow money for leverage.

Option traders benefit even more, however. Most of the time, leverage is a double-edge sword, and you can lose at the same rate you gain. That's not true for options. Call options can make an unlimited amount, so the leverage works for you when you're right. But they can only lose a small, fixed amount when you're wrong, so the leverage doesn't work equally against you. By purchasing calls, you can participate in all future stock price increases, but only have a small fixed loss if you're wrong. Options are the perfect risk management tool.

Intrinsic and Time Values

We just showed that if the stock reaches $130 at expiration, the $120 call will be worth exactly $10. But what if it reaches $130 prior to expiration? If that happens, the $120 call will still be worth at least the $10 intrinsic value, but it will also contain additional value. It may, for example, trade for $11. As long as the option hasn't expired, traders are willing to pay something for that remaining time.

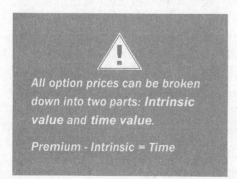

All option prices can be broken down into two parts: Intrinsic value and time value.

Premium - Intrinsic = Time

Any additional value over the intrinsic value is called the *time value,* or *extrinsic value.* If the stock is $130 and the $120 call is trading for $11, then $10 is the intrinsic value and $1 is the time value. The intrinsic value plus the time value always equals the option's premium. In this example, $10 intrinsic + $1 time = $11 premium.

To figure out the time value, you must always first calculate the intrinsic value. Just take the option's premium and subtract out the intrinsic value. You're left with the time value:

Premium – Intrinsic Value = Time Value

If Apple is trading for $130 prior to expiration and the $120 call is worth $11, so you could sell the contract for $11, for a 120% gain. Only the time value erodes with the passage of time. At expiration, all time values are zero. If you get all the way to expiration and the stock is still $130, the $120 call would be worth just the $10 intrinsic value. If there's any intrinsic value at expiration, it remains with the option. It's only the time value that goes to zero.

What happens if the stock's price fell to $120 or lower? For call options, if the stock's price below the strike, it's *out-of-the-money*. There's no intrinsic value. Nobody's going to pay anything for the right to pay $120 for the shares when they can buy them for less in the open market.

If the stock's price is ever trading for exactly the strike (or very close), it's called an *at-the-money* option. But at expiration, traders are only worried about whether the option is in-the-money or out-of-the-money. At expiration, an at-the-money option is just as worthless as out-of-the-money.

If the option expires worthless, then you've lost the premium – you've lost your $5. But your benefit is that the call option limits the downside loss to just the premium paid. By purchasing this $120 call, the most you can lose is $5. There's no way you could guaranteed to limit losses to just $5 by purchasing shares – not even with stop orders. Call options give traders unlimited potential for gains, just like stock buyers, but limited potential for loss. Option buyers have the advantage when uncertainty strikes. That's why options are necessary for today's investors.

Understanding how to break an option's price down into intrinsic and time values is crucial for success. All option strategies make use of one value or the other, and in some cases, both. Just as an accountant needs to know how much of a business expenditure is due to cost and how much is due to tax, options traders must be able to break option prices down into the two component parts of intrinsic and time values. Most trading software will clearly show the intrinsic and time values, but you have to know how to interpret it.

Breakeven Point

New traders often wonder how to choose from the big list of strike prices. Each strike price creates a different risk-reward profile. Each one has a different probability for expiring in-the-money. To help with strategies, it helps to know how to calculate the *breakeven* point. For call buyers, that's found by adding the strike price to the premium. In this example, the $120 strike plus the $5 premium equals $125. That means you need the stock to reach $125 at expiration just to break even. With the stock at $125, the $120 call would be worth exactly the $5 intrinsic value, which is exactly the price you paid, and you'd just break even. By using different strike prices, option traders can alter their breakeven points to give them more or less leverage and different probabilities of success.

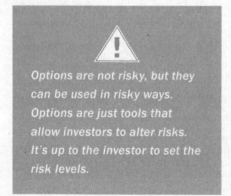

Options are not risky, but they can be used in risky ways. Options are just tools that allow investors to alter risks. It's up to the investor to set the risk levels.

Options are not risky. Each expiration and strike carries a different probability for success. When you hear stories of options losses, it's usually because the trader was buying short-term, out-of-the-money options that had virtually no chance of making money. If you bought the $195 call for 10 cents, you'd need the stock to reach $195.10 in 90 days. With it currently at $120, it's highly unlikely for that to happen. That's a risky option. At the other extreme, we can look at lower strikes, such as the $100 strike, and it will behave much more like shares of stock rather than an option. We'll show you how to make an option act like shares later in this book. For now, recognize that the various strikes are what give you the many choices for managing today's risks.

Put Buying: A Bearish Outlook

Once you understand how call options work, it's easy to understand puts. They work in exactly the same way – just in the opposite direction. Call buyers make money if the stock price rises. Put buyers make money if the stock price falls.

If you buy a put option, you have the right, not the obligation, to sell 100 shares of the underlying stock, at a fixed price, over a given time. The definition is identical to that of calls; the only difference is it that put buyer has the right to sell. Put options got their name because the buyer can "put shares back" to another investor. It's as if you're saying, "I don't want my shares anymore. I'm putting them back over (selling) to another investor."

To understand put buying, let's stick with our Apple Computer example, but this time we're going to assume you think the stock is going to fall. How can you make money by using put options?

The Apple Jan. 2016 $120 put is trading for $4.80. For technical financial reasons, at-the-money calls will usually cost a little more than puts. So while the $120 call was trading for $5, the $120 put was trading for $4.80. If you thought Apple's price was going to fall, you could buy this put option to profit from that outlook.

Now you know what to do: Find the January $120 put on the platform, click on buy, and you own the put option. That trade will cost $480 plus commissions, and that's the most you could ever lose.

Now that you own the put, you have the right, not the obligation, to *sell* 100 shares of stock at the fixed price of $120 per share at any time between today and expiration. Just as with calls, you don't need shares, and you're not required to ever sell shares. If you buy the put, you just have the right to sell shares. Because you have the right to sell, as the stock price falls, your fixed higher selling price becomes more valuable. Put buyers benefit from falling prices.

For instance, let's say that Apple falls to $110 per share at expiration. Because you have the right to sell for $120 per share, your put option is worth the $10 difference, or intrinsic value. That's because you could buy shares in the open market for $110 per share, exercise your put and sell them for $120, and capture the $10 gain. Because you could definitely capture $10, the market will automatically price the $120 put at $10. So just as with call options, put buyers do not ever need to own shares or exercise to sell shares to capture profits. Instead, they just buy and sell the contracts in the open market.

Therefore, you could sell your put for $10. Because you paid $4.80, you'd bank the $5.20 difference as a profit. Just like call options, put options provide leverage. Here, the stock fell 8% but you more than doubled your money. Just as with calls, if there's time remaining on the option, it will sell for more than the intrinsic value. If Apple is trading at $110 prior to expiration, the $120 put would be trading for more than the $10 intrinsic value. The additional amount would be the time value. You could sell your put for more than $10.

Of course, if you owned the shares of stock, you could exercise the put, which means you'd sell your shares and receive the $120 strike, or $12,000 less commissions. If you didn't own the shares but exercised the put, you'd end up with a short stock position, which for some investors, may be part of their overall strategy. There's nothing to fear with using put options; they're just another way to sell shares of stock.

Put buyers have the advantage of profiting from falling stock prices. Anybody who's been investing for any length of time has certainly seen how quickly – and how far – stock prices can fall. People are generally very risk averse, and as stock prices fall, everyone rushes to sell, and that can send prices plummeting.

Stocks generally rise slowly but can crash quickly – it's the staircase up but elevator down as traders like to say. As a stock investor, the only way you can profit from falling stock prices is to short shares of stock, which is one of the riskiest positions you can take in the financial markets. There's no upper limit on how high a stock's price can rise, so your potential loss is unlimited. For this reason, most traders never short stocks, and miss out on half – and often the best – opportunities in the market.

By purchasing puts, however, you can profit from falling prices, but do so with limited risk. The most you can lose is the amount paid. To find your breakeven point for puts, just subtract the premium from the strike. Here, your breakeven here is $120 - $4.80 = $115.20. If the stock falls to $115.20 at expiration, the $120 put has $4.80 of intrinsic value. If you sold your put for that price, you'd just break even. If the stock closes at or above the $120 strike, the put just expires worthless and you'd lose the premium. Again, that's the worst that can happen. The put option allowed you to short shares of stock but with limited risk. Options are just tools for controlling risk.

Put Buying as Insurance

As you just found out, put options can be used to speculate on falling prices. Just buy the put, and if prices fall far enough, sell at a profit. However, puts can also be used conservatively, and you can use them as a form of insurance.

Let's say you owned 100 shares of Apple which is currently trading for $120 per share. To protect against losses, you buy the $120 put for $4.80. If the stock falls to $110 per share at expiration, your put option is worth the $10 intrinsic value. You lost $10 on the stock, but gained $10 on the put. The put acted as an insurance policy to offset some of your losses.

However, it didn't completely keep you from losing. As with any form of insurance, you don't get the premium back, so you'd lose the $4.80 paid. However, by purchasing the put, you know for a fact that the $4.80 premium is the most you could lose on your shares. No matter how low the stock price may fall, your selling price is locked at $120. You may choose to sell the put and take the profit to offset your losses, or you could exercise the put and sell your shares for $120 per share.

You can probably now see that put options are identical to call options; they just work in the opposite direction. Option buyers – calls or puts – have rights. They do not have obligations to do anything at any time.

The Option Buying Advantage

New traders often focus on the limited risk that options provide as the big benefit. It's much more than that. It's that one key word – right – that makes all the difference in how you can manage risk. By having the right to decide, you get to wait and see what happens with the stock's price before making any decisions.

Imagine that you're at a horserace, and everyone is placing bets. You, however, have a special deal with the track owner. You get to watch the horses come thundering down the track, and when the race is almost over, you then get to decide on how to bet. Sounds ridiculous, right? It would be too big of an advantage. But that's exactly what option traders get to do. Option traders get to wait and see how the stock price is shaping up before making a commitment. That's the big benefit received for the premium paid.

By controlling the shares, the buyer has the choice – or option – to decide whether or not to buy or sell the shares. The buyer gets to wait all the way until expiration to see how the future turned out. If it's not favorable to buy or sell, the option buyer can just walk away from the deal and lose only the price paid for the option.

Stock buyers can't do that. Instead, they continue to take the fall – dollar-for-dollar – all the way down to zero. While that's unlikely, it's not impossible – just ask former employees who held shares of Enron in their 401(k) plans.

The option trader limits losses. Options are the perfect risk-management tool. For option buyers, the benefit is that they get to delay decisions – days, months, or years – and see how the stock price behaves. They get to decide on which shares to buy based on tomorrow's news. If it sounds unfair, now you see why we call it the option advantage.

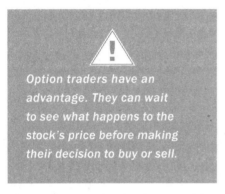

Option traders have an advantage. They can wait to see what happens to the stock's price before making their decision to buy or sell.

Naturally, that benefit doesn't come for free. You must pay for the option, and it's possible you could lose the relatively small amount paid. But that's exactly the benefit. You're guaranteed to limit your loss to a small, fixed amount, yet be able to participate fully if you're correct about the stock's direction. That is something that cannot be done if you buy shares of stock.

Call and put buyers have a unique advantage in today's markets. You can buy calls to profit from rising prices, but only have a small, limited loss if you're wrong. By purchasing puts, you can profit from falling prices and place a cap on your losses if you're wrong. Options allow you more choices because there's less fear. That's why we like to say options give you options. You can easily see the benefits of buying options. How can you benefit from selling options?

Option Selling: Getting Paid to Accept Obligations

Option buyers pay a premium and have rights. Option sellers receive the premium from the buyer and have obligations to fulfill the contract – only if the option buyer decides to exercise. The obligations are easy to figure out once you realize the buyer and seller are opposite of each other. If the call buyer has the right to buy, the seller must have the obligation to sell. Obligations are opposite of rights, and sellers are opposite of buyers. Option sellers are sometimes called *writers*, just as it is in the insurance world. If you write an option contract, you're the seller.

Now try it for put options. If you buy a put option, you have the right to sell. The put seller, therefore, must have the obligation to buy shares. Just as with options buying, there's nothing to fear from selling options. They're just ways of buying or selling shares of stock – exactly the same things you've been doing all along.

If you have trouble remembering what option sellers do, start by thinking about the buyer's rights – then just flip terms:

	CALLS	PUTS
BUY	Right to Buy	Right to Sell
	⬇ ⬇	⬇ ⬇
SELL	Obligation to Sell	Obligation to Buy

Option selling is very easy to do. Rather than clicking the "buy" to purchase the option, you just click the word "sell." Cha-ching! You've got cash. You're the seller. However, that doesn't mean you can close the account and walk away with the cash. You have a potential obligation to fulfill. Let's see how that works, and how you can benefit from selling options.

Call Selling: The Obligation to Sell Shares

If you sell calls, you'll receive cash up front, but in exchange, have the obligation to sell the underlying shares at the fixed strike price. Let's go back to the Apple $120 call, but this time we'll sell it:

Sell 1 Apple Jan. 2016 $120 call for $5

When you sell (or write) an option, it is a short contract, which means you've sold something that was not in your account. It will show up with a minus sign as one of your positions:

Apple Jan. 2016 $120 call: -1

If you sell this $120 call, you'll receive $500 cash up front into your account. Whenever you sell an option, the premium received is the most you can make. By selling the call, you have the obligation to sell shares. If you sold this call without any other assets to back it up, such as the actual shares of stock or another call option, it's called an uncovered, or naked, position.

You have the obligation to sell 100 shares for $120 between now and expiration (at the call buyer's discretion) and the only way you could do that would be to buy the shares in the open market. There's no telling how high that price may be, so you have unlimited risk if the stock price rises. Selling naked calls is never a good idea, but there are many strategies that allow investors to sell calls without such risks.

But just so you understand how short positions work, we'll continue with the example as a naked position, and then we'll show you safer ways for selling calls.

Call Selling: Three Ways to Exit

By selling this call, you have three ways to get out of the contract. First, and probably the easiest, is for the call option to expire worthless. If the stock price closes at expiration at $120 or below, the option is worthless. There's nothing you would need to do. The Monday following option expiration, the short option would just disappear from your account. You've fulfilled your obligation to deliver the shares. Because it was never advantageous for the call buyer to exercise, the contract is over and you keep the $500.

The second way to get out of the short contract is to buy it back in the open market. Just as you can buy a call to get into a contract, you can also buy it to get out of a short contract. During the option's life, its price will fluctuate depending on a number of factors, but mostly due to time and stock price. Let's say that the stock price falls a little, or that time passes, and the option's price is now less, say $2.

You could place an order to buy the contract, and that would offset, or flatten, your short position. You sold the call for $5 and bought it back for $2 thus capturing a $3 profit. Think of buying back a contract like your cell phone contract. Most carriers allow you to get out of the standard two-year agreement by purchasing the contract back at a fixed price, usually $250. You're paying a fee to relieve yourself from the future obligations. That's exactly what happens in the options market. The difference is that the market decides on the price of the contract. Buying back the contract gets you out from underneath your obligations.

Of course, the share price may rise. Let's say Apple rises and the contract is now worth $7. If you buy back the contract, you'll lose $2. You received $5 but had to spend $7 to get it back. Regardless, you're out of the contract.

The third way to exit from the contract would be to deliver the shares, but that only happens if the long call buyer decides to exercise. You'll get a notice from your broker, which is called an *assignment* notice. You'll receive the strike, or $12,000 cash (less commissions) and have to deliver 100 shares. If you don't have the shares, you'll have to place an order in the open market. Now you can see the risk of selling a naked call. There's no telling how high that price may be. Yes, you received $12,000, but what if the stock is now worth $150? You'd buy the shares for $15,000 and sell them for $12,000 and end up with a $3,000 loss. Regardless of the loss, you're out of the contract because you fulfilled your obligation to deliver 100 shares for $120 per share.

Because there's no telling how high a stock's price may rise, selling naked calls is a strategy we never recommend. It may be good for some institutions or hedge funds with very deep pockets, but it's rarely advisable for individual investors.

Still, there are many times you can sell calls and gain a better risk profile than just using shares alone. One strategy would be to buy the shares of stock first. That way, your purchase price is known ahead of time. If you buy the shares today at $120, it's as if you're buying them and stashing away as inventory. No matter how high the price may rise, you now know for sure that you'll have shares at the $120 price. Now that you have the shares, let's go sell the $120 call for $5.

This is a common strategy called the *covered call*, which we'll detail in Rule #21 – along with an interesting twist for today's markets. If you own 100 shares of Apple and sold this call, you would always be able to deliver the shares since they're already in your account. No matter how high the stock price may rise, you know that you'll be able to deliver the shares. The upside risk with the naked call is now "covered" by having the shares in your account.

Understand, however, that you're not guaranteed to sell your shares. When you sell any option, it's always a potential obligation. The sale is triggered only if the call buyer decides to exercise. It's the buyer's right to decide, and it's your obligation to sell the shares if that choice is made. If the buyer exercises, there's nothing you need to do. You'll just look into your account one day and the shares will be gone. The cash will be there. It's automatic. What are the benefits?

Let's say you just bought Apple shares for $120, but then sold the January $120 call for $5. By receiving $5, your cost basis is effectively lowered from $120 to $115. It's as if you paid $120 for the stock, but received a $5 rebate. By selling the call, you immediately have less downside risk. You could afford to have the stock price fall to $115 and just break even. Had you not sold the call, you'd be down $5. By selling the call, the cash acts as a hedge against falling stock prices.

If the stock price stays relatively quiet, you may not make much on your shares, but the $5 cash is always yours to keep. Just as when an insurance company sells a policy, they keep the premium. When you sell calls, you're acting as the insurance writer. You keep the premium no matter what happens to the stock's price.

If the stock price remains below $120 per share at expiration, there's nothing you need to do. The option contract expires worthless, and you're free to write another call on Monday (or later) if you choose.

If the stock's price is the same at expiration – $120 per share – your return is $5/$115, or about 4.3%. Because this is a three-month call, your annualized return is over 17%. Not bad for the stock price going nowhere. Had you not sold the call, your return would be flat. Call sellers can make consistent income – even in flat markets. Month after month, many traders do nothing but write calls to generate income.

What happens if the stock price rises above $120 on expiration Friday? You have a couple of choices. First, do nothing. You'll most likely find that you got assigned and find your shares are "called away" on Monday morning. Option sellers get assigned only if the option buyer exercises. As the option seller, you can't call the broker and request an assignment. Remember you don't have a right. That right belongs to the option buyer. If you find your shares are called away, there's nothing else you need to do. The terms of the agreement have been fulfilled. You earned at the rate of 17% per year, even though the stock's price may have only risen a few pennies.

There's another choice you could take. You could choose to buy the call option back and not have to worry about losing your shares. For instance, let's assume that Apple has risen to $124 at expiration thus making the $120 call worth exactly $4. You could buy the call back for $4, and that short call position is now gone from your account. Remember, you started off with a minus position. When you buy it back, it flattens that position. Are you worse off because you had to buy back the option?

Not at all. In this example, you sold the option for $5, but bought it back for $4, so you're still up one dollar. You paid $120 for the shares, which are now worth $124. Your stock is up $4, and you're up $1 on the option – you're still up $5. The true risk to the covered call writer is for the stock price to fall. This is why Pete and I stress to clients why it's important to identify stocks that are in good consistent uptrends before using covered calls. If you want to collect monthly income, you want to be sure your stocks are fundamentally and technically sound. Selling options against weak, volatile stocks is a big mistake among new traders.

We even have free proprietary tools at www.investitute.com. Just click the "Research Lab" link and you'll be able to identify excellent stocks for income generation. You won't find these tools anywhere else, and they're built on the same principles Pete and I used to create decades of successful investing.

As you get more advanced, new strategies emerge. Call sellers don't need to necessarily buy shares. Instead, they can buy a different call as a substitute for shares. Because that long call will be so much cheaper than the stock, the returns are magnified even more. If 17% per year looked good, watch what happens if you buy a call instead of the shares. So rather than using a covered call, as professional traders, Pete and I would be more inclined to use other strategies called *vertical spreads* or a *diagonal spreads*. With a vertical call spread, we'd buy a call option, but sell a different call against it.

For instance, the January 2016 $115 call is trading for $8.50. If we bought this call, we could write the January 2016 $120 call for $5 thus making our total cost $3.50. That's much better than the $115 required when using shares of stock. Notice that we've purchased a lower-strike call: $115 is a lower price than $120.

This means we have the right to buy shares for $115 and the obligation to sell for $120 – a $5 maximum gain. Because we spent $3.50, our return is bolstered to over 43%, or 168% annualized. We just need the stock to remain at $120 or higher by expiration to get that. And because we've only spent $3.50, that's the most we can lose.

The covered call writer in our example was exposed to potentially $115 points of downside risk. That's the problem with owning shares in today's markets. The risks are too great to have that kind of downside risk. Unfortunately, every single stock strategy is going to leave you wide open to the lightning speed of today's information. Options greatly reduce that risk and give you better returns to boot.

We can make it even more interesting by using a diagonal spread. We could, instead, buy a January 2017 $115 call as a substitute for the stock. It currently has 440 days to expiration, so just over one year until expiration. It's trading for just over $15. Rather than writing the $120 call one time, we could write options month after month for over a year and accelerate those gains even more. By paying $15, we're controlling 100 shares for over a year – but are paying $1,500 rather than $12,000 to do so.

These strategies are not going to be crystal clear to you, but remember that our intention is to only show why selling calls can be beneficial – even though they create obligations. Obligations are not bad; they're just part of buying and selling shares of stock. When you sell calls against shares of stock, you're getting paid to accept an obligation you were willing to accept anyway. It makes it a less risky position, and that's one of the many benefits of selling calls.

Put Selling: The Obligation to Buy Shares

Call selling has advantages for those who are willing to sell shares. Conversely, put sellers can benefit if they're willing to buy shares. Put sellers receive cash up front today and have the potential obligation to buy 100 shares of stock for the fixed strike price in the future. The premium received is the most you can make from the strategy; that's always true whether you're selling calls or puts. Just as call sellers are not guaranteed to sell shares, put sellers are never guaranteed to buy shares. They only buy shares if they get assigned, and that's up to the put buyer.

While selling the put does create an obligation, if you were willing to buy the shares anyway, why does it hurt to receive money in exchange for accepting that obligation?

In our put buying example, we found the Jan. 2016 $120 put was trading for $4.80. Rather than buying this put, you could choose to sell it. All you do is go to the platform and click "sell" rather than "buy." You're instantly credited with $480 cash. If you look in your account, you'd see a minus sign for your position:

Apple Jan. 2016 $120 put = -1

In exchange for that cash, you accept the obligation to buy 100 shares for the $120 strike between the day you sell the put and expiration.

Put Selling: Three Ways to Exit

As with call selling, you have three ways to exit a short put contract. The easiest to understand is if the contract expires worthless. If Apple rises above $120, the put buyer has no incentive to exercise. Nobody wants to exercise and receive $120 per share when they could sell shares for more in the open market. So if Apple is above $120 at expiration, the contract will go unexercised, and you've fulfilled your potential obligation to buy the shares. Of course, you won't buy the shares, but at least you have $480 to show for it. If you choose, you can always write another put. Each time you do, you're lowering your cost basis on the shares you may eventually purchase. For instance, if you sold a similar put three times, you'd collect $14.40. If you got assigned for $120 at that time, your cost basis is $120 - $14.40, or $105.60.

The second way to exit the contract is to buy it back, which you're free to do at any time. If Apple is trading for $115 at expiration, you may decide you'd rather not buy the shares. In that case, you'll have to buy back the short put to close out the position. With the stock at $115 at expiration, the $120 put will be trading for the $5 intrinsic value. Just buy the put back by spending $5. However, because you received $4.80 from the sale, you only lost 20 cents on the deal. Had you purchased the shares for $120 rather than choosing to sell the put, you'd be down $5. The put premium received still protected you by reducing losses. Option selling provided a good hedge.

Prior to expiration, the put's value will fluctuate and you may decide to buy the contract back. If you sold the put for $4.80, you may find it trading for $2 at a later time. You could choose to buy it back and you'd profit by the $2.80 difference. In other words, you sold for $4.80 and bought it back for $2 and pocketed the difference. You're also out of the contract. If the contract is trading for a higher price, you can still buy it back at a loss. For example, if the stock falls significantly prior to expiration, the put may be trading for $6. You sold it for $4.80 and bought it back for $6, so you lost $1.20 on the deal – but you are out of the contract.

The third way to exit the contract is if you get assigned. In this example, if Apple fell below $120, you *may* get assigned. Remember, it's the buyer's right to decide to sell the shares. Just because an option is slightly in-the-money doesn't guarantee you're going to get assigned. The only way to know for sure is to wait for Monday morning and see if you've purchased the shares. However, if you do, the $4.80 cash from selling the put reduces your cost basis to $115.20. Selling puts put you in a less risky position.

Just as with call options, if you sell a put by itself, it's called a naked position. While selling naked puts may seem like a good deal for stock investors, we generally don't recommend it. All too often, stocks can end up taking an enormous unexpected drop, and the put sellers regret it. Once you understand options, you'll find there are better ways to sell puts to capture premiums.

We can show some far more fascinating – and far more profitable positions – rather than just selling naked puts. Remember, our goal for this section is for you to understand the option advantage. It's not designed to teach you all the ins and outs of strategies. Instead we want you to understand what it means to buy and sell options. The possibilities are endless, but they all begin by understanding the option advantage. You must know your options.

The Option Selling Advantage

Option sellers benefit by receiving a fixed premium today, in exchange for some potential future obligation. If the obligation is something you're willing to do anyway, it's not really a risk to you. That's one of the advantages of the options market. Investors are just trying to find out who's in the best position to accept risks, but they don't need to know each other. Instead, they just need to know prices. If you're willing to accept certain risks, you can simply sell an option.

The premium serves to reduce risk. Once you've sold an option, you can exit by purchasing the contract back, having it expire worthless, or taking the assignment and actually buying or selling shares. But if you were willing to buy or sell the shares anyway, the cash from the sale acts as a hedge against adverse price movements. Investors can also use option selling strategies to create monthly income. You can alter the risks to suit your needs, and the option premiums are often much larger – and more frequent – than dividends.

Who's the Watchdog?

Now that you understand buying and selling options, you're probably wondering about the integrity of the market. After all, if you decide to exercise an option, who's to say that the option seller will comply?

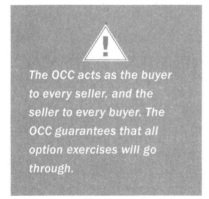

The OCC acts as the buyer to every seller, and the seller to every buyer. The OCC guarantees that all option exercises will go through.

That's where the Options Clearing Corporation, or OCC, steps in. The OCC is the largest derivatives clearing firm in the world with strict oversight by the Securities and Exchange Commission (SEC) and Commodities Futures Trading Commission (CFTC).

Technically speaking, when you buy an option, you're buying it from the OCC, and when you sell an option, you're selling it to the OCC. The OCC acts as the buyer to every seller, and the seller to every buyer. The OCC ensures the market integrity – it's the market watchdog. Since 1973 when options began trading, not a single exercise has ever failed to go through. If you ever wish to exercise a call or put to buy or sell shares, you can be sure the exercise will go through. The OCC guarantees it.

It's a new world of investing. If you wish to invest for bigger profits, less risk, and fewer headaches with the day-to-day market turmoil, you have to understand the new rules of investing. You must know your options.

Investitute Takeaway

Option buyers spend far less money than stock traders. They have less to lose, and better returns on their investments. Because option investors have more cash, they can diversify their investments. For any portfolio size, option buyers can control more positions and diversify risks better than if they just invest with shares of stock. Option buyers have more ways to profit: They can make money whether stock prices rise, fall, or even remain flat. Option investors can create monthly income by writing options. You only get these advantages if you know your options. They're essential for managing today's risks.

RULE 3

Understand Your E.I.

Today's markets are managed by A.I. – artificial intelligence.
To compete, you must begin by knowing your E.I. – emotional
intelligence. Most people can imagine the extreme dedication, focus,
and training that's required to compete in professional sports. Just
watch any ice skater nail the quadruple Lutz, and you can only
imagine the number of hours spent training – and falling. Perfection
didn't come from a weekend course.

People can also appreciate the number of hours required to become
a great scientist, mathematician, or engineer. Just watch any videos
sent back by NASA's rover *Curiosity*, and it's hard to believe you're
looking at Mars. That knowledge wasn't acquired from a YouTube
video. It was a process: Conquer the mountains, then the moon,
then Mars.

We could go on giving examples, and everyone would agree that
every profession takes time to master – until you get to options.
That logic immediately goes right out the window. For some reason,
people think they can take a weekend course to learn a strategy,
and now they've mastered the markets. It doesn't work that way.
But because of today's computerized trading, new traders think
there's no skill involved. All they have to do is buy an option, and if

the price moves in their favor – they win. Options are not a one-armed bandit in a casino. You don't pull the handle and either win or lose. They're tools, and there are methods for using them – some right, some wrong. Options allow you to alter risks and rewards, and it's up to you to understand how to control and manage them. If you can master options, you can master the market risks.

To do so, you must have the emotional intelligence to realize it's a process and there are things to learn. There's a beginning, a path, and a method you must master. One of the surprises for today's new traders is the instant feedback we get from computer trading. There are no more delays waiting next month for your statement to arrive, or later in the day for your broker to call to let you know how your portfolio has performed. Instead, you now see every tick of the market – delivered in real time to your computer or cell phone. You'll see how you've performed today, since inception, or at any time period you want. You'll have immediately red and green blinking lights to show what's happening.

If you don't have the right training and mindset, it's easy to get whipsawed out of positions that otherwise would have been winners. If you're willing to take time to learn the right steps, there's money to be made in the new markets – and lots of it. Before you can battle the A.I., you have to enter with the right E.I.

Mastery Takes Options Knowledge

Mastery takes more than discipline. You need knowledge – *options* knowledge. Although option prices are tied to stock prices, they work differently from stock. If you have the right knowledge, you can make an option behave almost like shares of stock, but you can also make it behave like a highly leveraged lottery ticket.

You can make an option's price respond a little, or you may choose to make it move a lot. You can switch your outlook from bullish to bearish, or bearish to bullish – while the stock is moving. You can make your option's price rise if the stock price stays still. You can create profitable strategies regardless of the stock's direction.

Options are more than just a way to profit from rising or falling stock prices. With the right knowledge, you can get rid of risks you don't want to take – and get paid for ones you're willing to accept. Stock investors don't get those choices, which is exactly why options traders can outperform stock traders – if you know how to make them work for you.

You must have the right E.I. so you'll be patient through the process. Using options is not enough. Knowledge makes them usable.

Mastery Takes Technical Knowledge

Emotional intelligence also includes knowledge of the technical processes. There's a system of bids and offers, expiration dates, types of orders, and regulatory trading rules. Will you get caught with ex-by-ex, PDT labels, early exercise, or the need to beta weight your portfolio? If none of that made sense, it shows you need more technical knowledge. Don't worry, as we'll explain them later in this book. The only thing you need now is the understanding that mastery takes time and coaching. Not only does it require options knowledge, it requires knowledge of the technical process. Understanding the covered call or iron condor strategies alone isn't going to cut it. They aren't magical lanterns with genies that hand over money for nothing. They're tools that create different risk profiles. If you understand how to find the opportunities and how to manage the risks then profits appear.

Handing you a paintbrush isn't going to make you Rembrandt. Handing you a strategy isn't going to make you money. You have to understand the technical processes that make strategies work. Technical information is easy to teach. You just need to begin with the right E.I. and agree to take the time to understand.

Mastery Takes Market Knowledge

Emotional intelligence is also more than just the technical process. You have to understand how markets work. Financial markets are a continuous live auction, much like eBay, but it's filled with buyers and sellers all trying to figure out what financial assets are worth. It's not you against the market makers. It's not you against the banks. It's you against all other investors and traders. If you want to compete, you need to understand what the market is and how it works. You need to know what everybody else knows.

Unfortunately, new traders seem to think this doesn't matter. It's an easy misperception with today's computerized networks. But remember that it's all the same operation: It's just people buying and selling securities based on information. Computers don't allow shortcuts; they just allow the information to flow faster, so it's even more critical to understand the process. You shouldn't feel too confident flying a fighter jet at mach speeds just because the information is computerized. You need to know what makes it tick. This is why Pete and I spend a great deal of time with clients showing them exactly how markets and exchanges operate. It takes time, and you have to realize it's a necessary part of the process.

Markets Look Forward

Markets are forward looking, which just means the market anticipates prices. If a $100 stock is believed to be worth $110 next month, it will trade for $110 today. To succeed with investing, you must anticipate where prices are moving – not chase after them.

In football, a wide receiver will miss every single pass if he waits for the ball to be thrown and then chases after it. Instead, the receiver must anticipate where the ball is going. The quarterback must anticipate where the receiver is going. It's harder than it looks, but with training and understanding it can be executed flawlessly. For the same reasons, in the financial markets, you can't wait for news to come out and then buy options to make a profit. That's chasing information. Information drives prices, so to catch those price swings, you must anticipate where the information is going – not wait for it to come out.

And just like a beautifully completed football pass, it's harder than it looks. If you wait for information to be released and chase after it, it's too late.

Success depends on more than that. You also must anticipate how the market will react to the news. Pete and I see this a lot with some of our protégé traders. A company may be expected to release great earnings tomorrow, and the trader wants to buy call options today to profit from that news. It's probably too late. The ball has already been thrown. The market expected great earnings three months ago. If you buy a call option expecting prices to go up, the rest of the market is waiting for that information to be announced – and ready to sell. Even if the information is good, chances are, the price will fall.

The only way to profit from buying a call right before earnings is if the numbers are a true surprise. In other words, the collective market missed it. That's not going to happen too often. If you think that earnings will be stellar, chances are, so does everybody else. Other complications can occur. The earnings may be great, but the market may think they weren't great enough. Or the company may announce on its conference call that it can think it doesn't replicate those earnings in the future. Lots of things could happen to send that stock's price into a tailspin – even though the earnings number was good.

You'll buy at the high, sell at the low, and wonder how the market seems to always go exactly the opposite way you thought. The markets not going in the opposite diction, you are. You're chasing information. It's not a misunderstanding of options. It's a misunderstanding of markets. To succeed, you need to understand how markets work.

Once you understand markets, you can use volatility, which we'll talk about later, to determine if the entire market thinks the option's price is high or low – before you buy. Without the understanding of how markets arrive at prices by using volatility, you'll never know if that option represents a good price or not. You'll always be chasing after the ball after it's thrown. With training and practice, though, you can anticipate where prices are going. That requires you to have the right E.I. to realize it's not just option strategies you're after.

Options are information neutral. You don't profit from options just because the news or information was good. You profit because you correctly anticipated the information – and how the rest of the traders would react. All of the training requires emotional intelligence.

Emotional intelligence has joined the ranks of "multiple intelligences" recognizing soft skills beyond the original I.Q., or intelligence quotient. Emotional intelligence can be described as the ability to identify and manage your own emotions and those of others by appropriately concentrating your feelings and focus to think more clearly.

Think of emotion as e-motion, or energy in motion. People have a wide range of ways of expressing emotions. When things are tense, some will scream while others go silent. Ironically, it's not as much the emotion itself that causes the reaction, but the person's inability to withstand the strong feelings of emotion in their body that causes their reaction.

You need the ability to maintain equilibrium when surprise profits – or extreme market meltdowns – occur right in front of you. It will save you from irrational actions. This ultimately *saves* you money and makes you money by allowing you to make better, more rational, trading choices.

Options mechanics, technical details, and market structures are all facts. Out of all the details above, the only unknown is discipline. You're the wildcard. Do you have the time and discipline to learn, or are you just eager to jump in for fun? Jumping in doesn't work for football, ice skating, or NASA. It doesn't work for options either. There's a process. Everyone can get it, but it takes time and education.

Pete and I can definitely pass decades of information to you with precision. We just need to know that you have the proper mindset – the proper E.I. – to catch it.

Investitute Takeaway

Options are the only tools that will allow investors to successfully navigate the new markets. However, there is a process you must follow. Before you jump into options or new strategies, make sure you have the discipline to take the necessary steps. Today's computerized trading does make it seemingly easy to invest. Just click a button and anyone can send an order – even from their phone. Sending orders is not investing. Anyone can do that. If you want to accomplish your financial goals in today's risky markets, you have to use options, but you have to understand there is a process to follow. It doesn't just take intelligence to master the markets. It takes emotional intelligence. Know your E.I.

RULE 4

Price is Not Risk

Some people see the glass half full. Others see it half empty. Comedian George Carlin said he sees a glass that's twice as big as it needs to be. People have different ways of seeing things, and all may be correct at certain times. When it comes to options trading, though, traders have a way of viewing risk that's not only wrong, it's dangerous for today's markets.

Most traders see the option's price as the risk. If an option costs one dollar, they may say, "I'm only risking a dollar," which sounds like it's low risk. On the other hand, if they see a $20 option, they immediately think it's high risk since they could now possibly lose $20. Price is not risk. And if you teach yourself to see price as the risk, you're going to see the markets in exactly the opposite way they actually work.

What is Financial Risk?

When someone talks about investment risk, it means the probability of losing some or all of your money. If you put $1,000 into an investment and there's no chance of losing it, such as with a government T-bill or bank CD, it's a risk-free investment. A risk-free investment, however, just means it's free from default risk – you'll always get your money back.

All investments, even risk-free ones, are subject to inflation risk. Inflation risk means your investment may lose value because of inflation. If you earned 2% on a bank CD but inflation was 3%, you're actually worse off by 1% – even though you have more money. You can buy fewer things with it, so your investment lost money in terms of buying power. That's inflation risk.

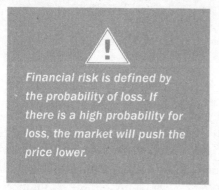

Financial risk is defined by the probability of loss. If there is a high probability for loss, the market will push the price lower.

On the other hand, if you have a high probability of losing that money, such as with junk bonds or penny stocks, it's a high-risk investment. Placing $10,000 into a T-bill is not high risk, even though you have a lot of money tied up into it. There's no risk because there's no chance of losing it. If you buy $1,000 worth of a penny stock, you shouldn't say it's low risk just because it only cost a small fraction of the T-bill. Risk isn't defined by the amount of money you have into the position; it's defined by the probability of losing it. If risk was defined by price, your state lottery would be the best investment on the planet: It only costs a dollar – and you might make millions.

Why do so many traders see the price as risk? It's because they don't understand that the financial market is a continuous live auction. Rather than having rare art or memorabilia for sale, it has financial assets – stocks, bonds, futures, options, and many others. It's up to the market to decide what each is worth, and those values change based on new information. The new information may reveal that a stock, for example, is going to have exceptional future growth. You may see the stock price rise on that news. On the other hand, the information may reveal that there's additional risk in the stock, and now you may see the price fall.

One you see how markets price things, you'll see there's a connection between the true risk of the investment and the reward you may get.

Let's say you're at an auction that has a unique offering – mystery boxes of cash for sale. Of course, being an auction, you must bid on them. The auctioneer has one box for sale, and it's guaranteed to have $100 cash inside. The crowd recognizes the box is worth $100 because the cash inside is known. It's a guaranteed deal. In response, the auctioneer will receive close to $100. There's no reason to expect much less.

If one person bids one dollar for the box, it would be a free $99 to that person if the bidding stopped there. Somebody will surely compete and bid two dollars to capture the $100. Others will join in and the bids will rise to $3, $4, and so on. That process continues quickly, with each bidder competing against the next until the bidding stops close to $100. There's no reason to fear bidding higher amounts. It's free money to the highest bidder. However, if the bidding stops at $99, the reward is only one dollar. The guaranteed known cash gave bidders the incentive to bid high and, in response, left the winner with a low reward.

However, let's say the auctioneer puts two boxes up, but only one contains $100; the other is empty. The high bidder gets to select one box. Now the auction is only for a possible $100. It's not guaranteed, so bidders will push the price down. The auctioneer may only get $30 for this deal. If the high bidder selects the correct box, it's a big reward – he wins $100 by paying $30. But it wasn't guaranteed. The winning bid could have just as easily been lost.

Businesses are priced the same way. You'll pay a lot more for a McDonald's franchise than a small mom-and-pop coffee shop. A McDonald's restaurant produces far more cash – and far more consistently. There's more money to get, and a higher chance of getting it, so it will carry a higher market price.

All financial assets are priced the same way. Financial assets have possible payoffs – hidden cash – and it's up to the market to decide how much that package is worth. The crowd places bids depending on the amount of potential cash and the probability of receiving it.

When the government puts a $10,000 T-bill up for auction, investors know it's a package that contains exactly $10,000. In response, the market will bid very close to $10,000, say $9,950. By placing a high value on the asset, it leaves a small reward. Just because it has a high price and small reward doesn't mean it's a bad investment. That relationship is due to the guaranteed nature of the T-bill. Markets don't like risk. When things are risk-free, people bid aggressively and leave very little reward as a result.

Now let's look at the penny stock. Is it possible the company could end up being worth millions or billions of dollars? Yes, it's possible – just don't count on it. The market realizes there's probably not much cash in this company, and no matter how much cash it may potentially be worth, there's a low chance of that value being realized. Even though it's possible the penny stock may be worth more than the T-bill, the market isn't willing to pay much for it. The crowd may bid one dollar per share. By placing a low price on the asset, it potentially leaves a very big reward if it pays off.

However, if you see price as risk, you'll be led to believe the T-bill is high risk since it costs $9,950 while the penny stock is low risk since it only costs a dollar. Now you can see why that's a dangerous way to view risk. High price doesn't mean high risk. Low price doesn't mean low risk. Instead, price is formed in response to the risk. If an asset has high risk, the market will bid low. Low price equals high risk. High price is a result of low risk.

The T-bill's high price is a direct reflection of its zero-risk quality while the low-priced stock is a result of the perceived high risk.

The options market works exactly the same way. Options are just disguised boxes of cash. The $100 call for example, will be worth $1 if the stock is $101 at expiration, $2 if the stock is $102, and so on. The amount of cash the option could be worth is unknown, but the more cash that could be in the option at expiration, and the higher the probability for getting it, the higher the price market is willing to pay.

IBM is currently trading for $134.10 and a few of the 30-day strikes are listed below:

STRIKE	CALL PRICE
110	24.15
115	19.25
120	14.00
125	9.52
130	5.75
135	2.62
140	0.87

New traders feel the $110 strike is riskier since it costs $24.15. They feel there's more money to lose, so it must be riskier. Many would lean toward buying the $140 strike for 87 cents thinking it's lower risk. From their perspective, that's the most they can lose, so it therefore has less risk.

That's exactly the opposite of what's happening. Instead, the market recognizes the $110 strike will most likely contain cash – intrinsic value – at expiration. In other words, it's far more likely to be in-the-money in the next 30 days. Because it's unlikely for IBM to fall below $110 in the next month, the market feels there's definitely going to be quite a bit of intrinsic value in this option. Traders are therefore willing to pay a higher price.

New traders may look at the $110 strike and wonder who'd ever pay $24.15 for an option. It seems risky. But price isn't risk. The breakeven point is $110 + $24.15 = $134.15, which is just five cents above IBM's current price. That option really isn't even an option any more – it's acting like the stock. The market is essentially saying that this option is definitely going to have intrinsic value at expiration. In response, the market bids high. It's actually a low-risk option, which is why the price is relatively high.

On the other hand, the market recognizes the $140 strike is probably going to be out-of-the-money. Its breakeven point is $140 + $0.87 = $140.87. While it's possible for IBM to reach that level in 30 days, the stock would have to climb over 5% during the month, and that's highly unlikely – at least that's the way the market sees it now. If the market felt it had a great chance for being above $140, it would push that price much higher than 87 cents. Even if the call does end up in-the-money, it's probably not going to be by much, so it wouldn't be worth a whole lot. Traders sense there's not going to be a lot of cash in that option, and a very good chance they'll lose all their money. It's risky. In response to the higher risk, they bid the price lower to 87 cents.

Options traders are often tempted to trade the out-of-the-money strikes on the belief they're less risky. To succeed, you have to realize that price is not risk.

The mistake new traders make is to assume that all options have an equal chance of making money. They don't recognize the options market is a live auction and traders are bidding on the prices of these assets according to what they think they'll be worth in the future. If traders feel the options could be worth a lot, they'll bid higher. If they feel they're not going to be worth much, they'll bid lower. High prices are therefore associated with less risky options while low prices are associated with higher risk – exactly the opposite of how most traders see it.

Of course, it's true that you could lose more money by purchasing the $110 strike for $24.15, but that doesn't mean it's riskier. One hundred shares of IBM will cost a lot more than a lottery ticket, but that doesn't mean you should "invest" in lottery tickets to control the amount you could lose. All you're doing is setting yourself up for guaranteed failure. If you set yourself up for failure, don't expect your investments to do well. You must see risk for what it is, and price is not risk.

Price is the Equalizer

Because of price, there's another curiosity about investments that's counterintuitive. All investments are technically the same in terms of risk. In other words, because of price, all investments are equalized. Price accounts for the risk. All things being equal, higher risk investments are less desirable. In response, the market bids less for them. The low price leaves potentially higher rewards. There is a commensurate reward to balance that high risk. On the other hand, all things being equal, low-risk investments are more desirable, but their prices are bid higher as a result. The high price leaves a smaller reward, but that smaller reward is commensurate for the low risk. The price shows the amount people are willing to pay for potential cash in a financial asset. The lower the risk, the higher the market is willing to pay and the smaller the resulting reward.

Think of price like a point spread on a football bet. Next week, the Carolina Panthers play the Washington Redskins. The Panthers are 9-0 for the season, and heavy favorites to win. Does that mean you can bet on Carolina and make easy money?

Not at all. The markets recognize the benefit in betting on Carolina. The betting crowd would recognize it's easy money to bet on Carolina, and anyone has the advantage in selecting that team. But that advantage gets factored in because you have to pay for any advantages. If it's a straight-up bet – my $10 against your $10 – nobody would bet on Washington. You'd have no market. To create a market, you have to create a way to balance the buyers and sellers. You have to have a way to make it fair for both sides. That's why Vegas will build in point spreads.

They may start the betting off with a one-point spread. If they find they have more people willing to bet on Carolina than Washington, Vegas increases it to two points. The process continues. Eventually, the point spread will reach a level where you'll get an equal number of buyers and sellers. For this game, Vegas settled on a 7.5 point spread. By subtracting 7.5 points from Carolina's final score, the betting crowd couldn't figure out which side of the bet was favored.

The point spread equalized it. In the eyes of the crowd, it was now fair. There's no reason to think that one side has an advantage, and there will be an equal number of bettors for both teams. A buyer can be matched with every seller.

That's exactly the role of price in the markets. Prices act to equalize buyers and sellers. Because of price, you can never say for sure that the buyer or seller has the advantage. It's exactly like saying the person who bets on the favored team must always have the edge. The point spread removes any advantage. Likewise, in the financial markets, price accounts for all advantages – and makes the asset fair to the buyer and seller.

The Highest Bidder Determines Price

Because the financial markets create prices by a competitive bidding process, the current market price is viewed as fair by buyers and sellers. That doesn't mean that the prices can't be volatile. First, new information can change investors' perceptions of just how much cash may be in that asset. But more interestingly, the market price is determined by the highest bidder. If an option is priced at $5, it doesn't necessarily mean that's the highest price that someone thinks it's worth. Instead, all it shows is the price at which the second highest bidder was not willing to cross.

Think of it like bidding for something on eBay. You're *willing* to pay $100, but right now you're the high bidder at $50. Everybody sees the auction is priced at $50 right now. Why isn't the price at $100, which is the highest price you're willing to pay? It's because the second highest bidder isn't willing to cross your current $50 price. The only way to get you to increase your price toward $100 is if another bidder is willing to pay more than your current $50 bid. So the current price doesn't really show the highest price that someone is willing to pay. It just shows the price at which the second highest bidder isn't willing to cross. For this reason, you can see quick jumps in all prices, but especially options because they're relatively low priced to begin with.

The Risk of Today's Markets

To succeed with options in today's markets, you can't see risk in the wrong way. As markets become more volatile, new traders will naturally gravitate to lower-cost options thinking they're taking less risk. They're not. The better way to approach the markets is to know your options and create profiles that hedge the unwanted risks but leave ample profits open. It never makes sense to put yourself into a guaranteed losing position – just so you can limit losses. Yet that's how many traders will end up if they see price as risk.

Once you understand how markets work, you'll see that all investments are priced according to risk. You can't say that one is necessarily better because any benefits have been priced into the asset. Instead, each strike and strategy is just a different set of risks and rewards. If you want to make money with options, find the strategies that allow you to accomplish your goals for the least amount of risk. Don't try to find the magic strategy that has high returns for no risk; they don't exist. Instead, match the risk to your goals and you'll find success is much easier by using options since they allow you to alter risk-reward profiles in ways stock traders cannot.

No matter how you choose to approach trading and strategies, you have to understand that price doesn't represent the risk. But there is a big risk in seeing the role of price the wrong way. Traders who think price is risk will be doing exactly the opposite of what they need to do to survive. There are many new risks in today's markets, and you don't need to make things worse by seeing risk in the wrong way. Don't make risk twice as big as it needs to be.

Investitute Takeaway

It's easy to think that a low-priced option means it's low risk. Always remember that options are priced by an auction, and traders are bidding up the price according to the amount of rewards it may produce along with the probability of receiving it. If you're using high-risk options believing they're low risk, you're going to set yourself up for failure. When those options fail, you'll turn to even cheaper options thinking you're reducing the risk. That's heading the wrong way. To succeed, you have to take some risk, but don't add to the risk unnecessarily. Low-priced options are not low-risk. They're high risk, which is why the market pushed the price lower. To succeed in today's markets, you must have a clear perception of risk.

RULE 5

Know Your Option Price Boundaries

Investors may know no boundaries of what they feel an option is worth, but options have price boundaries that can't be broken. Most traders would think that an option's price can be anything – it just depends on the supply and demand. While supply and demand certainly play an important role, they can only drive option prices so high or low before other option pricing boundaries begin to take control. To survive the new markets, you need to use the right strategies. And they'll only work if you understand the boundaries that option prices must follow.

You Must Pay for Advantages

In the financial markets, advantages must be paid for. If one financial asset has an advantage over another, the market will recognize the advantage and compete more aggressively for it. The result is that the assets with perceived advantages will end up with a higher price. All advantages get baked into the price. This doesn't just happen with financial markets; it will happen with any auction-style market. Again, think of eBay.

If you place a Timex watch and a Rolex watch on eBay, you can be sure the Rolex will fetch more money. The market recognizes there are advantages in the Rolex compared to the Timex, so it will automatically put a higher price on the Rolex. The market takes care of that all by itself. It doesn't need any coaxing or prompting from anyone.

For exactly the same reasons, the options markets recognize that some options strikes or expirations have advantages over others. In response, traders push those prices higher. The new rules of investing require you to know the rules of pricing. If you've traded options before, you've probably wondered how to determine which strikes, expirations, and strategies are right for you. Strategies are used to take advantage of pricing discrepancies, but they'll only work once you understand the boundaries that option prices must follow.

All Options Must be Worth at Least Their Intrinsic Value

For any financial transaction, the cash value is always the minimum value. If you're an analyst trying to value Apple Computer and find it has $200 billion in cash, it has to be worth at least that much. Cash is cash, and if there's no risk of not getting it, one dollar has to be worth one dollar. That's exactly how options work too.

If you have a $100 call and the stock is $110, the call must be worth at least the $10 intrinsic value. That's the amount of guaranteed cash sitting in the option right now. The call holder knows for sure that the call could be exercised for $100 and the stock could be immediately sold for $110, which would leave the holder with $10 cash. Because that intrinsic value is instantly guaranteed, it has to be the minimum call value. If there's any time remaining, traders will be willing to pay more than $10 for the $100 call. But one thing you know for sure is that if the stock is $110, no matter how much or how little time may remain on the contract, it must be worth at least $10.

If the market valued it less than $10, it provides an opportunity for free money, which is called *arbitrage*. If the $100 call was trading for only $9, traders could buy the call for $9, exercise the call and pay $100 to get the shares. That's a total of $109. Then they could instantly sell the stock for $110. Because traders could make an instant free dollar, they'll continue to buy the $100 call and push its price higher. When it trades for at least the $10 intrinsic value, the free-money opportunity stops. What you need to understand is that all in-the-money calls must be worth at least their intrinsic value.

All in-the-money put options work the same way for the same reasons. If you have the $100 put and the stock is $90, the put must be worth at least the $10 intrinsic value. The put gives you the right to sell shares for $100 when they're only worth $90 in the market. That's guaranteed cash. All you'd have to do is buy the shares for $90, exercise the put, and collect the $100 exercise price. You're guaranteed to be left with the $10 cash.

Because in-the-money options are guaranteed to always be worth the current intrinsic value, the market values all options for at least the intrinsic value. The market recognizes that cash is 100% guaranteed at the time of purchase, so it must be reflected in the price.

Here are some IBM call and put prices with the stock at $138.50:

IBM = $138.50		
IBM JAN 2016 (55 DAYS)		
CALLS	STRIKE	PUTS
23.75	115	0.26
19.10	120	0.45
14.55	125	0.71
10.00	130	1.28
6.02	135	2.42
3.12	140	4.52
1.31	145	7.72
0.50	150	11.95

With the stock at $138.50, the $115 strike is $23.50 in-the-money. That's the intrinsic, or cash value. Because of that, you know the option must be worth at least $23.50, and the above table shows the market has valued it at $23.75. The remaining 25 cents is time value. The $120 strike is $18.50 in-the-money, so it must be worth at least that much. The table shows the market has valued it at $19.10. The additional 60 cents is the time value.

Any call strikes above the current $138.50 stock price are out-of-the-money, so there's no intrinsic value minimum. It's up to the market to decide what the time value's worth. For the $140 call, there's no intrinsic value, so there's no guaranteed cash in it. It's out-of-the-money, and the $3.12 price is all time value.

Likewise, all in-the-money puts have to be worth at least their intrinsic value. The $150 put is $11.50 in-the-money. Because you now realize that all options must be worth at least their cash value, you know that put must be worth at least $11.50. The market has valued it at $11.95. The additional 45 cents is the time value. Any put strikes below the current $138.50 stock price have no intrinsic value, so their prices are all time values.

The $130 put, for example, is out-of-the-money, so there's no intrinsic value, or immediate cash that can be extracted from the put. Its $1.28 premium is all time value, and it's up to the market to decide that price. All options, calls and puts, must always be worth at least their intrinsic value at all times.

Lower-Strike Calls and Higher-Strike Puts are Worth More Money

Different strikes will be worth different prices, but is there any relationship between the strikes and prices? Yes, the lower strike calls and higher strike puts have to be worth more money.

This relationship is pretty easy to understand if you think about the rights that options convey. If you buy shares of stock, you'd rather have a lower cost basis rather than a higher cost basis. In other words, you're better off paying $50 per share rather than $55 per share. Lower purchase prices are always better than higher ones, all other things being equal. But when you put that same principle in terms of option strikes, new traders get it wrong the majority of the time.

If you buy a $50 call, you have the right to buy shares for $50 per share. However, if you buy the $55 call, you'd have the right to pay $55 per share. The market recognizes the $50 strike is a more advantageous purchase price, and in response will place a higher price on the $50 call compared to the $55 call. The advantage in the $50 call has been priced in, and it now carries a higher price.

It may help to visualize this relationship another way. The $50 call can always capture more intrinsic value compared to the $55 strike. Pick any stock price above $50, and you'll see that the $50 call always has more intrinsic value. If the stock is $60, the $50 call has $10 of intrinsic value, while the $55 calls has only five dollars. If the stock is below $50, both options are out-of-the-money, but the $50 is closer to the stock price. It has a better chance of becoming in-the-money, so it still has an advantage over the $55 strike. No matter where the stock's price may be, the $50 call always has an advantage compared to the $55 call, so it will always carry a higher price. Lower strike calls are like throwing a bigger cast net into the water. It's more likely to come up with fish. Lower strike calls are more likely to catch intrinsic value. Traders recognize the advantage and respond by bidding prices higher.

Put options work in the opposite way, and higher strikes must be worth more money. If you buy a put option, you have the right to sell shares for the strike price. When you sell shares of stock, higher selling prices are more advantageous. All things being equal, you'd rather sell your shares for $55 rather than $50. So for put options, the pricing will be reversed, and higher strike puts will carry greater prices than lower strikes.

The previous table on page 63 shows that as the call strikes
get lower (smaller numbers), the option's price gets higher.
The opposite relationship holds for puts. That's not a
coincidence. It's just the markets at work, and traders are
automatically pricing the advantages into each strike. With
IBM at $138.50, notice that the $115 strike's breakeven price
is $138.75 – just 25 cents higher than the stock. The $115
strike is really more like shares of stock, yet new traders will
view it as an expensive option. They'd be tempted to buy
strikes near the bottom of the list. If they buy the $150 strike,
the breakeven point is $150.50, almost 9% above the current
stock price. With only 55 days remaining, it's highly unlikely
that the $150 call will ever materialize and be worth anything
at expiration. It's not at all acting like shares of stock. It's far
riskier, and that's why it's cheaper. As call strikes get lower,
the options are behaving more like shares of stock. For puts,
as strikes get higher, the options are behaving more like short
shares of stock.

Calls and Puts Have Maximum Values

Call option prices get larger as the strikes get lower. If you
could push a strike price all the way to zero, it would always
capture 100% of the stock's intrinsic value. If there was such a
thing as a zero-strike call, it would be worth exactly the stock's
price. It can't be worth more because the very best you can
do is to exercise the call and get the shares. It can't be worth
less, because you're always capturing 100% of the stock price.
This often seems counterintuitive. New traders think that if you
have a low strike call with an infinite amount of time, it would
be outrageously expensive. Instead, it would be worth exactly
the stock's price. This is one way to show that options are not
necessarily risky compared to shares. You can make them behave
exactly like shares if you choose. What makes stock trading
riskier is that you have no choice but to accept losses all the
way down to zero. Options traders get to choose much smaller
maximum losses.

For put options, the maximum price is the strike price. Put options get more valuable as the stock price falls, but the lowest price a stock can fall to is zero. If you own the $50 put, the very most that option could ever be worth is $50. Of course, that would be very rare as it means the stock price must be all the way to zero. In most cases, you're going to see the put price trade at a premium far less than the strike price.

This is an important point for traders buying puts on low-priced stocks. Sometimes traders look at a $10 stock and buy a $5 put option thinking they can make a lot of money if the price falls on upcoming bad news. The most the $5 put could ever be worth is $5, and the chance for any stock to fall to zero are pretty slim, especially in a fairly short time. Before you buy puts on low-priced stocks, recognize the maximum boundary and see if it's worth trading.

Calls and puts have maximum values. For calls, the maximum value is the stock price. For puts, it's the strike price. No matter how good or bad things get, those are the limits.

At Expiration, All Options are Worth Either Zero or Intrinsic Value

At expiration, all option time values become zero. If there is any intrinsic value, it remains with the option.

All options eventually expire. As time passes, the option will lose a little bit of time value each day. One thing certain about option prices is that all time values must be zero at expiration. The only reason for paying time value is because time remains. Once time has expired, all time value must be gone too. However, that doesn't mean all option prices are zero at expiration. New traders often hear that all options expire worthless. That's not true. If there's any intrinsic value, it remains with the option. It's only the time value that becomes zero at expiration. Looking at the previous call and put prices with 55 days

to expiration, the $130 call is worth $10. You can break that down
into $8.50 intrinsic value and $1.50 time value. Recall the time-
value formula:

Premium – Intrinsic Value = Time Value

In this example, $10 premium - $8.50 intrinsic value = $1.50 time value

Assuming the stock's price remains at $138.50, as time passes, this
option will slowly lose $1.50 worth of value and be worth $8.50 at
expiration. It will not lose the entire $10 strictly from the passage
of time. Don't confuse that to think this option is guaranteed to be
worth $8.50. You could lose the entire $10 premium, but only if the
stock's price fell below the $130 strike. The passage of time only
affects the time value.

However, if the option is out-of-the-money then it will expire
worthless. There is no intrinsic value for it to maintain. For
example, the IBM $140 call was trading for $3.12. That's 100%
time value. If IBM doesn't rise above the $140 strike at expiration,
the $140 call will lose all of its value and expire worthless.
However, if IBM rises to $142 at expiration, the $140 call would
be worth exactly the $2 intrinsic value at expiration.

Put options work exactly the same way: At expiration, they lose
100% of their time value, but will keep any intrinsic value that
may be present. The $135 put is trading for $2.42, but will be
worthless at expiration unless the stock falls below $135.

At expiration, all options either expire worthless or are worth just
the intrinsic value. There are no in-between values.

Understanding the relationship between intrinsic and time values
shows that options are a race against time. If you buy the $140
call for $3.12, you'd need the stock to rise to the breakeven
price of $140 + $3.12 = $143.12 at expiration just to get your
money back. At that price, the $140 call would have gained
$3.12 worth of intrinsic value but lost $3.12 in time value. You'd

just break even. The stock price rose, but it didn't rise fast enough to create a profit by expiration. Options not only need direction to profit, they need speed. However, by selecting different strikes and expirations, traders can control the amount of speed necessary to profit. To understand the strategies, you have to understand the option's relationship with intrinsic and time values.

Longer-Dated Options Are More Expensive

When it comes to options pricing, just remember that more time means more money. For any given strike, the longer the time to expiration, the more expensive the calls and puts will be.

Think about the insurance market. If you call your auto insurance company and ask for a six-month quote and a one-year quote with the same terms, the one-year policy will cost more. For the same reasons, option sellers will only sell longer-dated options if they can get higher premiums.

In the financial markets, time is risk. The more time allowed, the more time there is for the stock's price to move – up or down.

Option sellers only receive a one-time, fixed premium from the sale, just like insurance companies. After that, they're at risk of stock price movement. The more time allowed, the further the stock price could work against them, so they'll only sell if they can get higher premiums.

While price movement is a bad property for sellers, it's good for buyers. Buyers are just on the opposite side of the trade. They pay a fixed premium, but have no limits on the profits if the stock price moves. Option buyers want to see lots of price action. More time gives buyers a better chance for the stock to move in their favor, so time is an advantage. It is true that more time will also give the calls or puts more time to fall out-of-the-money, but there's only a limited loss in that direction. Option buyers benefit from seeing big price moves.

Buyers are willing to pay more money, and sellers are going to command more. The result is that longer-dated options – calls or puts – will cost more money. Comparing the previous IBM calls with the April 2016 expiration having 146 days to expiration, you can see that longer-dated options cost more money:

	55 DAYS	146 DAYS
STRIKE	CALLS	CALLS
115	23.75	24.50
120	19.10	19.75
125	14.55	15.90
130	10.00	12.00
135	6.02	8.70
140	3.12	6.00
145	1.31	3.92
150	0.50	2.40

You'll find the same relationship for put options. Remember that price is not risk. All too often, new traders believe longer-dated options are riskier because they cost more. The market is pricing the longer-dated options with higher values because option buyers recognize the benefit of time. They're just paying for that advantage.

Square-Root Pricing Rule

While longer-dated options will cost more money, they won't cost as much as you might think. In fact, when you consider the amount of time you're getting, longer dated options are actually cheaper than shorter dated options.

Traders often think that if a one-month option costs a dollar, a two-month option must cost two dollars – twice the time, twice the price. It sounds right, but it's not. It turns out that it takes about four times the amount of time to double an option's price. If a one-month option costs one dollar, the four-month option will be priced at two dollars:

TIME TO EXPIRATION	OPTION PREMIUM	COST/MONTH
One-month	$1	$1
Four-months	$2	$0.50

It's called the square-root pricing rule because it takes four times the amount of time in order to double an option's price. In the table above, there's four times the amount of time between the options. The square root of four is two, which becomes the multiplier for the price. The four-month option will only be only two times the value of the one-month option – not four times as it may seem. Because the one-month option costs one dollar, the four-month option will be twice as much and cost two dollars. Even though the longer-dated option has four times the amount of time, its price is only doubled from one dollar to two dollars.

Options are priced according to volatility, which is proportional to the square root of time. It's counterintuitive, but that's the science of stock price movement.

Even though the four-month option is more expensive in total ($2 vs. $1), when you consider the time you're getting, the cost is sharply reduced. In the previous table, the four-month option costs 50 cents per month while the one-month option costs one dollar per month. For new traders, it appears that the four-month option is twice as expensive as the first, but it's actually half as much once you consider the amount of time you're getting for your money. There's a pricing relationship at work that makes longer-date options a better deal for buyers, and a progressively worse deal for sellers. That's why professional traders generally buy longer-dated options and sell shorter-dated ones. For options buyers, this pricing relationship plays an important role in selecting expirations for strategies. Just remember that option prices are proportional to the square root of time. Longer-dated options will cost you more money, but they're actually cheaper per unit of time, such as per month or per day.

The Difference Pricing Rule

Because there are limits on option prices, there must be relationships between strikes: For any two calls (or any two puts) the difference in their prices cannot be greater than the difference in strikes. Looking at the previous IBM quotes, if you select any two strikes, you'll see that the difference in those options prices is less than the difference in strikes:

55 DAYS		
STRIKE	CALL PRICE	DIFFERENCE
115	23.75	$4.65
120	19.10	
125	14.55	
130	10.00	
135	6.02	$2.90
140	3.12	
145	1.31	
150	0.50	

Take a look at the $115 and $120 strikes. That's a five-dollar difference, but the difference in the prices is $4.65 – it's less than five dollars. Comparing the $135 and $140 strikes, again that's a five-dollar difference, but the difference in prices is $2.90.

You don't just have to use adjacent strikes. Comparing the $120 call and $130 call is a $10 difference, but there's only a difference of $9.10 in prices. Why can't the difference in prices ever be greater than the difference in strikes?

If you buy the $115 call, you have the right to purchase shares for $115 per share. On the other hand, if you purchased the $120 call, you have the right to buy the shares for $120. If both options control the same stock for the same amount of time, the only advantage the $115 call provides over the $120 call is a $5 benefit – that's it. By purchasing the $115 call, you have the right to pay $5 less than if you owned the $120 call.

You know the lower-strike $115 call has to be worth more money than the $120 strike, but should now see that it can't be priced by more than the $5 difference. Yes, you must pay for any advantages conveyed in an option, but you shouldn't expect to pay more than what the advantage is worth. The market's not going to pay $5.01 – or more – for $5 worth of a benefit. If the $115 call is priced at $23.75, the very minimum the $120 call could be worth is just $5 less, or 18.75.

This difference pricing rule says the *maximum* difference between two option prices is the difference in strikes. Prior to expiration, however, you'll usually see the difference is less.

Let's break the $115 and $120 strikes down into their intrinsic and time values. With IBM at $138.50, the $115 call has $23.50 intrinsic value and 25 cents time value. The $120 call has $18.50 intrinsic value and 0.60 time value:

STRIKE	PREMIUM	INTRINSIC VALUE	TIME VALUE
115	23.75	23.50	0.25
120	19.10	18.50	0.60

However, you also know that once expiration arrives, all time values

become zero. That means the $115 call will just be worth exactly
the $23.50 intrinsic value and the $120 call will be worth exactly
the $18.50 intrinsic value, and the difference in the prices is now
exactly five dollars. As long as there is any presence of time value, the
difference in the prices cannot be greater than the difference in strikes.

You have two basic conditions where any two options will start to
converge to the difference in strikes. First, if both options are in-the-
money but with very little time to expiration.

If IBM was $121 – just barely above the $120 strike, but there's only
a day or so to expiration, you may see the $115 call priced at $6.10
and the $120 call priced at $1.20. The difference is $4.90. It's close
to the five-dollar difference, but not quite there. That's because
there's still a tiny bit of time value on both options. But if the stock
price stays the same and time continues to tick by, the time values
eventually become zero. The $115 call will be $6, and the $55
call will be $1, and there's now exactly a five-dollar difference. As
long as both options are in-the-money, but there's not much time
remaining, you may see the difference in prices being close to the
difference in strikes.

The second condition where you may see two option prices
converge to the difference in strikes is when there's a lot of time to
expiration, but both strikes are very deep in-the-money. Let's say
IBM shoots up from $138.50 to $150 over the next 25 days. There
was 55 days to expiration, but now there's only 30 days remaining.
Even though there's still quite a bit of time, both options are very
deep in-the-money, so the market is pretty sure they'll both expire
with intrinsic value. The time values will be low. You may see the
$115 call trading for $35.30 and the $120 call priced at $30.50.
The difference is now $4.80, but if the stock price is still $150 at
expiration, all time values become zero, and the difference in the
options will be exactly five dollars.

Options may be may appear to have no rhyme or reason to their
prices, and it's easy to think that option prices could be any
value at all. But once you understand the intricate relationships

that go into options pricing, the quote board becomes a matrix of patterns, shapes, and symmetry. It's also your hunting ground for opportunity. Winning with options is not just about understanding strategies. Strategies allow you to take advantages of pricing discrepancies, but you have to apply prices provided by the market. There are definite patterns to understand. The new rules of investing require you to know the rules of pricing. The machines know them well.

Investitute Takeaway

Option prices are not just random numbers appearing on your screen. They're bids and offers from other traders in a live auction. When you understand the rights and obligations that options convey, you'll see option prices have to remain within certain boundaries. Sometimes prices are a little high; other times a little low. If you just see a board filled with numbers, you'll see disorder. But if you understand these pricing relationships, you'll see opportunities.

RULE 6

Balance Fear & Greed

It's a fine line between man and machine. It's an even finer line between fear and greed. Greed propels markets higher, causing opportunities for fortunes to be made. Since 2010, Apple shares increased from about $8 per share to $120 for an average return of 32% per year for five straight years. Going into the close of 2015, Amazon.com and Netflix doubled - and the year wasn't even over.

Fear, however, sends markets crashing down, causing huge losses. Who would believe that Blackberry – at one time more dominating than Apple's iPhone – would fall from $66 to $6 in a couple of years? Enron, once considered the king of all stocks, fell from $90 to nothing in a matter of months. Fear and greed cause stock prices to rise and fall dramatically. Today, however, we have other concerns to compound the fears.

Most trades are executed by computer, and they can cause positive feedback loops. In other words, if a stock price begins to fall, computers may see the hordes of sellers lining up and begin shorting shares to capitalize on the impending drop. As share prices fall more, it triggers stop orders for yet more investors. That causes computers to send even more orders thus sending share prices plummeting even faster. The more prices fall, the more they accelerate. When this happens, the results can be dramatic.

For example, on May 6, 2010, traders were traumatized by the Flash Crash, where the Dow fell nearly 1,000 points, or about 9%, within minutes wiping out nearly one trillion dollars in stock market valuations. While most of those losses were recouped within 36 minutes of trading, for many investors, the damage was already done. Stop orders were triggered, and losses were realized that never should have occurred. Whether it should have occurred or not is not the issue. The issue is that the investors who lost had no recourse. Despite their best efforts to invest money into good quality stocks, they ended up on the losing side. It doesn't have to be your fault in order to lose money. It just has to occur in your account. And that's now a big possibility with today's electronic trading.

Another bizarre incident occurred in August 2000 when Emulex, which traded under the ticker EMLX at the time. A press release came out in the morning which said the CEO was stepping down because of an SEC investigation and that past earnings reports were going to be revised downward. Of all the bad things a company could possibly report, it doesn't get much worse than that. It's not the type of news shareholders like to hear. But there was nothing you could do because the exchanges halted trading. Shares can be halted during the day if the news is deemed to be significant enough to materially alter the stock's price. The exchanges want to give people time to digest the news and think about it before everyone begins selling and creating chaos. Instead, trading halts usually serve to let people stew and agonize. Traders will instantly line up at the gates just waiting to sell upon the halt being lifted.

That's exactly what happened. After the halt was lifted, Emulex dropped from about $104 to $43 – a 58% loss – within 16 minutes. It instantly wiped out $2.2 billion in market capitalization. The stock continued to trade because Emulex was headquartered in California – three hours behind the east coast, so nobody from the company could be contacted. The stock just crashed, and investors lost millions. Occasionally, stocks do crash in reaction to news. That's not necessarily a problem. It's just the market doing its job and trying to figure out what the shares are worth.

This time, there was just one small problem…

The press release was a hoax. It was sent by a former employee of Internet Wire, who knew how to format the story to appear real. There was no reason for the news outlets to not believe it. He shorted shares hoping to profit from the fall. Once the story was confirmed to be a hoax, the stock quickly recovered most of the losses – but not without leaving devastation in its wake.

Yes, the offender did serve 44 months in jail, gave up his $250,000 profits, and was also fined $103,000. Big deal. The state made that money. None of it made its way back to the shareholders who potentially lost millions. It's a risk of being in a market where information can flow quickly. Just imagine if that happened today. It would have been on Twitter and the entire world would have known in seconds. The selling pressure could have been much worse. It's a risk of today's markets, and you have to know ways to defend against technology glitches – and fraud.

Option Rights to the Rescue

Option traders, however, survived the scare. They were never unfairly triggered out of positions. They had the right to decide to buy or sell. The market doesn't make that decision for them. Because they're locked into fixed strike prices, there's no reason to rush the decision. Option buyers get to wait until expiration to see the outcome – and then make decisions. Having the right to decide, and the ability to wait, was a big advantage.

Many Emulex call options went nearly worthless instantly. With the stock down 58%, they were far out-of-the-money. There's no reason to sell the calls as you wouldn't get anything for them anyway. You might as well hang on and hope for the best. You can't do any worse, but you might do better. That's the option coming to the rescue and reducing its value when stock prices fall. Stock traders, on the other hand, took the ride down – dollar-for-dollar – and either sold or got triggered out with stops. Once the stock rebounded quickly, they weren't holding profits, just regrets. That didn't happen to a single call option owner.

That's important for today's markets. It used to be enough to follow a company's P/E ratios or other fundamental data to determine if the stock is under or overvalued. Not anymore. The world is now one big market, and investing has changed. Just 20 years ago, the markets used to be on edge while waiting for the Fed to release the M1 and M2 money supply numbers. Today, few investors even know what those numbers are. Anybody remember the semiconductor industry's book-to-bill ratio? That used to cause some of the biggest market swings ever. Not anymore. Investors can no longer survive by just watching U.S. economic indicators or trying to decipher hints from the Fed.

Markets are now global, and all depend on each other. In 2014, our markets went into convulsions in response to Greece collapsing, China devaluing the yuan, the banking crisis in Cyprus and Portugal, the meltdown of Argentina's peso, Russia invading Crimea, and even a passenger jet shot down in the Ukraine. The terrorist attacks of 2001 embedded deep reminders of just how connected we really are to the world. Our markets no longer just depend solely on our values; they depend on what the world thinks too. Everything is now connected to everything else.

The rules of investing have changed. Not only must you balance between fear and greed, but you have to be ready for today's potential crashes and market manipulations that will become increasingly easy to pull off. Those very technologies, however, are what provide the potential for big profits. You must be willing to let winners run – but be able to cut those losses short before they get too big. Sounds easy enough, so what's the problem?

Investors Hang Onto Losses – And Cut Winners Short

The problem is that investors are notoriously risk averse. They find it excruciatingly painful to accept losses. In response, they end up trying to gamble their way out of losing positions. Those rarely turn into wining positions. They usually just turn into bigger losses.

It's a curiosity that investors find it more satisfying to hang on to losing positions even though it means it will probably turn out to be a bigger loss. They just can't bear the thought of taking that for-sure loss. They find more satisfaction in hanging on and hoping for the best. That's not the worst of it, because the problem gets compounded.

Because investors despise taking losses, they end up selling stocks at the first sign of profit. The result is it they may end up with many small gains – but a few really big losses. That's not a plan for success. At best, it's plan for tax losses. Any strategy that involves selling shares at a predetermined level of profit – 20% for example – is just a bad idea. To succeed, you must let your winners run.

Still, traders love countering, "You can't go broke taking a profit." It sounds comforting, but it's probably the most dangerous standard for investors. You can go broke by consistently taking very small profits in the stock market. It wouldn't make sense for Exxon to go into the oil drilling business, spend billions of dollars for rigs and fields, and stop the oil flow once one rig is just above breaking even. Yet that's how most investors approach the market. They'll spend $10,000, $20,000 or more on shares of stock and sell for a hundred-dollar gain. It makes no sense. It's not a big enough profit relative to the risks. Time will surely send that approach into losing territory.

The problem for stock investors is that shares of stock are usually expensive. It's easy to get nervous when lots of money is on the line. That's why stock investors end up selling at the first sign of profit, but it's exactly the opposite of what they should be doing for success.

Whether it's an oil rig gushing out tons of oil, or a stock price gushing out gains – you have to let them run. It may be that one rig – or one stock – that provides all of your profits. Successful stock investors can always tell you what they made their money in. It's usually just one, or perhaps a few stocks. You'll never hear them say they made millions by picking up nickels in front of bulldozers.

Unfortunately, you'll never know which stocks are going to be the big winners, so the best approach is to treat them all equally and let the market determine that. You'll know which ones are the winners – after they occur. But you need to be sure that your trading plan allows you to let profits run.

Most investors never get to experience those gains because they're tempted to sell at the first sign of profit. People are wired to be risk averse. It's a safety mechanism for survival, but it's the very thing that will kill you with investing. It causes traders to gamble their way from losing positions and to sell winners too soon. They become their own worst enemy.

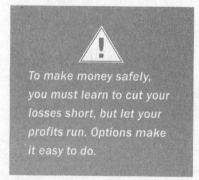

To make money safely, you must learn to cut your losses short, but let your profits run. Options make it easy to do.

The trick is to do the opposite. That's why Wall Street says to "Cut your losses short, and let your profits run." That, of course, is easier said than done when you're dealing with expensive stock. Who wants to let them run? That's exactly where options will help.

If you buy a call option, you're going to spend a small fraction of what you would spend for shares. That instantly gives you a big advantage because the most you can lose is that small amount paid. Call options force you to manage the downside risk.

By purchasing options, you're forced to cut your losses short. The instant you buy a call option, you know your maximum loss – that's good risk management. If you bought shares of stock instead, you don't know your maximum loss, other than it can't fall below zero – but that's a long way down. Are you willing to take that potential fall? Naturally, stock investors think they're going to sell the stock when it falls by a certain amount. They're sure they can limit the losses to a small, fixed amount. But once that price is reached, their instincts kick in to gamble their way from the loss. Cutting that loss is too painful.

That changes with options. Even if it's your first option trade, the call option will shield you from the temptation to gamble your way from a losing position. It won't let you lose more than what you have invested. The machines are programmed to cut losing positions short. Don't be fooled into taking the other side of the trade and letting losses run. Manage the risk, and there's no better way to do it than with options.

A Picture's Worth a Thousand Words

Options provide invaluable benefits for protecting the risks of falling stock prices. How do they help you to let winners run? Option traders can adjust their positions. There are many hedging, rolling, and morphing techniques that options traders can use to alter their risks and rewards – but stay in the position to allow profits to run further.

To appreciate rolling, you have to be able to read profit and loss diagrams, or risk profiles. These are invaluable tools for options traders, and the OptionsHouse platform will automatically draw them for you.

The graph below shows the risk graphs for shares of stock purchased at $100:

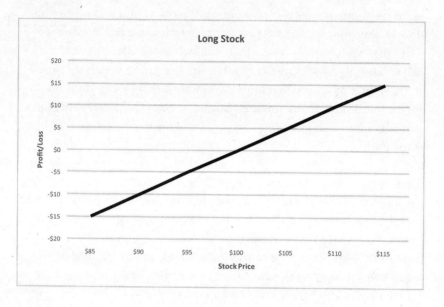

To read the graph, just pick a stock price along the horizontal axis, trace a line up to the graph, and then look to the left vertical axis for the resulting profit or loss. For example, if the stock price rises to $105, the stock investor makes a $5 gain as shown below:

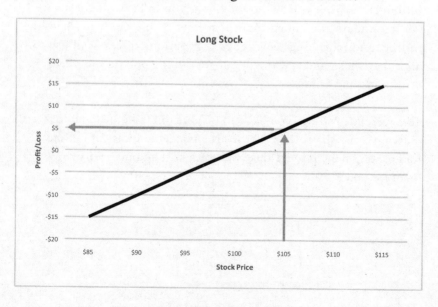

If the stock price falls to $90, the graph shows the investor loses $10. Wherever the line crosses zero, it's a breakeven point. Every strategy has at least one breakeven point. For the shares of stock, it's the $100 purchase price. If you paid $100 and sell for $100, you just break even. That's why the graph crosses zero on the horizontal axis at the $100 stock price.

A picture's worth a thousand words, and this one shows that stock traders can make dollar-for-dollar if the stock price rises, but lose dollar-for-dollar if the stock price falls. As a stock trader, you can make an unlimited amount of money at the risk of losing it all. That's an extreme outcome, and one you want to avoid. That's the big risk of owning shares of stock. You get one profit and loss diagram to choose from. It doesn't matter who you are or how long you've been investing. All stock traders share the identical profit and loss diagram – a straight line. Before you decide to buy shares of stock, always be sure to account for that unlimited downside risk. Are you willing to assume that risk in today's fast paced, electronic trading world? We didn't think so. Let's see how options will help. You'll see why they're one of the new rules of investing. A $100 call option purchased for $5 looks like this:

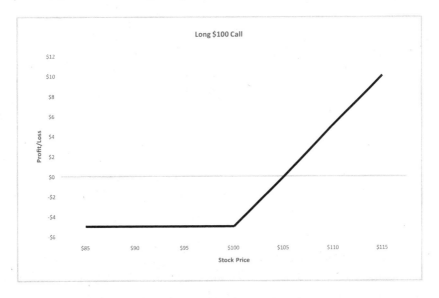

Notice that the long call option graph is shaped like a hockey stick. Option profit and loss graphs will always have a bend at the strike price. That's a graphical way to show that options allow investors to alter risks and rewards. The flat area to the left of the $100 strike shows that you can only lose a fixed amount of money – the $5 premium paid. No matter how low the stock price falls, that's the maximum loss, which is significantly less than the potential $100 fall faced by the stock buyer.

However, if the stock price rises, the $100 call option will capture the intrinsic value between the stock price and exercise price. For instance, if the stock is $110 at expiration, you'll capture the $10 intrinsic value, which is exactly what you would have captured by owning the shares. The profit and loss diagram shows that call buyers have *unlimited* upside potential if the stock price rises, but only have *limited* downside risk if the price falls. If we overlay the two graphs, it's easy to see the call option benefits. The call buyer greatly reduces the downside risk, but in exchange, gives up a small amount of the potential gains:

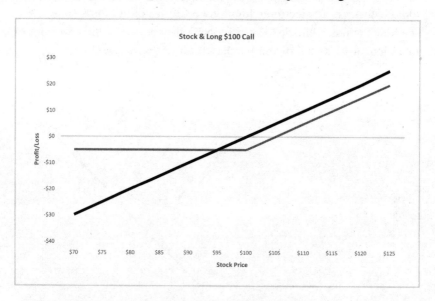

The long call is just one of many fascinating option strategies. The reason there are so many option strategies is that each one provides a unique shape to the profit and loss diagram. Each provides different sets of risks and rewards. Some will make you money if the stock price rises; others will make it if the stock price falls. Some will make you money in both directions. Others can make money if the stock price remains in a small range. Options are so much more versatile, and you can create the exact risk profile that you need to accomplish your goals. That's something stock traders simply cannot do. Let's explore some of the strategies you can use to allow profits to run – but guard the downside risks of stock investing.

The Roll-Up: Letting Winners Run Safely

Once you can read risk graphs, you'll appreciate one of the most powerful option techniques, which is called a roll-up. Jazz Pharmaceuticals (JAZZ) has had an amazing run from $20 to $190 in the past five years. Few stock investors would have been willing to hold onto shares for the entire ride. Option traders easily will by rolling up.

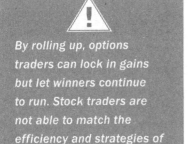

By rolling up, options traders can lock in gains but let winners continue to run. Stock traders are not able to match the efficiency and strategies of options traders.

With the recent market pullback in late 2015, Jazz was trading for $142.60. Let's say you think it's going to rally into the end of the year and want to purchase 100 shares.

Rather than paying over $14,000, you could buy one December 2015 $135 call, which is trading for $13.50, or $1,350 total. The call immediately gives you an immediate downside hedge. The most you could lose is the $1,350 spent on the call, which is much less than could be lost by placing $14,000 in the stock. Before the trade is even executed, you've already managed the risk by defining a smaller, limited potential loss.

You may be wondering why we're suggesting a call that is in-the-money. Why buy the $135 call when we could buy something closer to the current stock price like the $140 call? That's what most option traders are tempted to do. While an at-the-money will cost less money, the breakeven point is increased. At-the-money options require a faster move in the stock in order to be profitable. The deeper in-the-money you go, the more the option behaves like shares of stock. There's an entire art in selecting the right strike price, which the OptionsHouse platform can help to guide you by using the profit and loss diagrams, or by using strategySEEK.

To see why there's a difference in the amount of required stock price movement, consider the breakeven points for the $135 and $140 calls. The $135 call has a breakeven point of $135 + $13.50 = $148.50. With the stock currently trading for $142.60, that's only $5.90 away. You need the stock to move $5.90 by expiration just to get your money back. The option provides a classic hedge, or tradeoff: You're giving up some of the possible gains in exchange for not having unlimited downside risk.

What if you didn't want to give up that much in possible gains? Remember, options allow you to alter your profiles, and you can easily do that by selecting different strikes. If you purchase a deeper in-the-money call, the breakeven point will be reduced, but you'll pay more for the option. For instance, the $115 call is trading for $28, which has a $143 breakeven point. With the stock at $142.60, that's only 40 cents away. The $115 call is behaving almost like shares of stock. It's primarily intrinsic value, and has almost no time value. Even though it looks like an expensive option to new traders, it's really just cheap shares of stock.

The point to see is that option traders can make their risk-reward profiles anything they want. Once you master options, you can make them act virtually like shares of stock, or you can make them behave like long-shot lottery tickets – or any shade of risk in between. The choice is up to you, and that's why options give you options.

Let's stick with the $135 strike. Remember, you paid $13.50 for the call, or $1,350 total. Now let's assume that you're correct and Jazz rises a few points. If you were holding the shares for over $14,000, you'd be very tempted to sell and take the profits. That's the big problem with being a stock trader. The shares are so expensive, and stock traders are tempted to take the very quick profits. Risking lots of money to capture a small gain is not a good trading plan. How will you benefit by using the $135 call option?

Well, just as with the stock, you could sell and take a profit. It's what many options traders would do. Pete and I know firsthand that the real money is made by letting profits run – and that's how we train our clients. Selling a call at the first sign of profit goes against the philosophy of letting profits run. What if Jazz runs to $200 or more? Don't think it can't happen. That's exactly how it ran from $20 to $190 in the first place. Trends last longer than investors expect, so it pays to stay in positions longer – provided you can do it safely.

We want you to capture those big gains. However, just sitting on the option and hoping for the best isn't a good plan either. The stock could fall and you could lose the $1,350 investment. To get the best of both worlds – safety and more potential profits – we teach our traders to roll up the call.

Locking in Gains: The Roll-Up

When you roll up a call, you'll sell your current call but replace it with a higher strike call. In other words, you've "rolled the strike up." In this example, you'll sell your $135 call, but simultaneously buy a higher strike call, perhaps the $140 call. It's simple to do, as it's just one order that executes both trades. In the OptionsHouse platform, just a couple clicks of the mouse will set up the trade for you.

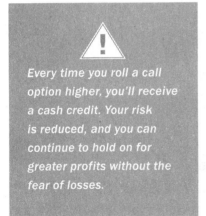

Every time you roll a call option higher, you'll receive a cash credit. Your risk is reduced, and you can continue to hold on for greater profits without the fear of losses.

Now that you know some option pricing principles, you should understand one of the immediate benefits. The $135 strike must cost more than the $140 strike. Therefore, if you sell the $135 call and buy the $140 call, you'll put cash in your pocket – but still control 100 shares of Jazz. By rolling from the $135 to the $140 call, it's called a five-dollar roll since that's the difference between the strikes. You also know that the maximum difference between these strikes is five dollars. Because there's still time to expiration, that difference will be somewhat smaller. One of the rules we teach our investors is to roll when you can capture about 80% of the difference, so we'd suggest rolling when you can capture about 80% of the $5 difference, or a $4 credit.

The trade will look like this: Sell one Dec. $135 call, and simultaneously buy one Dec. $140 call for a net credit of $4. You can even place this order ahead of time – days or weeks – and the computer will execute the roll for you when that moment arrives. That way, you don't even have to be in front of your computer. It couldn't be easier. Use computer trading to your advantage.

When that order executes, you'll have an instant $4 credit per contract, or $400, credited to your account, less a few bucks for commissions. There's one key reason for the roll: It immediately reduces the amount you have at risk – but it still keeps you in the position.

Originally, you paid $13.50, but after getting $4 back, you now only have $9.50 at risk. You've captured some profit, and that can never be taken away if the stock price falls. It's cash sitting in your account, but you still control the same 100 shares of stock. Congratulations, you've reduced the risk but still control 100 shares for bigger future gains. Now you're following the new rules of investing. The roll shifts your profit and loss diagram higher. Your initial $135 call is shown by the shaded dotted line. Your new $140 call is the solid line:

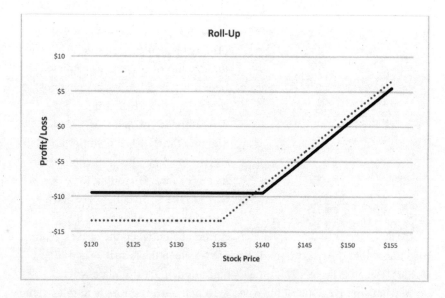

The roll accomplished something that a stock trader cannot do. You still control 100 shares of stock and can continue to profit. You initially spent $13.50 but just got $4 back, so your cost is lowered by 30%. You've managed your risk.

The very best that stock traders can do is to sell some of their shares as the stock price rises. Eventually, however, they'll run out of shares. They'll eventually miss out on gains. That will never happen to the options trader. Jazz can run to a thousand dollars, and you'll always control the 100 shares of stock but continually sweep cash into your account.

These are just a few basic rolls. There's also over-rolling and hard-rolling, and both will give great advantages depending on the opportunities.

Options are not risky. Instead, they're the perfect risk management tool. You knew up front the maximum you could lose. But that amount gets reduced if you're correct about the stock's direction. As the risk is reduced, the fear of loss is reduced, and that allows you to stay in the position for longer periods – and capture greater profits. If you're impressed with rolling, we're just getting started. Remember, options give you options, and there are new rules of investing.

The Free Option: Your Reward for Continued Rolling

Once you purchased the initial position for $13.50, your first goal is to get that amount back by rolling. Once you do, you're effectively holding an option for free. It's mathematically the same as if someone paid you to take the call option. That doesn't mean you should be careless with the position. It's still your money, and you could always convert that to cash by selling, but at least you've recovered the initial outlay. That's a big step. Now there's no fear of losses, and that's going to give you more confidence to let those profits run.

For example, your first $4 credit reduced the cost from $13.50 to $9.50. The next $4 roll will reduce it to $5.50. With two more rolls, you'll have a $2.50 credit, and you're holding a free option. Your profit and loss curve has shifted entirely above zero. No matter how low the stock's price may fall, the worst that can happen is that you made a $2.50 gain on your $13.50 investment, or 18% in a short time.

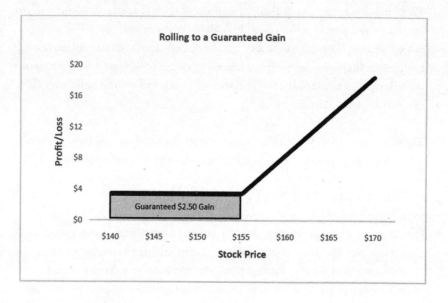

Rolling is perhaps the biggest reason why option traders can outperform stock traders. Option traders have the ability to stay in positions much longer and let those profit run.

Options are more cash efficient than stock. As a stock investor, if the share price rises, all you can do is watch your unrealized gains increase– paper profits they're often called. Those gains are meaningless until the shares are sold and converted to cash. Options traders get the best of both worlds. We can convert unrealized gains to cash as the stock rises, but we always maintain control of 100 shares of stock – an impossibility for stock traders. The lower downside risk and greater cash efficiency come from having the right to buy shares of stock rather than having to fully pay for the shares. When you have rights to buy or sell, it changes the way you invest. Things have changed, and you must change the way you invest. You must use options to manage the new risks.

Rolling Down – Protecting Put Options

For every call option strategy, there's always a corresponding put strategy. If you buy put options anticipating a decline in the stock's price, you can roll down your strikes. It's exactly the same concept as rolling up – just in the opposite direction. If you buy a $100 put and the stock price falls, you can roll down by selling your $100 put and buying the $95 put. You just continue to chase the stock's price down. Because higher-strike puts are worth more money, each roll-down produces credits. You roll down for exactly the same reasons as the roll up. You're just doing it in the opposite direction. The credits reduce your risk, and allow you to hang on for bigger profits.

Increase Your Profits by Rolling Out

All good things eventually come to an end, and options are no exception. Eventually, your option will reach expiration. What can you do if the stock price is still rising and you wish to stay in the trade? Well, you can execute a roll-out. A roll-out is similar to a roll-up in the sense that you're executing two trades at once. In this case, however, you're selling your current expiring option and replacing it with a longer-dated one. You're keeping the strike price the same, just increasing the amount of time on your option.

For example, assume you've been rolling the Jazz Dec. $135 strike several times and are now holding the Dec. 2015 $150 strike. But now the $150 strike is about to expire. All you have to do is place a simultaneous order to sell your Jazz December 2015 $150 call and by a longer-dated call, perhaps the January 2017 $150 call. This will definitely cost some money since longer-dated options with the same strikes will be more expensive.

However, if you're using in-the-money options, that difference isn't going to be that much. The intrinsic value just gets rolled into the new option, and you're only paying the difference in time values.

For instance, if the stock is $165, your December 2015 $150 call may be trading for $15.20. It will be mostly intrinsic value and very little

time value since it's about to expire. The January 2017 $150 call must also trade for at least the $15 intrinsic value, but it will definitely have more time value. However, because it's deep in-the-money, it won't have a lot of time value, perhaps $2, so its total price will be $17.
The roll with therefore just cost the $1.80 difference. With just a few mouse clicks and spending a small amount of money, you can easily extend the time to expiration when your option is about to expire.

Rolling Up & Out

Rolling out will definitely cost money, but you can reduce the amount you're paying by also rolling up to a higher strike call. Rather than buying the January 2017 $150 call, you may decide to buy the January 2017 $155 call. The $155 call will cost less than the $150 call, so it reduces the amount you have to spend. If you roll up while you're rolling out, it's another adjustment called rolling up and out: You're rolling up the strike but out further in time. That can also easily be done in the OptionsHouse platform with a few clicks of the mouse. Once your option is about to expire, it's easy to add time to the clock. There's no reason to not stay in the trade. You can easily execute many types of rolls in the OptionsHouse platform with just a few mouse clicks:

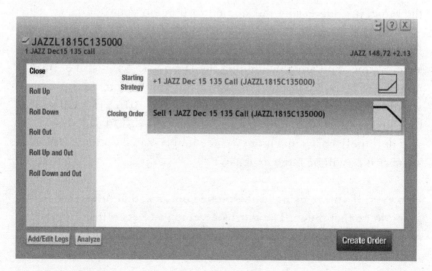

To make consistent money – and safe money – you can't follow the herd. You can't beat the averages by doing what the average person is doing. Cut your losses short. Let your profits run. It's too dangerous to do with shares of stock. The new rules of investing require you to do it safely by using options to balance fear and greed.

Investitute Takeaway

Option buyers have the right to decide to buy or sell. That means you can wait to see how stock prices unfold before making your future decisions. Don't underestimate this benefit. As news flows faster into the markets, options will be the only way you can make safe profits by confidently letting your profits run and cutting losses short. By rolling your options, you can efficiently balance fear and greed.

RULE 7

Manage Risk by Morphing

To change and change for the better are two different things. New information constantly arrives into the market, some good, some bad, some true, some false. Investors sift through the information and constantly change their opinions on stock valuations. That's why stock prices are so volatile. As information flows, stock prices change too.

Stock traders can't make changes as market conditions change. If you buy shares of stock, you're bullish – you want share prices to rise. If you're wrong, well, there's not much you can do. Yes, you could sell part of your position, but that doesn't change the risk profile – it's still a straight line. All that does is change the rate at which you'll gain or lose. You're still losing, just at a slower rate. That's not much of a benefit.

Option traders, however, are versatile and can make dramatic changes. Not only do options allow you to delay decisions about buying or selling, but they can also alter your risk-reward profiles – while the stock price is moving. That means you can switch from bullish to bearish, or from bearish to bullish. Surprisingly, you can create profiles that make money from big moves in either direction, and you can also profit from the complete lack of movement. If you're not making the kind of returns from stock investing that you'd like, part of the reason is that you're greatly limiting yourself in the many places money can hide. Options open up many doors, expand your universe of potential profits, and make investing easier.

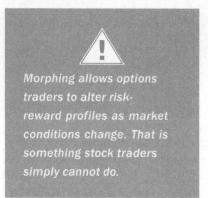

Morphing allows options traders to alter risk-reward profiles as market conditions change. That is something stock traders simply cannot do.

The ability to change your risk profile is yet another option advantage and something that stock traders cannot do. In the options market, when we change our risk profiles, it's called *morphing*, or a morph for short.

An entire book could be written on the many ways to morph positions, and they're often the topics of live seminars and webinars we provide to our clients. But right now we just want to show why the new rules of investing include morphing. Things change quickly, and you need to be able to alter your views. Once you master option strategies, you'll take command of your finances and not be fearful of today's market risks.

Let's say you're expecting a bounce in Home Depot's share price going into the end of 2015, which is about two months away. It's currently trading for $124 per share, and you want to buy 400 shares. That would cost nearly $50,000, and your risk profile is a straight line up – and a straight line down. You can make all the money in the world but you can also lose everything you've got. One of the first investing principles Pete and I teach clients is to avoid extreme outcomes, and stock investing is one of the most extreme outcomes you can put yourself into. With stock, you have unlimited gains in exchange for unlimited losses. Options give you better choices.

The January 2016 $120 call with 66 days to expiration is trading for $6.50, so that's the most you could lose per call option, or $2,600 for four contracts. That's much easier to manage than $50,000.

By purchasing this call, your profile looks like the standard hockey-stick shaped profile we saw in the last chapter:

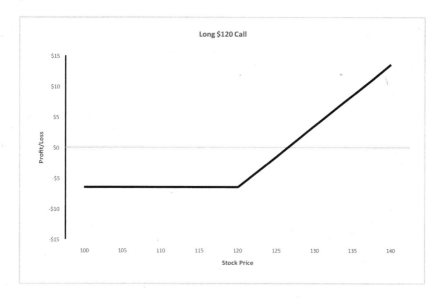

But now let's say things have changed. The stock has moved up one dollar to $126 over the past couple of weeks, but it's not moving as quickly as you originally thought. You still think it will move higher, but would like to reduce the amount of downside risk. This is a perfect time to morph the position by selling a higher-strike call.

With 52 days remaining, the $125 call is worth $4. By selling this call, your profile now looks like this:

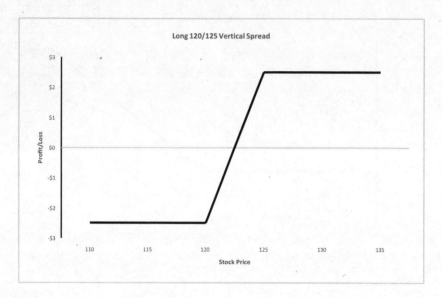

Notice that you've changed – or morphed – the diagram's shape. This is a different option strategy called a *vertical spread*. Vertical spreads are always named by the strikes, so we'd call this the 120/125 vertical spread. Specifically, this is a long 120/125 vertical spread since you paid for it. In other words, you spent $6.50 for the $120 call but received $4 for the $125 call. On a net basis, you paid $2.50 for it.

However, the profit and loss diagram no longer looks like a hockey stick. It can no longer make an unlimited amount if the stock price rises; instead, the profile is flattened on the right side of the chart above $125. What happened?

Think about your rights and obligations with the options. By owning the $120 call, you have the right to buy the shares for $120. By selling the $125 call, though, you have the obligation to sell shares for $125. If you can buy shares for $120 but must sell them for $125, the most you can make is the $5 difference. This morph has limited your upside to just $5. Why limit gains?

Well, that was done to limit risk. Because you received $4 from selling the $125 call, it great greatly reduced the amount you could lose. Originally, you spent $6.50 for the $120 call. By selling the $125 call for $4, the most you can now lose is the $2.50 difference, or $1,000 for four contracts. (Remember, each contract controls 100 shares, so $2.50 * 4 calls * 100 shares = $1,000). The original trade put $2,600 at risk. The morph reduced it to $1,000. So far, so good. What about the maximum gain?

The most this vertical spread can be worth is the $5 difference in strikes. Because you paid $2.50 for the position, if it ends up being worth $5, you'll make the $2.50 difference. The morph put you in a brand new position that cost $2.50 and can make $2.50. You can see that the graph lines up with -$2.50 at the maximum loss and at +$2.50 for the maximum gain. Even though you've reduced the amount into the trade, you can make a 100% return on that money. You're now in a position that allows you to hold on for more possible gains, but reduce your losses if you're wrong.

The morph, however, did something more intriguing. Notice that with the stock price at $126, both options are in-the-money. That means you don't even need the stock price to move in order to double your $1,000 investment. In fact, the stock can even fall one dollar back to $125 – and you'll still double your money.

Without getting into the details, what this morph has done is to change the strategy from a directional strategy (thinking that the stock would rise) to a premium collection strategy, which is a separate category of option strategies. It's an unknown door to stock traders. Premium collection strategies work because you're accepting cash today, or collecting the premium, in exchange for accepting some type of an obligation.

By selling the $125 call, you have the possible obligation to deliver shares at the $125 strike. However, that's not a risk to you since you have the right to buy shares for $120. You always have the right to purchase the shares for less money. If the stock stays above $125 per share at expiration, this 120/125 vertical spread will be worth the $5 difference. That's the most it could ever be worth. How do you collect your profits? Simply click on a button to sell the vertical spread and you've doubled your money. You have no stock to purchase or deliver since you've closed the contracts.

Options are versatile and the possibilities are nearly endless. Let's say you like the idea of reducing the downside risk further by using the vertical spread, but you're not wild about completely giving up all of the upside profit. Is there anything else you can do? Of course, that's the option advantage. Rather than selling four contracts of the $125 strike perhaps you could sell fewer, say three:

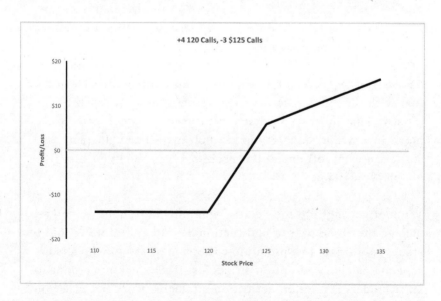

By selling three $125 calls at $4, your account is credited with $1,200 cash. The most you can lose is now reduced from $2,600 to $1,400. Your downside risk is now a little greater – $1,400 compared to only $1,000 when you sold four calls. But in exchange for that, you've now opened up the possibility for unlimited gains.

You have the right to buy 400 shares at $120, but the obligation to sell 300 shares at $125. That means you control 100 shares free and clear. You can still make an unlimited amount of money, but only on 100 shares rather than 400. The right side of the graph isn't flat anymore, but it's also not as vertical as it was when you owned four of the $120 calls by themselves. You're in a profit range between those two extremes. Options traders can create nearly an infinite number of risk profiles. Stock traders get one.

What if the news changes while you were holding the $120 call, and you now think the stock is heading for a big fall, perhaps because of an upcoming earnings report? Rather than selling the $125 calls, you could sell a lower strike call, say the $115 call. With 52 days to expiration, they're worth $11.50. By selling four of these calls, you've now changed your outlook from bullish to bearish:

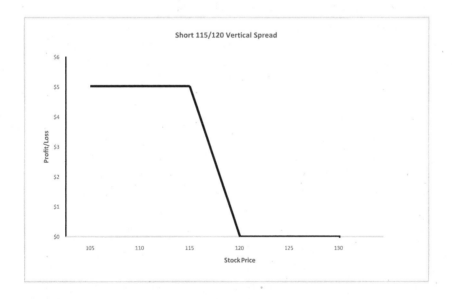

You've now morphed into a short vertical spread. It's considered short since you received money for it on a net basis. You sold the $115 calls for $11.50 but bought the $120 calls for $6.50. The net difference is a credit of $5.

The best part is that you can't lose on the position. You can make $5, or $2,000 for the four calls, if the stock falls to $115 or below. The worst that happens is you break even if the stock price is $120 or higher. Here's the math behind it: Because you sold a lower strike call, you have the obligation to deliver shares for $115 but the right to buy them for $120 – that's a $5 potential loss if the stock rises to $120 or higher. Your $5 credit exactly offsets that possible $5 loss. If the stock falls below $115, you'll make $2,000. But if the stock rises to $120 or higher, you just end up flat. It's doubtful that many people would be willing to hold 400 shares of stock to speculate on an earnings report, but look how much easier it is to do by morphing options positions. You created a new risk profile that can't lose, but you can make money if the stock price falls. Morphing into a position that can't lose doesn't mean you can just do this on command. The reason it worked here is that you took earlier risk and the stock moved in your favor. The new option prices created the opportunity. The opportunities are out there. You just need to know how to capture them.

Is your head spinning yet with amazement? We're just getting started. Remember, we could write an entire book on various morphs and trade adjustments. It's a key part of being able to manage the day-to-day market risks. Right now, we just want you to see the importance of morphing. Let's try one more to show how versatile you'll become once you master options.

What if you want to play both sides of the market and make money if the stock rises or falls? Maybe there's a good reason to think prices will fall, but there are also compelling reasons why they may spike. What can you do? As a stock trader, you can't profit from both directions. Go long if you're bullish, or short if you're bearish and hope for the best. You have to pick one side or the other.

Options are versatile, and you have lots of choices. One is to sell three $115 calls instead of four. Your graph will morph to a type of *ratio spread*, which is created when you buy and sell option contracts, but in different quantities, or ratios. If you buy more of the higher strike calls, you get a type of ratio spread called a *backspread*. Here, you sold three $115 calls but bought four $120 calls, and your risk profile morphs into a long $115/$120 backspread:

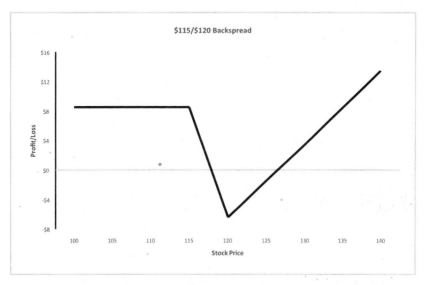

If the stock falls below $115, you can make a maximum of $850. If the stock price rises, however, there's no limit on how much you can make. Notice that the right side of the graph is no longer flat like it was with the 120/125 vertical spread. The tradeoff is that you can now lose some money if the stock stays between the $117.83 and $126.50 breakeven points. The maximum loss is $650, but that only occurs if the stock price lands exactly at $120 at expiration – an unlikely event.

Don't worry about the calculations and mechanics, as the OptionsHouse platform will show all of these morphs to you in real time. If you can click a mouse, you'll see all the potential profits, losses, and breakeven points. You'll even see the associated probabilities of them occurring.

Below is the Home Depot morph to make a possible $2.50, or $1,000
for four contracts:

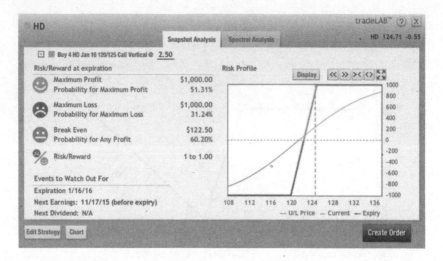

Stock traders can change, but the best they can do is reduce or
increase the number of shares. They can't change the shape of
the risk profile. Options traders can. As market conditions change,
options traders can change risks and rewards, and even change
directional outlooks. Stock traders can change, but options traders
can change for the better. That's not a new idea to options traders,
but it is a new rule of investing in today's uncertain markets.

Investitute Takeaway

Market prices change quickly, and you must be able to adapt.
It's no longer safe to sit on shares and ignore risk management
techniques. Options are the only tool that allows traders to alter
risk-reward profiles. Don't ignore them – learn them. Once you
learn to morph, you can alter those profiles while the market is
moving. The very technology that's causing concern for potential
market crashes is the same technology that allows you to see real-
time graphs of what's happening to your profits and losses, and
morph quickly and efficiently.

RULE 8

Create a Trading Plan

There's only one reason to invest – to make money. But if that's your plan, it's probably going to set you up for failure.

Your overall goal is not a plan. Knowing the obvious isn't going to help you make money. Instead, a true plan outlines details: How much are you willing to risk on each investment? What kind of returns are you seeking? Over what time? How much of a loss are you willing to accept? You need to know the necessary steps that get you to your goal.

Without a trading plan, all you have is hope. You can hope things move in your favor and to make a lot of money. That's no plan for today's volatile markets. In the process of hoping, you're going to find unusually volatile days – it's just what markets do now with all the instant feedback and immediate executions. You need to outline a plan for how you'll handle it.

Trading plans are important because you can outline them ahead of time when you're thinking rationally. You've got time to think clearly about what you're trying to do. Without a written plan, big market moves will make it too easy to take excess risk when things are moving your way – and to take excess risk when they're not. It's impossible to walk the fine line between fear and greed. Write out a plan, and treat it like a contract with yourself. Stick with it.

Doing so, you'll see how easy it is to make decisions. Let's say you have 100 shares of Costco (COST) which is currently $163. You purchased shares over one year ago for $130. You'd like to hold on for more gains, but are also fearful of losses. It's the classic battle between fear and greed that stock investors face. Most would say take the money and run. But remember, trends last longer than people expect. You need to learn to hold on, but protect the unknown downside risks. That's why you need to learn options. Now that you know something about options, is there something you can do?

Yes, there are lots of things you could do, but the best choice can be made once we know what you'd like to do. We need to know your trading plan.

I ask you a few questions and find your goal is to at least match the market returns; that is to at least match the S&P 500. Your bigger goal, however, is to not lose what you have. Now that we have a simple plan outlined, the opportunities become clear.

You could use a simple strategy called a *stock swap*, where you sell your shares and swap it out for a call option. Because the stock must always cost more than any call option, the strategy always produces a large credit to your account. You don't even need cash; it's self-financing.

For instance, the January 2017 $160 call (420 days) is currently $15. You could sell your shares for $163 and spend $15 on the call. You'll end up with a cash credit of $148. No matter how bad market conditions may get, that can't be taken away. You originally spent $130 for the shares, but now received $148 cash, so you've recouped your initial investment – plus a guaranteed 14% return – and you still control 100 shares for the next year.

The S&P 500 is only up 1.5% for the year, so you've vastly exceeded your goals, can't lose money, and might make more. It makes perfect sense to give up something that's unknown in exchange for surpassing goals and still possibly making more money. It was an easy strategy to select, but only because we knew where you wanted to go. You had a trading plan.

What's the cost? It's the time value. With the shares at $163, the $160 call is worth $15, which means $3 is intrinsic value and the remaining $12 is time value. That $12 is an opportunity cost, as it represents what you're giving up in the future. Remember, all time values become zero at expiration. But you're giving that up in exchange for a guaranteed profit and the chance for more. It's a classic hedge – give up some upside in exchange for removing the possibility of losses. That was easy to give up, but only because we knew what you're trying to do.

No matter what your goals may be, we could always come up with an options strategy to help you meet that goal. Maybe we'd use a stock repair strategy, sell spreads against long stock, use diagonal spreads, vertical spreads, or condors. The possibilities are endless, but the answers always depend on what you're trying to do.

Stock investors don't have the number of choices available, so they can't create the intricate plans of options traders. Because options traders have so many more choices, so many more strategies, and so many more profit and loss profiles to create, they have a bigger need for a trading plan.

Trading plans also touch on your emotional intelligence. You have to be disciplined enough to think in detail about what it is you're trying to do. Making money is not a plan.

Creating Your Trading Plan

A trading plan doesn't have to be anything formal, although it does help to write it down. When it's written, it becomes a document you can refer to for decision making. A trading plan should include the following elements:

Realistic: The financial markets usually return an average of 7% to 10% per year, depending on the time span being measured. By using options, you'll gain leverage and can certainly beat those marks. The more you deviate from those returns, the higher the risk you must take. Some investors think they can make 30% per month for taking little risk. That's not realistic.

We've also heard people say things like, "I'm not greedy. I just want to make $200 a day." That may be a goal, but it's not a plan. The market is not an ATM that lets you dictate just how much you'll take – or what dollar amount determines greed. Two-hundred a day may not be greedy to one person, but does that mean Warren Buffett can say he just wants a million dollars a day? The market is filled with investors just like you – all trying to do exactly the same thing. The only way you can earn rewards is to take risk. That's where options come in since you can find better risk-reward profiles than by using any other asset. It's a dangerous misperception to think you can consistently grab a few loose dollars lying around each day. No investor will leave free money behind. Make your plan realistic.

Specific & Measurable: Put specific numbers on your goals and time frames. A plan is not to make a lot of money quickly. Instead, say you want to make 20% per year, for example. Once you've made your plan, stick with it. If you have a goal to make a certain amount for retirement in 20 years, determine how much you need to earn each year to accomplish that goal. Stay focused on the goal. Sure, bigger money could be made – but so could bigger losses. There's no sense in taking additional risk to accomplish the same goal. You'll only know what creates additional risk if you make your plan specific and measurable.

Keep it Simple: Staying with the plan is far more important rather than the actual plan. Keeping it simple allows you to stick with it. Lots of plans can work, but to have your best chance of meeting your goals, make your plan simple. A complex plan may sound good

on paper, but it can also set you up for failure. Don't think you
have to create a complex plan to accomplish big goals. Legendary
investor Warren Buffett's plan is as simple as it gets: He searches
for undervalued companies and keeps them for his favorite holding
period – forever. Too many times we see traders creating plans that
allow them to wiggle around at every twist and turn in the market.
Their trading plans become so intricate and complex that it's hard to
keep track of the plan, much less follow it. Keep it simple.

Identify Risk Levels: How much risk are you willing to take?
Remember that risk is defined as the probability of losing money.
Just because you put a lot of money into an investment doesn't
necessarily mean it's high risk. Remember, price isn't risk. A
trading plan shouldn't say that you're only willing to "risk"
$5,000 per trade, for example. Putting $5,000 into lottery
tickets is risky; putting $100,000 into treasury bonds isn't. Risk
has to be defined as the probability for loss, which is why the
OptionsHouse platform will spell out the expected probabilities for
gains or losses. It's the only way to truly identify risk. Without
these levels, it's easy to overstep your risk boundaries and try
to gamble your way out of losing positions. Losses will happen.
Success depends on you staying with the plan, and to do that,
you have to properly identify risk.

Disciplined: Plans only work if you can stay with them. You need
a set of rules that allow you to reach your goals – not set you up
for failure. That's part of having them realistic, but it also means
you must stay with the plan. Make sure your plan is outlined in a
way that allows you to carry it out. If you don't have the time or
the discipline to carry out the plan, it's not a plan. Discipline is what
connects plans to your goals.

Comfortable: Make sure you understand the strategies you're using.
Lots of ways can be used to make money. All can work. The key is to be
sure that your plan is comfortable for you so that you're willing to stay
with the plan. If you're not familiar with condors and butterfly spreads,
for instance, don't make them part of your plan just because your friend
says they've worked great for him. He may have a different set of goals,

risks, and rewards. Staying with the plan is of paramount importance, and you're more likely to do it if it's comfortable for you.

Cost Efficient: A financial plan is always much easier to carry out if you're making things affordable. Too many times, investors set up automatic deductions from checking accounts to invest into stocks or mutual funds each month. However, as stock prices rise, they often end up having to increase those dollar amounts in order to keep with the plan. The irony is that a rising market – exactly what they were hoping for – may exactly be their undoing. It may cause the plan to fail. A similar situation occurs with investors working out of a tax-advantaged account who have made the maximum contributions for the year. They're not allowed to put more money into the account.

When investors find they can't afford their preferred investments, they end up buying cheaper stocks. Being forced to select your second or third favorites is not an efficient plan. Stay with the investments where you have the most confidence.

Cost-efficient plans will not allow you to dig yourself into such holes. This is exactly why options are becoming more important for today's investing. With so many different strategies to choose from, you can always find a way to invest in any company of your choice that will fit your budget.

Consistent: Make your plan something you can consistently replicate. Don't make it so complicated or costly that you can't stay with it. Remember, staying with the plan is far more important than the plan itself. Be sure it's something you're willing – and able – to stay with. Consistency counts.

Fits Your Expertise: Understand the underlying and strategies. Today's investments can get quite complex. Don't put money into a triple-levered ETF if you don't understand what it is and how it works. It may sound great that you get three-times the returns, but you also have to understand tracking errors and other problems that can arise. Options can provide all the leverage you need, limited risk, and unlimited gains, but by sticking with the investments you know best. Stay with familiar companies that fit your knowledge. Stick with strategies that fit your expertise.

These are just some of the key points for any trading plan. They're additional things to think about other than just trying to make a lot of money. Investors today get lured by the computer, and think it's the road to riches. The computer will greatly help with investing, but it's just a tool. It will definitely help to speed up the process, but will only help if that process follows a sound plan.

Investitute Takeaway

Investing is more than just buying stocks and hoping things go up. Instead, you have goals to accomplish, risks to consider, and a process to follow. If you outline a simple trading plan, it creates a roadmap of how you're going to accomplish your goals. Treat it like a written contract with yourself. When you have knowledge of where you want to go, along with a plan for getting there, you're much more likely to get there. Trading plans have always been a great idea, but they're required to navigate today's uncertain markets.

RULE 9

Learn to Spot Fair Values

What's fair is fair. It's fair and square. Give something a fair shake. A fair-weathered friend, and you've got more than your fair share.

Okay, fair enough.

There are many expressions about fairness, but when it comes to surviving the new markets, there's another expression you'll have to understand – fair value. Whenever you're faced with an opportunity to make money under uncertainty whether it's a bet, casino game, or financial investment, there's a fair value associated with it. You may have even heard the term used on CNBC when they may say, "The S&P 500 futures are trading 12 points below fair value." What exactly does fair value mean? And why do we care?

Fair value is the price that doesn't favor the buyer, and it doesn't favor the seller. The price is not too high for the buyer; it is not too low for the seller. It's the value that's just right. The idea of fair value is well known to professional traders, but you must understand it to survive the new markets.

For new traders, it's puzzling. How can a price be fair? Isn't somebody going to get the better end of the deal? Sure, it's possible. The idea, though, is that you shouldn't consistently expect that it will be the buyer, or consistently expect it will be the seller. If buyers always had the edge, sellers would back away and price would rise. The increased price will take away the buyers' edge. On the other hand if sellers always had the advantage, buyers would back away and price would fall. The lower prices would reduce the sellers' advantage. At some point, a price has to be reached where the buyer and seller can't quite tell who has the edge. That's because the edge is gone. The deal is priced at fair value.

If you continually bought or sold every financial asset priced at fair value, you would just break even after years of investing. If there's no edge, there's no long-term profit. For options traders, there's a fair value, and you have to understand how to find it. It's going to be a big source of profits for those who understand it – and losses for those who don't. The new markets are going to make traders greatly deviate from fair value, and that's where new opportunities will lie.

Heads I Win, Tails You Lose

Whenever you're deciding to accept a financial investment, the entire analysis boils down to figuring out how much money you think you can make versus how much you'll have to pay for it. Conceptually, the idea is very simple. In practice, it may not be so easy.

Let's start with a simple example. Let's say that Pete and I are going to flip coins. I offer to pay him one dollar each time it lands heads. How much should he be willing to pay me when it lands tails? In other words, how much is it worth to win one dollar at the flip of a coin?

Some traders think this has no value; after all, it's just a game or a bet. But if there is any opportunity to make money, there has to be a value to it. If someone offered to pay you one dollar at the flip of the coin – with no cost to you – there'd be no reason to say no. That's an easy way to show it does have value. The better question is how much. Here's a way to figure it out intuitively.

Assume Pete's willing to pay $1.50 each time the coin lands tails. Is that a low, high, or fair price? Half the time he'll win one dollar, but half the time he'll lose $1.50. On average, he's losing 50 cents every couple of flips, or about 25 cents per flip, on average. That price is too high and wouldn't be fair to him. What if he offered to pay 50 cents?

If I accept his offer of 50 cents, half the time he'll win one dollar, and half the he'll lose only 50 cents. Over the long run, he'll win 50 cents every couple of flips, or 25 cents per flip, on average. Fifty cents is a great price for him, but an unfair price to me.

If $1.50 is too high of a price and 50 cents is too low, there must be a price somewhere between those extremes that is neither too high nor too low – a price that is just right. A price that is fair to him. A price that is fair to me.

It turns out that one dollar is the price that he should be willing to pay every time he loses. If I pay him one dollar each time he wins, and he pays me the same when he loses, we'll just break even in the long run.

Over a short period of time, one of us could end up on the winning side. But if we were to continue flipping the coin long enough, we'd just break even.

It's the long run averages that determine the fair value, so one dollar is the fair value for this coin-flipping game. It's the proper price relative to the risks.

If a game is fairly valued, it does not mean that you can't lose. If we were to flip the coin a single time, it's obvious one of us will definitely lose. That's a short of a run as you can get, and one party can definitely win or lose a fairly valued game in the short run. It's possible one of us could win or lose after several tosses. That doesn't mean it wasn't priced fairly. It just means the game wasn't played long enough. Fair value is a long-run concept.

Below is a computer-generated chart of 1,000 coin tosses priced at fair value. That is, paying one dollar to win one dollar. You can see there are periods of gains, and periods of losses. But if we sit there long enough, we'll just come back to breaking even:

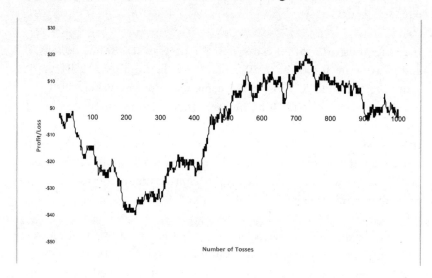

However, what if Pete decided to pay $1.50? What would his profit and loss look like for this game? Now you can see the negative edge working against him. By paying $1.50, he's paying more than fair value, and has no shot of winning in the long run:

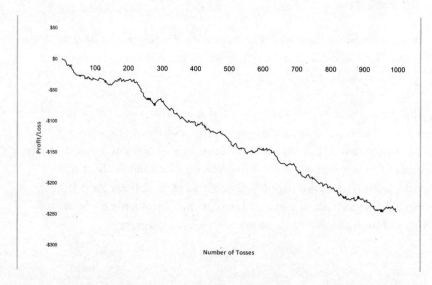

Look how accurately the math works out. If he's expected to lose 25 cents per flip, after 1,000 tosses, he should expect to lose about $250 – almost exactly what the chart shows.

On the other hand, if he pays only 50 cents for the bet, in the long run he'll have a big edge and will end up on the winning side. Notice that his expected profit is his 25-cent edge times the 1,000 flips, or about $250:

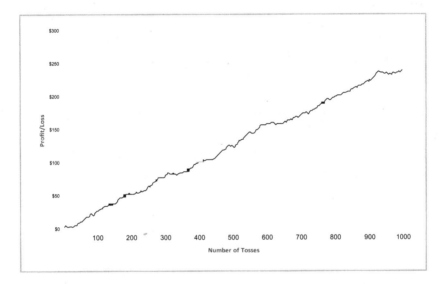

No matter what the probabilities may be for winning or losing, there has to be a price that exactly makes the buyer and seller break even over the long run. That's the fair value.

What Does Fair Value Have to do With Options?

Fair value is critical for options traders. Options are a financial asset and have the possibility of paying off cash – lots of it. Just like our coin-tossing game, if there's any possibility for a financial payoff, there has to be a price that doesn't favor the buyer of the seller. There has to be a fair value.

To find an option's fair value, traders look at a theoretical pricing model to gauge whether the option's price seems justified. It's very easy to do, and the OptionsHouse platform will show you these values.

As the new markets get more volatile, traders will be willing to pay greater premiums to get the hedges that options provide. If you know where to look, you're going to find many times where traders will price options far greater than what they're worth – much like paying $1.50 for the coin-tossing game. Novices are willing to do that and will end up with long-term losses. Astute traders will see the opportunities – and take the profits.

Most traders would never think that an option could have a fair value. In fact, most hear that option sellers have the advantage. In the long run, the buyer or seller cannot sustain a long-run advantage. On average, options are priced fairly – but there can be big discrepancies at times. Those discrepancies are going to get bigger in the new markets, and you have to understand how to find them – and trade them.

Against the Odds

Another mistake is often made by novice traders in the new, more volatile markets. New traders focus too much on the risk-reward ratios thinking they have an edge if they can "pay a little to make a lot." For instance, they may feel that if an options strategy costs one dollar but can pay off four dollars, they're risking one dollar to make four. In their view, they have a favorable risk-reward ratio. It looks like they're minimizing the risk and maximizing the amount they can make. That's dangerous. Price is not risk.

The coin-tossing game shows why. We can look at probabilities in a different way. With a coin toss, you have an equal chance of winning or losing. The coin has two sides, and you only win on one of them. Another way to say it is that for every one way you can win, there is one way you can lose.

This is a common way that professional traders will express the "odds" of winning. For the coin-tossing game, the odds are 1:1 –

you have one way to win for every one way to lose. When financial opportunities are expressed in odds, they're easier to value. With the coin-tossing game, 1:1 odds simply means you should pay one dollar in order to win one dollar. The risks and rewards are balanced so the price and rewards should be equal too.

You can work the odds backwards to get the probabilities. If you have a game with 1:1 odds, just add those two numbers together. That shows there are two things that could happen (heads or tails), and you win with one of them. You're winning with one out of two ways, or a 50% chance.

Now look at the hypothetical options strategy where you can pay one dollar to make four dollars. If you can pay one to make four, that's 4:1 odds apparently in your favor. But looks can be deceiving. The market's actually paying you more than what you can lose because the probabilities are against you. With 4:1 odds, there are five things that can happen, and you get to win with one of them. That means your chances for winning are one in five, or 20%.

Now work the problem backwards to check. If you pay one dollar and have a 20% chance of winning, you'll play four times before winning once. On average, you'll spend five dollars and earn five dollars. It's fairly valued. Even though "pay one to make four" risk-reward ratio sounds appealing, it's just a disguised way of saying you have a 20% chance to win. This is a tiny bit oversimplified because, with options, your money is not returned on the times you win like it is with a bet. The important point to understand is that you cannot survive the new markets by just looking for those opportunities where you pay a little to make a lot. Instead, you have to look at the fair values.

We're not saying that risk-reward ratios aren't important. Instead, we're saying that you can't misinterpret them. Just because it's cheap and can make a fortune doesn't mean it's safe. It means it's high risk. Successful trading means balancing the risks and rewards to accomplish your goals.

To win with options, you can't just look at the market price and attempt to determine if it's a high or low price. Price, by itself, tells you nothing. If you just looked at price for the coin-tossing game, you'd may have been lead to think it was a good deal to pay $1.50. After all, that's not a lot of money, so it seems like low risk. Now you see the danger. It's a terribly over-valued bet, even though it "only cost $1.50." The price tells you nothing. Instead, you need to understand what you're getting in return for that price – you're interested in the fair value. In order to understand the fair value, you must look at options in a different way from their price. There's no way to survive the new markets without it.

A Trip to the Casino

Okay, let's recap this section by doing a fun example of fair value and show why you cannot succeed with options if you focus on risk-reward ratios. Instead, you have to understand fair value. Let's take a trip to the casino.

Roulette is very simple to play. For American-style roulette, there are 38 numbers from which to choose. You place your chips on a specific number or group of numbers. If your selection is chosen at random by a spinning wheel, you win. Otherwise, you lose the amount you bet. Below are just a few of the types of bets you can make along with the payoffs:

BET	PAYOFF
Single Number	35:1
Two-Number	17:1
Three-Number	11:1
Four-Number (Corner Bet)	8:1
Five-Number	6:1
Red or Black	1:1

Of the many types of bets, let's consider one of the simplest to understand, the single-number bet. For the single-number bet, you place your chips on any one of the 38 numbers. If that number is selected by the spin of the wheel, the casino pays you 35:1, which means it pays $35 for every dollar you bet. If you bet $10, you'll win $350 if that number comes up.

Once again, notice the seemingly favorable risk-reward ratios. It seems like a favorable deal to win $35 for only "risking" one dollar, but just as with options, it's the wrong way to look at it. Whether the single-number bet or an option trade is a good deal or not has nothing to do with how small the risks are compared to the rewards. It has to do with the fair value.

For the single-number bet, the apparently favorable 35:1 risk-reward ratio is simply a reflection of the relatively high risk. Remember, as the risk increases so does the reward. The fact that you can make $35 per dollar bet only means there is a relatively low probability of winning. There's substantial risk.

Now that you understand odds, you can see how casinos make money. If there are 38 spaces on the wheel and you can win with only one, your chances of winning are one in 38. For every one space on the wheel acting in your favor, 37 are acting against you. The odds are therefore 37:1 against you. If it was fairly valued, you should win $37 for every one dollar bet. The casino, however, only pays $35. It pays off at less than fair value, and that's why you'll lose this game if you sit there long enough spinning the wheel. You're losing $2 out of $38, or a little over 5%. That's the casino's edge. Even though 35:1 appeared to be a favorable risk-reward tradeoff, fair value cast it in a not-so-fair light. Would you do better with a different bet?

If you select the two-number bet, you'll have two spaces on the wheel acting in your favor and 36 acting against. The odds are 36:2, or 18:1 against you. If the game was fairly valued, the casino should pay $18, but it only pays $17. You're being shortchanged one dollar, or again, about 5%. The two-number bet is no better.

If you run through all of the bets, you'll find they carry the identical casino edge of about 5%. The one exception is the five-number bet, which carries nearly an 8% casino edge. By understanding fair value, you're now in a better position to understand the risks. What appeared to be very good risk reward ratios are now obviously bad deals.

Fair value shows the only strategy you need for roulette is to avoid the five-number bet. With all the others, you're going to lose your money equally fast. Focusing on risk-reward ratios would have led you down the wrong path, leaving losses in its trail. You can't beat the casino by receiving less than fair value, and you can't beat it by spending more than fair value – no matter what strategy you try.

To make money in today's markets, you need to think like the casino. The casino is only concerned with its advantageous reference to fair value. It couldn't care less about the risk-reward ratios. If it did, it would never think to offer 35:1 payoffs. The reason they're offered is because they're not so great when viewed in terms of fair value. To survive the new markets, you can't get lured into bad trades just because they seem to have great risk-reward ratios. You have to understand how to find the fair values.

Spotting Fair Values

One of the big benefits we have with the new computerized trading is that we can spot when options are trading well above or below fair value. These create some of the best profits for today's traders. When you can gain a favorable edge, you're on the winning side. You don't get it by looking at risk-reward ratios. You don't get it by selecting cheap options. You get it by purchasing options that are priced below fair value and selling ones above fair value. When you learn to see the markets like this, you may be buying $10 options and selling one-dollar options – exactly the opposite of what you've probably been doing. The OptionsHouse platform is one of the easiest ways traders can see how fair values are stacking up. That's what we'll show in the next section. When you do, you'll have the edge. You'll have an unfair advantage over other traders. That's what successful investing is all about – acting on information before the rest of the crowd. As market risk increases, traders get more risk averse, and option premiums can trade far above fair value. At the same time, traders may turn to option selling to generate profits and end up driving prices below fair value.

Nobody said high-speed computerized trading would make things fair for everyone. We're just saying if you know how to use the information, you'll have the advantage. For any trade, you're either on the winning side of fair value, or you're on the losing side. You need to know which side of fair value you're on. It's a new concept for today's traders – and a new rule of investing. It may not seem like fair play, but all's fair in love and war – and trading.

Investitute Takeaway

New traders look at risk-reward ratios as a way to determine opportunities. The ratios mean nothing – until you compare them to fair value. For today's markets, you're going to see big deviations from fair value – above and below – and each creates a trading opportunity where you have the edge. Fair value is the one way to standardize risk. And when things get risky, you want to see risk clearly. You need to see it through the eyes of fair value.

RULE 10

Traders Will Find Value in Volatility

You've probably heard the old business school joke about the shopkeeper who sold all of his products at a loss – but tried to make up for it in volume. An equally flawed idea is the options trader who overpaid for calls and puts but tried to make up for it by making lots of trades, or using different strategies. Multiplying losses only creates bigger losses, and any strategy to make up for it is, well, a joke.

One of the biggest difficulties for new traders is to understand that options are not just directional assets like shares of stock. If you buy shares of stock, you just need the price to rise. It doesn't matter how quickly it rises, just as long as it rises. But when stock investors become option traders, they carry the same mindset to the options field. They assume a call option is just a straight substitute for shares of stock. They think that if the stock price is going to rise, just buy a call option since it's just a cheaper form of stock. That's a myth, and one of the biggest in options trading. You will not benefit in the least from trading that way – but the machines will. There are new rules, and you have to understand how options are priced. You need a way to figure out if an option is relatively cheap or expensive.

One of the first things we teach our clients is that options require speed from the underlying stock, which we've shown earlier in this book by considering the breakeven point. If you buy a $100 call for $3, you need the stock to rise to $103 by expiration to break even. That's 3% higher than the current price. However, if you paid $5 for that same call, you'd need the stock to rise to $105, or 5%, which is a more unlikely price.

However, that doesn't mean you can just directly compare prices and say that a $3 call is a better deal than a $5 call. It depends on the stock. Some stock prices have the ability to move much more than others. In financial lingo, they have more *volatility*. If a stock exhibits more volatility compared to another, the market will be willing to pay more for those options. There's a better chance for bigger profits, and traders are willing to pay for that advantage.

Inexperienced options traders are usually not aware of this relationship and are likely to overpay for options – or sell for too little – because they don't know how to judge an option's value.

Option prices can be too high or too low. The reason is that option prices are determined by what buyers and sellers think will happen to the underlying stock's price in the future. The more potential traders think the stock has, the higher the option's price will be. The market is a live auction with some traders bidding to buy options while others are offering them for sale. If a buyer and seller agree on a price, a contract is traded. Buyers are trying to buy low; sellers are trying to sell high. But a trade can only be executed if they meet somewhere between these two extremes. So just how much should buyers be willing to pay or sellers be willing to receive? It depends on what people think will happen to the stock's future price.

If traders believe a $100 stock won't move much in the future, maybe just a couple of dollars, a $100 call won't have much value. Buyers aren't willing to pay much for it since there's no real expected profit. Think about it: How much would you be willing to pay for a $100 call if you knew for sure the future stock price could only move a couple of dollars at best? There's no money in it, so buyers are not willing to pay much.

Sellers, on the other hand, also recognize there's not much reason to believe the stock's price will move. That's a benefit to the seller. Remember, when you sell an option, the most you can make is the premium received — but you could lose potentially much more. If traders think the stock's price isn't going to move much, they're not afraid to sell options. It doesn't pose much risk. If the overall market believes the stock's price will remain fairly quite during the option's life, you'll end up with a bunch of sellers and very few buyers.

If you managed to stay awake during your college economics courses, you may recall what happens in a market with lots of sellers and few buyers — price falls. Stocks that don't move much through the year — or are not expected to move much — will have relatively low option prices. That low price, however, doesn't necessarily mean they're a screaming good deal. It just means the market doesn't think there's much potential for larger future stock prices. Price is low for a reason.

However, what if investors think that same stock could make a really big move? What if it's rumored to be a takeover target by Apple? Now the opposite occurs. Everybody wants to buy, and traders compete with each other by bidding the prices higher. Sellers, however, are fearful. They don't want to receive a small fixed premium only to find the stock price has skyrocketed. That's selling inventory below value. Because there's a good chance of that happening, the market is filled with lots of buyers and few sellers. The option's price rises. High option prices don't necessarily mean they're overpriced. It just means there's a lot of potential future value. Economists may not agree on a lot of things, but one thing is indisputable: Prices are determined by the amount supplied and demanded. The reason you will see what appears to be great disparities in options prices is strictly because of the market's perception of what may happen with that stock's future price.

For instance, Alibaba (BABA) is currently trading for $80. The 30-day $80 call is $3.35. Exxon-Mobil (XOM) is trading for $81. The 30-day $81 call is $2.09. Both options are at-the-money, both expire in 30 days, and both stocks are trading for about the same price. Why the difference in option prices? Traders think Alibaba has more price potential over the next 30 days so are willing to pay more for it. The only way to find out if they're correct or not is to wait until expiration. But right now, that's the market consensus. Option prices depend purely on a perception of how far traders *think* the underlying stock will move.

New options traders often think that the cheaper $2.09 call is lower risk than the $3.35 call. Remember, price isn't risk. You can't just look at an option's price and determine if it's cheap or expensive. If Exxon goes nowhere over the next month, that was a very expensive option. If Alibaba rises $20, then its call was grossly underpriced. You have to learn to see option prices in terms of how the underlying stock may perform.

If you think Alibaba will rise over the next 30 days, you may decide to buy the Alibaba $80 call for $3.35. Your breakeven point is $83.35. If the stock is less than that at expiration, say $83, you were correct that the stock price would rise – but you still lost money. You overpaid for the option because you paid a price that suggested a higher stock price at expiration. Even though Alibaba's price moved higher, it didn't move quite as far as you expected, so you lost money. That's what happens when you overpay for options. Trying to make up for it in volume isn't going to help one bit.

To succeed with options trading, you can't just look at the price and determine if it's a good deal. New option traders often select a benchmark price – say $3 – and think any option priced below that is a good deal while any priced above are bad. A $3 option may sound like a good deal, but until you understand what you're paying for, it may actually be grossly overpriced. A $20 option may be dirt cheap. It depends on how much potential future stock price movement you can expect. But now for the $64,000 question...

How can you tell? How can you determine if an option's price represents a good deal or not? Experienced traders have had a long-time secret weapon – volatility. Volatility is a mathematical measurement about future stock prices, and it gives traders a great way to figure out if an option is relatively cheap or expensive.

If you've traded options in the past, but found you were losing money even though you were correct about the stock's direction, it's because you weren't taking volatility into account. The OptionsHouse platform makes it easy, and all you have to do is look at a simple graph. Computers make that easy; you just have to know how to interpret the information. The computers you're trading against are very well aware of this information, so it's not enough to buy a call just because you think the stock's price will rise. You have to have an idea of the option's fair value. You can see the market price, but does that represent a good deal? To answer that, you need to understand volatility.

While volatility will be important for options trading success, it will become even more important for the future. It will become a key profit source. All the world market uncertainty and speed of information that's causing unprecedented market risk are exactly the things that create new opportunities – if you know where to look. The more the uncertainty increases, the more you need options. The more you use options, the more you need to understand volatility. You can either use it, or lose it.

What is Volatility?

The dictionary defines volatility as instability, unpredictability, or explosive in nature – things like emotions, volcanoes, or flare-ups in the Middle East. Stock market volatility means the same thing. The only difference is that we're talking about the unpredictable nature of prices.

Stock market volatility is a simple idea. It's a way of measuring the fluctuations of stock or index prices. Anyone trading stocks knows that some stock prices move wildly throughout the day as if bouncing on a trampoline – companies like Netflix or Amazon.com. Others seem to be on tranquilizers and only move pennies per week. If prices move a lot, it's a high-volatility stock. Ones that don't are low volatility.

Volatility is Not Directional

A stock's direction has nothing to do with volatility. A stock moving up can exhibit the identical volatility as one moving down, or even sideways. Instead, volatility just measures the fluctuations around the stock price's trend.

Take a look at the following stock chart for AT&T (T) over a one-year period:

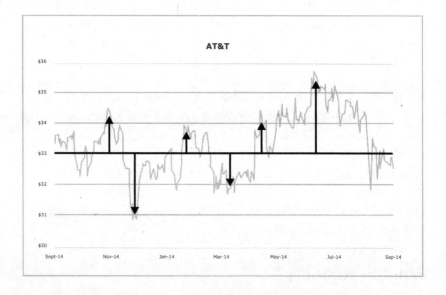

The price began and ended near $33 as shown by the horizontal bold line, so it was in a sideways trend. That's the average price. The stock price, however, didn't stay exactly at the $33 average for the entire year. Instead, it fluctuated around that price as shown by the arrows – that's the volatility. Sometimes the stock's price was above the trend; other times it was below. Volatility measures how far these variations are from the average trend.

As a rough volatility measure, the lowest price was $30.83, or 6.5% below the trend, while the highest price was about $35.70, or about 8% above the trend. All price fluctuations roughly occurred within 8% of the stock's average price.

Now take a look at Priceline (PCLN) over the same time:

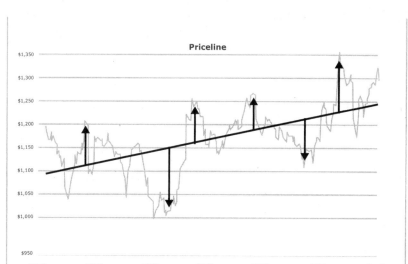

Unlike AT&T, the bold line shows Priceline was in an uptrend. Remember though, volatility has nothing to do with direction. Just as with AT&T, Priceline's daily prices didn't remain exactly on the bold trend line. Instead, daily prices fluctuated around that trend.

During the year, the average closing price was $1,168. The highest price was about $1,351, or 15% above the average. The low was about $998, or 15% below the average. All of Priceline's fluctuations occurred within 15% of the average. Now compare AT&T to Priceline: Priceline fluctuated within 15% of the average while AT&T moved within 8%. Priceline had larger fluctuations, so it was more volatile than AT&T.

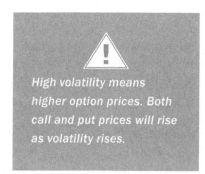

High volatility means higher option prices. Both call and put prices will rise as volatility rises.

Because Priceline has greater price fluctuations, its option prices will be higher – for both calls and puts. Bigger price fluctuations means the stock price could be much higher, so call buyers are willing to pay more. But those same big fluctuations also mean prices could be much lower, so put buyers are willing to pay more. High volatility means higher option prices – for calls and puts. Is that how the market responded to the higher volatility for AT&T and Priceline?

AT&T is currently about $33, and the one-month, $33 call is 42 cents. What can you get for 42 cents these days? Apparently, AT&T options. But now you should see that the "cheap" price doesn't necessarily mean it's a good deal. It just means that the market recognizes there aren't a lot of price fluctuations and therefore the $33 call is probably not going to be worth that much during the next month. Traders aren't willing to pay much for it.

Priceline, on the other hand, is about $1,330, and the one-month $1330 call is $33 – a big difference from 42 cents. Traders are willing to pay more for Priceline because there are more price fluctuations in the stock. It has a greater ability to rise or fall, so options traders are willing to pay more.

When you think of volatility, don't think of direction, or trend. Instead, think of how big the fluctuations are around the average trend. Volatility is actually a mathematical formula that measures the stock's price activity much like the Richter scale measures seismic activity for earthquakes. The greater the stretch between the highs and lows, the bigger the volatility, the bigger the stock price changes are expected, and the more valuable the option. Volatility is your key for determining if the option you're going to buy or sell will turn a profit.

Volatility is Annualized

Volatility is always reported as an annualized figure. Whether you measure the stock's closing prices over a three-month, six-month, one-year, or any other time frame doesn't matter. The volatility number is always reported as if it occurred over a one year period. The reason is simple. If AT&T was measured over a longer period than Priceline, it may appear that AT&T had more volatility, but that's only because more time was allowed for the price to move. To make fair comparisons, volatility is always annualized. For instance, a stock with 20% volatility is twice as volatile as a stock with 10% volatility.

The true volatility calculation was 15% for AT&T and 27% for Priceline over this one-year period. The higher the percentage, the higher the volatility, the higher the option prices.

Volatility is Risk

Volatility is also a measure of risk. In the world of investing, risk is defined as the probability of losing some or all of your investment. If you have a high probability of losing money, you're dealing with a high-risk stock. High-volatility stocks pose such risks because prices can move up or down by large amounts – and quickly. While it's true that Priceline could move up and make you lots of money, that's not a risk. The risk is to the downside. That's where you lose money. Priceline may be worth $1,330 today, but tomorrow morning it may be down $10, $20 – or far more. While we were writing this book, November 9, 2015, it fell $141.22, or 9.7% in a single day. And no, that's not a typo. That's volatility. That's why options traders are willing to pay $33 for a one-month option.

With high volatility stocks, you don't have a lot of confidence about the stock's value from day to day, so you have more risk. Priceline's nearly 10% drop in a single day is proof. Imagine what may happen with this stock over 30 days. That's why traders are willing to pay for these options.

On the other hand, if you hold a low-volatlity stock, you have a lot more confidence about tomorrow's price. If AT&T closes at $33 today, you can be pretty sure it will open at about the same price tomorrow. There just aren't a lot of price fluctuations from day to day, so you have more confidence that there won't be a drastic price change tomorrow. The stock has lower volatility. It has lower risk.

Volatility only occurs when stock price changes fluctuate *up and down*. If a stock's price was to do nothing but go higher (or lower), you have no volatility. For example, if Priceline increased by exactly 0.5% each day for the entire year, it's price chart would have looked like the following:

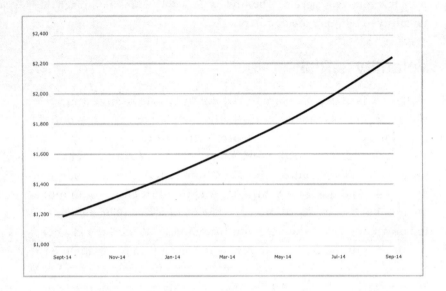

Because it started at $1,170 and ended the year over $2,200, new traders would think this means the stock had high volatility. Dramatic price increases (or decreases) don't necessarily mean high volatility. Notice the line in the chart: There are no fluctuations around it. It's a smooth line with each day posting successively higher prices. The volatility of this stock would be zero! That's because there is never a time when tomorrow's price is lower. So when you think of volatility, think of the back and forth whipsawing motion of a stock's price around its trend. Then you've got the idea.

Volatility matters because it allows options traders to get a handle on whether the price they're paying as the buyer, or receiving as the seller, represents a good deal. The only reason to make any investment is for an expected future profit. That's not only true for the stock market, but also if you're buying a business, home, rare art, collectible coins, or other investments. Your profit depends on the difference between the price paid and the unknown future price received, and that means the price you pay today may end up being too high. To succeed with options, you have to have a way to gauge if the price you're paying represents a fair deal. There's only one way to do that – volatility.

The Technical Side of Volatility

Up to this point, we just said that volatility is a mathematical measurement. Well, if you managed to also stay awake in any of your college statistics classes, you probably have a faint recollection of something called the standard deviation. The standard deviation is a mathematical measure of the fluctuations around the average. We're not going to get into the details, but just understand that what mathematicians call a standard deviation is exactly what traders call volatility. Volatility is just the standard deviation of those closing stock prices around the average stock price.

By using volatility, we can get great insights into a stock's future price. Let's say a stock is currently trading for $100. If the volatility is 20%, we multiply that by the stock's current price, which is $20. Because volatility is always annualized, this is a one standard deviation move over a one-year period. We can calculate a one-standard-deviation range by adding and subtracting $20 from the current stock price, which is $80 to $120.

According to the bell curve, 68% of all outcomes will fall within one standard deviation. So if we had thousands of stocks trading at the same price and volatility, 68% of them would have a closing price in one year between $80 and $120. Because this is one of many such stocks, we can alternatively say there is a 68% chance that this stock will have a closing price in one year between $80 and $120. If we guessed that the closing price would fall between $80 and $120 in one year, we'd be correct 68% of the time – and wrong 32% of the time.

What if they want more confidence in predicting the future price? We could calculate a two-standard-deviation range. If one standard deviation is $20, two standard deviations must be $40. Our expected range is now $60 to $140. Under a bell curve, 95% of the area lies within two standard deviations, so we're 95% sure that this stock's price will fall between $60 and $140 in one year. Who would have thought statistics would actually ever be useful? Don't be concerned over the calculations; the OptionsHouse platform will easily show you these ranges – and any range you select. You just need to know how to interpret them to make good decisions.

The graph below shows Priceline has a 95% chance of closing between $1,120 and $1,480 over the next month:

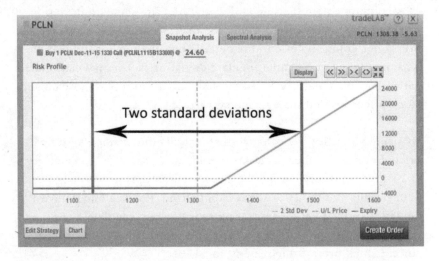

Using Option Pricing Models for Better Results

Professional traders have always used option pricing models, or calculators, to get a feel for whether an option's price represents a good deal or not. It all comes down to volatility. Remember, you can't look at an options total price, $3 for example, and make a judgment as to whether it's a good deal or not. Yet, that's how most options traders make their decisions. Instead, you need to consider volatility.

Let's say a stock is trading for $100. What should you pay for a one-month, $100 call option? To answer, we need to turn to a pricing model. The most famous is the Black-Scholes Model, which takes five factors: stock price, exercise price, days to expiration, risk-free interest rate, and volatility:

FACTORS		$100 CALL VALUE
Stock Price	$100	
Exercise Price	$100	
Days to Expiration	30	$2.30
Risk-Free Interest Rate	1%	
Volatility	20%	

After entering the five factors on the left, the calculator comes up with a $2.30 call value. This is the option's fair value, also called the theoretical price.

This means that if you were to buy (or sell) thousands of options just like this, in the long run you'd just break even.

However, notice that in order to price this option, the calculator needed to know volatility. If you look closely, you'll see something interesting about it. It's the only true *unknown* factor in the model, which is why volatility is so important for successful options trading. Why is it unknown?

If you had many traders all trying to figure out the fair value of this option, everyone would use $100 for the stock price, $100 for the exercise price, 30 days to expiration, and 1% for the risk-free interest rate. There's no room for argument – they're just market facts. However, when the model asks for volatility, what it really needs to know is the volatility that will occur during the option's life. That's called the *future volatility*, and because that's something we don't know, we can never be 100% sure what an options fair value is until we get the expiration.

If we don't know the future volatility today, our next best guess is to use the historic volatility as a substitute. It's exactly this disparity that allows us to see if an option is priced reasonably fairly or not. For instance, we used 20% for the volatility to derive a $2.30 call option

price. But let's say we look up the current market price and find the
option is trading for $3.50. Why is there a discrepancy? We thought
it was worth $2.30, but the market has priced it at $3.50. Who's right
and who's wrong?

All we can really say for sure is it that buyers and sellers
have agreed to trade for $3.50. Because we know the true
market price, we can work the pricing model backwards and
solve for the volatility. In other words, what volatility number
is necessary to make the option pricing model produce a
theoretical value of $3.50?

FACTORS		$100 CALL VALUE
Stock Price	$100	
Exercise Price	$100	
Days to Expiration	30	$3.50
Risk-Free Interest Rate	1%	
Volatility	30%	

The model tells us that 30% volatility is required to produce a $3.50 call
option price. Now we have something we can work with. While we can't
say if $3.50 is too high or too low just by looking at it, we can make that
judgment about volatility. The reason is that volatility is very predictable.
About the only constant in options trading is that volatility moves
sideways over time.

Volatility Moves Sideways

Market prices may rise and fall, but volatility just drifts sideways. No
matter how high or low a stock's price goes, if you look at the volatility,
it just oscillates back and forth. This is due to another mathematical
concept called *mean reversion*. In statistics, the average is called the
mean, so mean reversion just shows the data are moving toward, or

reverting to the average. It's easy to understand by considering some easy examples.

If a professional golfer shoots his absolute lowest score ever, he shouldn't expect his next round to be even lower. It's probably going to move back up toward his average. If a professional basketball player is seven feet tall, he shouldn't expect his children to be taller. Seven feet is already many standard deviations above the average, so the better guess is that his children will be shorter. Any time you're faced with an extreme outcome, it's not a good idea to expect the next occurrence to be more extreme. Instead, it's probably going to move in the other direction – lows get higher, and highs get lower. They gravitate around some average point.

That's exactly how mean reversion works. Stock prices are subject to supply and demand, analyst recommendations, earnings, and other types of information. But no matter how good or bad things get, volatility is only going to be so high or low. Each stock has a typical range for its volatility. If you look at volatility charts, you'll see that the volatility numbers just oscillate back and forth between two extremes. Below is a 1990 to 2015 chart of the Volatility Index, or VIX, which is a popular index that measures the volatility of the S&P 500. Even though the index has risen substantially over this time, it's evident that volatility just moves sideways:

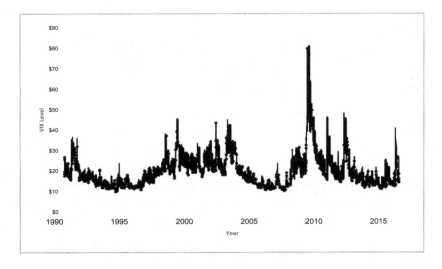

Here is a comparison chart of Priceline's implied volatility and historical volatility from the OptionsHouse platform:

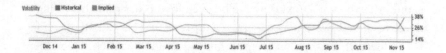

Whether looking at the overall market volatility, or the volatility of an individual stock, it's easy to see that volatility just moves sideways. Notice that the chart also gives a quick visual reference between historic volatility and implied. When the implied volatility is much greater than the historic, you have to realize that option prices are relatively high, and that must get factored into your strategies.

By looking at the OptionsHouse chart above, it's easy to see that the implied volatility is trading below the historical. The implied volatility is 23% while the stock is trading at 38%. In other words, the stock is producing price changes at the rate of 38% volatility, but options traders are only paying for 23% volatility. Traders are getting more volatility for the money, so options are relatively cheap. With just a quick glance at the chart, it's easy to see that the market is actually underpricing these options now. Even though the call's price was $33, when you consider the volatility you're getting, it's actually a cheap price. You can see how new traders are lured into thinking this would be an expensive option. To find profits in today's markets, you have to have the tools for seeing value. You need to see volatility.

Why did this happen when Priceline just took a big nosedive recently? Well, that crash was after an earnings report. If you look at the above chart, the implied volatility was already high – traders were bidding up option prices into the earnings report. After the report, the news was out, so nobody was willing to pay for the volatility anymore. The implied volatility fell, but the historic volatility rose. That's why you're seeing the two lines cross at the far right side of the chart. Once you understand how to read volatility, you can determine if option prices are relatively cheap or expensive with just a quick glance.

Four Types of Volatility

When option traders talk about volatility, we have to be careful to disclose what type of volatility we're referring to. Although the concept of volatility is always the same, we can measure it, or refer to it, across different times.

Think of how you'd respond if someone asked for information on the weather in your area. You could answer what the weather is typically like this time of year. You could say what it actually is today. And you could also say what it's *expected* to be over the next week. Your answer depends on the time frame. Likewise, we have four basic measures of volatility: historical, future, forecast, and implied.

Historical volatility is what we've been talking about so far. It's a measurement of the stock's volatility (standard deviation) over a given time. Naturally, depending on the time, we can get different results. A stock may have 20% volatility over the past three months but 15% over the past six months. Historical volatility is found by a rigid, mathematical calculation that leaves little room for interpretation. Because of this, it's also called *actual* volatility, *statistical* volatility, or *realized* volatility. Historical volatility measures the truth about past price fluctuations.

Future volatility is unknown. It's the volatility that will take place in the future. What is the future volatility of Priceline over the next month? Nobody knows. But at expiration, it will be the historical volatility. Then we'll know for sure.

Forecast volatility is an opinion about the future volatility. While Pete and I do not know what Priceline's future volatility will be over the next month, if we believe it will be 25% then that is our forecast volatility. Obviously, different traders will have different forecast volatilities. That's just a technical way of saying they have different opinions on how high or low the stock price may go.

Implied volatility is the most important and probably the most confusing to understand. It's found by *inferring* the future volatility from option prices. That's what we did in the earlier example assuming the call's market price was $3.50. By knowing the actual market price, we worked the pricing model backwards, and found the volatility number that is required to produce a $3.50 price. It turned out to be 30%, which is the implied volatility. In other words, because the market priced the option at $3.50, the crowd is implying the future volatility will be 30%. Otherwise, traders wouldn't be willing to buy and sell at that price.

When a pricing model asks for the volatility number, it's really asking for the *future* volatility. While we may have a good idea of what the future volatility will be (forecast volatility), it's something we can never know for sure and that's why it's impossible to say what an option's fair value really is. The best we can do is to gauge whether an option's price *appears* to be reasonable or not. Having that knowledge though is better than nothing and that's the all-important edge gained by understanding volatility and theoretical prices. The Black-Scholes Model is an option trader's cloudy crystal ball.

Volatility Will Be a New Profit Center

Not only is volatility important for understanding how to price options, it will play an increasingly important role in the future. As the speed of information increases, it's going to become increasingly difficult to react to market information. However, if you understand volatility, the very technology that's casing difficulties for stock traders will open up new doors for options traders.

We can use volatility in a different way by looking at each day's closing price and comparing it to a short-term moving average of volatility.

Take a look at Amazon.com over the past year:

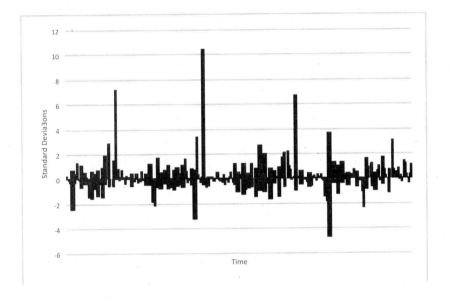

We're comparing each day's net change to a 20-day moving average of volatility. For example, if the stock closed up 1% today, we'd compare that to the volatility of the previous 20 days. According to the bell curve, nearly every day should fall within three standard deviations.

But look at the chart: You have one day that crossed four standard deviations, two that crossed six standard deviations – and one that topped 10 standard deviations. The odds for the stock to jump up six standard deviations are over a billion to one, and would be expected to happen by chance every couple million years. The 10-standard standard deviation mark is nearly incalculable. How are these moves possible?

The answer is that traditional pricing models are poorly equipped to model today's price changes. It's an error in pricing models. It can be the biggest thorn in your side – and it can also present the biggest opportunities. You just have to know where to look, how to trade it, and how to manage the risk.

Below is a chart of Priceline. You can see the six standard deviation move of the recent $141-point drop on the right side of the chart:

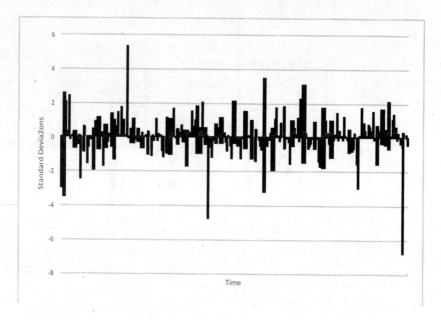

For the options trader, success depends on taking these potential volatility changes into account. If you buy options during high implied volatility, you need to know that at the time of the trade — otherwise you'll probably be looking at unexpected losses. It's easy to do if you just read the volatility chart showing when spikes are high and when they're not. If you just look at the stock price chart, you'll never see them.

Volatility is a critical concept for options traders whether new or experienced. By understanding volatility, you can quickly assess if options are cheap or expensive. There's no other method that allows traders to make relative comparisons. You must know volatility. When the new markets are creating four, five, six — and 10 – standard deviation moves, you can't ignore it. Value hides in volatility, and the new rules of investing say you must be able to uncover it. The machines may create the volatility, but the true options traders will profit from it.

What is Volatility Trading?

Volatility trading is just one of many styles of investing. For many professional traders, it's the only strategy that makes long-term financial sense mostly due to the theoretical edges it provides. While stock investing can be quite complex, volatility trading only requires you to compare implied and historical volatilities. In OptionsHouse, you can even compare implied volatility to historic implied volatility. Volatility trading will be more profitable as market uncertainty increases.

Volatility trading works because you're just looking at relative highs and lows. Volatility moves sideways over time, and there are ranges where it trades. In many cases, it's much easier to detect opportunities in volatility than direction in the stock's price. High volatility creates higher options prices, and that creates larger breakeven points. Rather than having to predict if the stock price will rise or fall, you're just figuring out if the crowd has overpriced the options. It's much like a point spread on a football bet. It may be difficult to figure out which team is going to win, but if Vegas puts a 20-point spread on one team, you're better off betting on the other. Historically, that's a really big spread and probably won't be beaten. That's exactly what we're doing with volatility trading.

One of the benefits of volatility trading is that you don't necessarily have to be concerned with the direction of the underlying stock as when you trade stocks. Even though stocks are a one-dimensional asset – you're betting the price will either rise or fall – there are a lot of complications that come about with trying to predict direction.

Stock investing is difficult because, no matter how much research you do, if it's public information, it's priced into the stock. New traders often make the mistake of reading a positive article about a company and think they can make easy money by purchasing the shares. But a dilemma arises once you realize that you're trading on information that is widely known by all other investors. Chances are that news is not brand new; it's probably been circulating for a while and is finally making it to the major news sources. Any perceived increase in value of the company has probably already been priced into its shares. If you're using options, you're probably faced with higher implied volatility.

The same is true for technical analysis. Just because a technical indicator may be giving a buy signal, remember that you're not the only one using that information. The best traders — whether technical or fundamental — are the ones who can successfully *anticipate* where those buy and sell points will occur and beat the rest of the market to the punch. It's the trader with the newest information that has the advantage.

You can't expect to beat the market by using the same information and acting at the same time as everybody else. Prior to the popularity of the computer, few people had access to stock quotes other than by looking in the newspaper. Back then, if you had access to real-time quotes, you'd have an edge by being able to identify short-term trends before other traders. So why don't you hear traders talking about the benefits of using real-time quotes? Because today, everybody has access to real-time quotes. Traders realize there's no additional value in real-time quotes. There's a penalty for not using them, but there's no advantage in using them. All benefits have been washed away.

Likewise, all traders are looking at technical indicators such as MACD, RSI, stochastics, and other common studies. If you believe these indicators *alone* have value then how much you'd pay for a monthly subscription service that provides the information to you?

Information only has value if it has the ability to change your decision.

You wouldn't pay a thing because that information is available to everybody who wants it for free. Information only has value if it has the ability to change your decision. This is why traders who make their sole decisions based on news or technical indicators often underperform the market.

This doesn't mean you shouldn't use technical analysis. To the contrary, technical analysis will become an increasingly important part of decision making. The difference is that the value doesn't lie in the indicator. Instead, the rewards will go to those who can extract information from the signals that is not already known by the market. And to do that, knowledge of options will become increasingly important. Traders who understand volatility will be able to see the collective opinions of the market.

As information flows faster, it will become increasingly difficult to profit from it. We hear a lot of traders thinking it will be easier because we have lightning-fast computers and information. Yes, but so does everybody else. To profit from options trading, you must have more information than the rest, and more importantly, you must be able to interpret the information correctly.

You Must Anticipate What the Crowd Thinks

Another problem we see with new traders is that they focus on one side of the argument that supports their outlook. It's fine to have an outlook; that's what investing is all about. To succeed, though, you have to filter through the information better than the rest of the crowd.

For example, during the terrorist attacks of September 11, 2001, many traders predicted that airline ticket prices would fall since the demand for airline tickets would fall. As one trader put it, "You don't need to know economics to figure that one out. If nobody wants to fly, prices must fall."

The truth is you do need to *not* know about economics to trade on that limited statement. Yes, it's true that prices will fall if demand falls, but that's assuming the supply doesn't change. But if part of your analysis says that people won't want to fly, why should you assume the airlines want to? After the attacks, airlines will certainly reduce the number of flights, or the supply of seats, just as passengers will surely reduce their demand. If the airlines do not want to fly, then the supply of airline seats is not constant and the problem becomes a question of which force – the reduction in passenger demand or the reduction in the supply of airline seats – is greater.

In other words, falling demand has *downward* pressure on price but falling supply has *upward* pressure on price. The resulting level for price depends on this tug-of-war between supply and demand. If the airlines reduce supply more than passengers reduce demand, you actually have a relative increase in demand and will see prices rise. Surprisingly, that's exactly what happened following the attacks – the cost of airline tickets went up.

Although basic economics can easily account for why prices rose, you will hear traders comment that the rising prices were a violation of economic principles because prices should fall if demand falls. These people are simply neglecting the fact that supply did not remain constant and that's what caused them to guess the price direction incorrectly. You must remember that any price is the result of two forces – supply and demand – but it's easy to only focus on the one that validates your view and forget about the other.

So even though the news appeared to predict falling airline prices, history shows that reacting to news is probably more difficult than most traders realize. But let's take it a step further and assume you did guess that airline ticket prices would rise. Does it follow that profits must go up?

No, because the total number of miles flown was sharply reduced. The airlines got a lot more money per mile, but they didn't fly nearly as many miles and the net result is a decrease in profits. The point is that it's nearly impossible to understand everything that's happening within a company and worldwide to make a consistently good educated guess as to what will happen to the stock's price based on current news. Keep in mind that, today, you must also factor in world events, currency fluctuations, commodity prices, and others. When the information flows at the speed of light, you need more than just a little bit of information suggesting the stock's price may rise.

As markets get more complex, faster, and riskier, you're going to see more opportunities in volatility trading. It never gets factored out like other information because traders and investors are inherently risk averse. They do everything they can to avoid risk. With options, however, traders get limited risk but unlimited reward risk profiles. They have less fear in bidding up options prices to lofty levels. And it's this strong tendency – and mistake – that allows us to profitably trade volatility.

This is why volatility trading will play an increasingly important role in today's markets. The above difficulties inherent in stock selection provide one of the strongest motivations for volatility trading since it's much simpler to understand and predict. You just need to know when volatility is relatively high or low. As volatility traders, we leave the guesswork on the stock's direction to the speculators. We just wait for times when speculators are overly optimistic or pessimistic and bid the options to unrealistically high or low time premiums. Before you can trade it and profit from it, you have to understand volatility. For today's markets, traders who do will find value in volatility.

Investitute Takeaway

Volatility is a mathematical formula that measures the degree of stock price fluctuations. Volatility is non-directional, so a stock moving up, down, or sideways can have high or low volatility. Volatility is always measured as an annualized percentage, and the greater the percentage, the greater the price fluctuations. Volatility is the only way to judge if the price you're paying or receiving represents a good deal. If you overpay for options, or sell for too little, you can end up losing on the trade even though you were correct about the stock's direction. Understanding volatility – and how to profit from it – is key for success in today's markets.

RULE 11

Follow the Inside Money

"If you're not inside, you are outside." That's the money-making advice Gordon Gekko gave to his apprentice Bud Fox in the hit movie *Wall Street*. He was, of course, talking about trading on inside information – information that only top-tier management would know. It's valuable information. It's smart money. There's just one problem – it's illegal to trade on it.

Inside information is defined as any material, non-public information. By "material," it means that it's significant information that would likely move prices – for better or worse – if released to the market. If you know your company is going to be acquired, it's material information. If you know your company is launching a new product line next season, it's not.

Anyone in possession of inside, material information can be prosecuted for trading on it – or leaking it to others who trade on it. The Securities and Exchange Commission (SEC) believes that trading on inside information allows a few insiders a big benefit at the expense of many, which would undermine the integrity of the financial markets. If investors felt they were going to be taken advantage of in the markets, nobody would invest, and that destroys the country's ability to raise capital. Who'd want to buy

shares of stock if you felt that only the insiders were going to make
all the money?

You'd probably feel snubbed if you sold your shares, only to find
that a few days later the junior executive just made $10 million
dollars from buying up shares because he knew the company was
being taken over. If you had that information, you'd have waited.
In an attempt to make things fair, the government tries to level the
playing field by making it illegal to trade on inside information.

Probably the most recent famous case was with Martha Stewart who
served five months in prison and paid several hefty fines for trading
on inside information. Insider information cases are often difficult
to prove, and hers was one of them. The Feds, instead, ended up
busting her for lying during the investigation about her sales, which
is why she didn't spend that much time in the slammer.

She sold shares of her ImClone stock the day before it dropped 16%
after its drug Erbitux failed to get FDA approval. ImClone's founder,
Samuel D. Waksal served seven years for selling shares ahead of the
information too.

The irony is that Stewart avoided a $46,000 loss by selling about
4,000 shares. As a billionaire, it would have been better to let that
serve as a tax write-off rather than a way to serve prison time.
Still, people can't avoid trading on inside information. It's money in
the bank, and seems wasteful to ignore it. It's as if the broker was
saying, "All you have to do is push this sell button, and you'll be
better off by $46,000 tomorrow." Who could say no?

As with all arguments, you have two sides to the story. Some
economists have argued in favor of trading on inside information.
All things being equal, we'd like to see free-flowing information
rather than having valuable information held back. One of the
key purposes of the financial markets is to determine the value of
shares, and what better way for people to make that determination
than to be in possession of all available information?

Trading on inside information may unfairly *benefit* insiders, but banning it can also unfairly *harm* investors. While many insiders benefited by selling ImClone shares ahead of the news, other investors bought shares and instantly lost 16%. If the FDA information been allowed to flow freely into the markets, investors whose untimely purchase ahead of the news would have been spared the large losses.

Regardless of the pros and cons, trading on inside information remains illegal. It's an instant source of big money. It's tempting, it's too big to resist, and insiders do it all the time. When they do, however, they're not buying shares of stock. Why buy expensive shares, when you can get big leverage from options? That's where the money is.

Every criminal knows to follow the money. When notorious bank robber Willie Sutton was asked by a reporter why he robbed banks, he replied "That's where the money is." His answer gave rise to Sutton's Law, which is used when diagnosing or solving problems – start with the obvious choice first.

If you're a corporate insider and have decided to make money illegally, follow Sutton's Law – go for the obvious choice first. The money is on the inside, and it's on options. Put down a couple of bucks on out-of-the-money call options, and when the stock's price pops, collect all of the intrinsic value – on many thousand more shares than you could have purchased otherwise. It's not a risk when you know the outcome.

Even Gordon Gekko couldn't resist. Once he figured out that Anacott Steel was being acquired, he instructed Bud to buy 1,500 July $50 calls. It's no surprise that they were short term and out-of-the-money. That's where the leverage is. It's where the smart money hides.

Trading on Inside Information – Sort Of

Anyone can make an investment based on publicly available information. In fact, even if you synthesize publicly available information and conclude that a company's going to be acquired, that's not illegal either. Everyone has access to that information at the same time. Rewards, however, come to those who know how to interpret the information better than the rest. It's only when you trade on inside information that it's illegal.

The options market gives everyone tremendous insights into future stock prices, so options can be used as a form of technical analysis. If you know where to look, you can see where the crowd is lining up. Spotting insider trading, however, is entirely different from acting on insider information. As long as you are using publicly available information to make your decisions, it's perfectly legal. As the markets get more sophisticated and information flows faster, insiders will get in possession of inside information sooner. Big money will be made by traders who understand how to spot insider activity. It's a new rule of investing. The new markets are making this a more viable way for fast money.

Spotting Illegal Activity: Volume and Open Interest

Experienced traders know how to spot potential insider trading by looking at the *volume* and *open interest*. Volume shows how many contracts were traded that day. When Bud bought 1,500 July $50 calls, he added 1,500 to that day's volume. If you bought 10 of the same calls later in the day, you'd add another 10 contracts to that day's volume. Whether you're buying or selling, each executed order gets tabulated in that day's volume.

Open interest is related, but a little different. When you're opening a contract, you're either initiating a position or increasing the size of an existing position. On the other hand, if you're closing a position, it's just the opposite. You're either completely exiting that position, or you're reducing the size of an existing position.

If you don't have any Anacott Steel July $50 calls and you buy 10, that's an opening transaction since you're initiating a position. If you buy five more at a later time, that's also an opening order because you've increased your position size from 10 to 15. If you decide to sell five of your July $50 calls, your position size is reduced from 15 back to 10. That's a closing transaction. If you sell the remaining 10, that's also a closing transaction since you've completely exited the position.

Open interest shows how many contracts are open for delivery. When contracts are first listed, open interest begins at zero. If one trader buys 10 contracts to open while another sells 10 contracts to open, then open interest increases by 10. Both traders are opening, so that's why open interest increases.

However, at a later time, if one trader sells five contracts to close, while another buys five contracts to close then open interest would be reduced by five contracts. Both traders were closing.

Finally, if one trader is opening while another trader is closing, then open interest remains unchanged. Those traders are just effectively swapping positions with each other. One is opening the position but the other is closing, so there's no effect on the overall open interest.

The only time that open interest increases is if the buyer and seller are placing opening trades. The only time it falls if both sides are closing. During each day, the Options Clearing Corporation (OCC) tracks the open interest and reports the level on the opening bell each day. Even though open interest changes during each trading day, you won't see the new information until the following day when reported by the OCC.

For any given expiration month, at-the-money options will usually have the highest open interest. For any given strike, open interest begins at zero and peaks at about the half-way point of the option's life. After that, it begins to decline.

New traders often focus too much on volume and think something may be going on with a particular stock if there's high option volume. Volume is important, but it doesn't show if those are opening or closing transactions. You could have a lot of volume for the day but actually decrease the amount of open interest if most of the traders are closing. The real way to spot potential insider activity is to consider radical changes in volume compared to the average while also monitoring the open interest.

Even with open interest, you have to filter out possible extraneous noise. You may see a sudden spike in open interest at one strike, but find a nearly identical open interest at a nearby strike. That may be a spread order, which means the trader is buying a call and selling a call, so the profit is limited. That information isn't going to carry the same significance as when insiders are buying straight call options. Gordon Gekko didn't buy spreads; he bought calls. There's no sense in hedging your bets when you know what's going to happen.

While most open interest occurs at-the-money, you may see a lot of traders suddenly lining up at an out-of-the-money strike. For instance, if the stock is $100, the $100 calls would usually have the largest open interest. If you see that the $105 or $110 calls have a quick spike, especially if that spike is large relative to the average volume, you have to wonder why. There's a good chance it's insiders jumping in prior to the news.

Speculative Trading Must be Part of Your Plan

Pete and I have actively searched for insider information for most of our career. We developed sophisticated tools for searching for unusual option activity, and came up with ways of filtering out the noise. We even have scanning tools that allow OptionsHouse traders to click a button and see an instant listing of all the unusual option activity.

Searching for inside information is a way of searching for a few — but very large home run hits. Naturally, all unusual activity is not going to turn out to be inside information. It is somewhat speculative. We say "somewhat" because you're probably never going to get hurt too badly from placing these trades. Usually the worst case is that they just don't turn out as good as expected.

For any portfolio, however, you must have some speculative capital invested. That's just good portfolio management. You don't want everything in guaranteed investments – even Warren Buffett doesn't do that – and you don't want everything in lottery tickets. Instead, you should use a well-balanced portfolio, one that is in line with your risk tolerances, but that's also free to take a good speculative trade when the rewards greatly outweigh the risks.

The best opportunities don't present themselves often, so when they do, you need to be ready to act. Options provide a big advantage because of the leverage, and you can invest very little money. It doesn't take much to gain some exposure to a few trades that may define your success. Is it worth the risk of missing out on some of the biggest stock price moves you'll ever see?

We have always taught clients the right times to speculate. For example, after you've rolled some options and are sitting on some nice profits. Take some of those gains and use to speculate if an opportunity arises. If it turns out to flop, those losses can be used at tax time to offset the gains from the rolling. If you speculate at the right times, you'll find that a large part of that risk sits with the government's taxes – not your money. If the speculative trade does turn out to be a homerun, you'll have more taxes to pay, but it's only because you made more money. Speculating at the right times can put you into a win-win situation.

For the times you want to speculate, what could be better? Do you want to take a shot on some unknown penny stock? Or just pick an out-of-the-money option and hope for the best? We have tools today that allow traders to do much better than that. We can scan thousands of optionable stocks, and when the entire world is trading in one stock market, somebody surely knows something. Information flows much too quickly – and secretively – for someone to not be in possession of that knowledge. Some will take advantage, and trade on it for quick profits.

We can use technology too, but in a different way. We can use it to spot them. We'll capture the identical gains by indirectly – and legally – using their inside information. Gekko was right, you're either on the inside, or you are outside. But by using sophisticated scanners, we can trade the inside information from the outside. Let the insiders take the risk. Their old ways of thinking have created a new rule of trading.

Investitute Takeaway

Inside information is illegal to trade on. But it's not illegal to use publicly traded information in an attempt to identify illegal insider activity. Speculation can always be part of any portfolio, provided the rewards are good relative to the risks. Computerized trading makes it so easy for information to instantly flow worldwide. Somebody will know something – and many will not be able to resist. We have ways to identify these opportunities, so you now have a way to trade them.

RULE 12

Learn to Speak Greek

The story of the Trojan horse is one of many epic Greek myths. It shows how things are not always as they appear, and that risks can hide in unusual places.

Options also contain hidden risks, and traders turn to Greeks of a different kind to see them. With options, the biggest risk is the way that prices can change. One day your option responds slowly to stock prices. Another day it may change quickly. Those changes, of course, are the very qualities that provide opportunities – provided you can see them.

For that, options traders turn to several mathematical measurements called the Greeks – each designated by a Greek letter. They're easy to use, but most new traders either don't know about them – or choose to ignore them. To manage your money in the most efficient way, select the right strategies and expirations, you have to understand how option prices change. Risks can hide in unusual places.

Insights into Option Price Changes

Option traders have rights to buy or sell shares of stock. Because of the right, not the obligation, option prices don't respond exactly the same way as shares of stock. If you buy 100 shares of stock for $50 per share, you'll make one dollar for every dollar the price rises, and lose one dollar for each dollar it falls. That should make perfect sense: You own the shares, so of course they rise and fall with itself.

Now consider an out-of-the-money call option, say the $60 call trading for 10 cents. With the stock at $50, it has a long way to go before that option is going to be worth anything at all. It's most likely going to expire worthless. If the market feels there's not much of a chance for it to have any intrinsic value at expiration, it's not going to respond too well with changes in the stock's price. If the stock rises one dollar, should you expect the $60 call to also rise one full dollar and be worth $1.10? If the market responded that way, it would be too good to be true, as that means you could own the shares of stock for 10 cents rather than $50.

To understand how option prices change, recognize that the market is a live auction, and buyers and sellers are placing orders to buy or sell based on the likelihood that the option will become shares of stock. If the $60 call is worth 10 cents, it's doubtful anybody is going to be eager to spend much more – even though the stock is now $51. Chances are it's still going to expire worthless, so the $60 call's price won't budge. The $60 call's price won't be too sensitive to changes in the stock's price.

Now think about a deep in-the-money call, say the $30 call. Because the option is so deep in-the-money, the market feels it's probably going to remain in-the-money by expiration, which means it would be worthwhile for someone to exercise it and convert it to shares of stock. So if the market feels this option is definitely going to become shares of stock in the future, it will treat it like shares of stock today. If the stock rises one dollar right now, the $30 call will rise close to one full dollar as well. The deep in-the-money call will be highly sensitive to changes in the stock's prices.

A Simple Pricing Model

To understand why options don't usually respond dollar-for-dollar with the stock, let's look at a simple pricing model. Let's say we have a stock trading for $100 that can only rise or fall five points. It's an unrealistic assumption, but that's done to provide some sense of volatility. Just how far can the stock's price go? We need to account for that. We'll also assume that all stock prices are equally likely, which is definitely not true in the real world of stocks. If the stock is currently $100, there's a better chance for the price to rise or fall by one dollar rather than five dollars. But this assumption is done to make the math easy. Below are the possible $100 call prices at expiration:

STOCK PRICE	$100 CALL
105	5
104	4
103	3
102	2
101	1
100	0
99	0
98	0
97	0
96	0
95	0

If the stock price closes above $100 at expiration, the $100 call will just be worth the intrinsic value and nothing otherwise. What's this call option worth? Because we assumed that all stock prices are equally likely, the call is worth the average price. If you add up all the numbers in the second column and divide by 11, you'll get $1.36. That represents the option's fair value. Remember, fair value means the price at which there's no inherent advantage to the buyer or seller. It's a price that's fair to both traders. Now let's make the stock price rise one dollar to $101. The possible values for the $100 call now range from $1 to $6:

STOCK PRICE	$100 CALL
106	6
105	5
104	4
103	3
102	2
101	1
100	0
99	0
98	0
97	0
96	0

Remember, we assumed the stock could rise or fall by five dollars, so with the stock at $101, it could rise as high at $106, or fall to $96. You can see that we've added the possibility for a $6 payoff. That wasn't available with the stock at $100. Because the stock has moved to $101, we're adding higher potential payoffs to the option. What's the $100 call worth now? Just add up all the numbers in the second column and divide by 11, and the answer is $1.90.

Now compare the two tables. We moved the stock price from $100 to $101, and the option's price moved from $1.36 to $1.90, or about 55 cents. This is a very rough way of showing why at-the-money options do not move dollar-for-dollar with the stock

In-the-Money Options

If we went through the exercise again, but this time assumed the stock was $106, there would be no possibilities for zeros for the option's price. The range of stock prices would be a high of $111 and a low of $101, which means the $100 call is always in-the-money as shown in the table below:

In-The-Money Call Option			
Stock Price	$100 call	Stock Price	$100 call
111	11	112	12
110	10	111	11
109	9	110	10
108	8	109	9
107	7	108	8
106	6	107	7
105	5	106	6
104	4	105	5
103	3	104	4
102	2	103	3
101	1	102	2
Sum	66		77
$100 call	66/11 = $6		77/11 = $7

The sum of the entire column is 66, which means the call's value is $6. If the stock rises one dollar to $107, the call's value increases by exactly one dollar to $7. This helps to show why deep in-the-money options move dollar-for-dollar with changes in the stock's price. They're so deep in-the-money that the market believes there's no chance for any "zero" outcomes in the option's price. No matter where the stock rises beyond that point, the call will track the stock dollar-for-dollar. Once again, at that point, the call option is no longer an option – it's stock.

Out-of-the-Money Options

Now let's take a look at how out-of-the-money option prices move, and you'll see why they're so slow to respond to changes in the stock's price. Let's say the stock is $96 so the $100 call is four points out-of-the-money. If the stock can only rise or fall by five dollars, the best the $100 call can be worth is one dollar. Out of 11 possible values, the average value falls to just nine cents:

Out-Of-The-Money Call Option			
Stock Price	$100 call	Stock Price	$100 call
101	1	102	2
100	0	101	1
99	0	100	0
98	0	99	0
97	0	98	0
96	0	97	0
95	0	96	0
94	0	95	0
93	0	94	0
92	0	93	0
91	0	92	0
Sum	1		3
$100 call	1/11 = .09		3/11 = 0.27

If the stock rises to $97, now the $100 call may be worth one or two dollars at best, so the average rises to 27 cents. Notice, however, that even though the stock rose one full dollar from $96 to $97, the call only rose from nine cents to 27 cents. Out-of-the-money options are not responsive to changes in the stock's price.

Just in case you're thinking that the percentage change is great – moving from nine to 27 cents – remember that this basic model assumed that all stock prices were equally likely. In the real world, this option would remain at nine cents, especially after accounting for bid-ask spreads and commissions.

Option prices are always rising and falling in response to people's perceptions on how likely it is for the option to expire in-the-money. These example are fairly easy to understand by considering extreme out-of-the-money and in-the-money options. As you deal with near-the-money options, those with strikes closer to the current stock price, it's not so easy to understand how their prices will respond. When you buy or sell options, you'll want to know just how sensitive your options are to changes in the stock's price. For that, you'll need to understand the Greeks. Risks – and opportunities – can hid in unusual places.

Introducing the Greeks

The Greeks are mathematical measurements that are outputs from a theoretical pricing model. The OptionsHouse platform will clearly show the Greeks in real time. Each Greek letter designates some relationship – usually between the option's price and another variable. There are five Greeks you'll need to know: delta, gamma, theta, vega, and rho.

Delta has several interpretations:

1) Percent change
2) Probability for expiring in-the-money
3) Share equivalent

Probably the easiest way to think about delta is that it shows how the option's price will change for a one-dollar change in the stock. Let's say a $50 call is trading for $3 with a delta of 0.50. If the stock rises one dollar right now, the option's price will increase by delta, or 50 cents. The call option's price will rise from $3 to $3.50.

In other words, the call option isn't going to pick up the full dollar change in the stock. With few exceptions, most options are not going to move dollar-for-dollar with the stock. Delta shows the percentage by which it tracks the stock's changes. With a delta of 0.50, if the stock had risen 50 cents instead, the call will rise 50% of that, or 25 cents. The call's price would rise from $3 to $3.25.

Delta works in reverse too. If the stock price fell from $50 to $49, the call would lose 50 cents and trade for $2.50.

Technically speaking, delta represents the percentage change for a small change in the stock's price, not a full dollar. If the stock price changes by a small amount, say 10 or 20 cents, delta will be accurate. If you see a price move greater than one dollar, delta will underestimate the move a little bit, and your option's price will actually change by a little bit more than delta.

However, to make it easy, most traders consider delta the amount by which the option's price will change for a full dollar change in the stock's price. That's actually a little too big of a jump, so delta will not be perfect. Still, it's an easy way to understand what it means.

Put options have negative deltas. That just means their values rise when the stock price falls, or falls when the stock price rises. If you have a $50 put trading for $3 with a delta of -0.50, it will increase to $3.50 if the stock price falls one dollar. It will fall to $2.50 if the stock price rises one dollar.

The delta of an at-the-money option is approximately 0.50 (or -0.50 for puts). Delta rises as the option moves in-the-money and falls as it moves out-of-the-money. Keep in mind this can be tricky when dealing with positive and negative numbers. A put with a delta of -0.50 is increasing if it moves to -0.40. The easier way to remember how deltas move is to forget about the negative sign for puts, and just remember that the number gets bigger as options move in-the-money. Delta always ranges between zero for deep out-of-the-money options and 1.0 for deep in-the-money options (-1.0 for put options). The very highest call delta is 1.0, which means the option is behaving just like stock and therefore moves dollar-for-dollar. For puts, a delta of -1.0 means it's behaving like short shares of stock. Delta can never exceed 1.0 because, ultimately, all the option can be converted into is shares of stock. Once it's so deep in-the-money that the market feels it will definitely expire with intrinsic value, the delta becomes one.

The second interpretation of delta is that it shows the approximate mathematical probability for the option to expire in-the-money. That makes intuitive sense if you think about it. If you had hundreds of at-the-money options, half of them would expire in-the-money and half would expire out-of-the-money. If there's a 50% chance for the option to expire in-the-money, the market will pay 50 cents on the dollar for that next dollar move.

Now think about the rules of probability. If there's a 50% chance for an option to be in-the-money, there must be a 50% chance for it to be out-of-the-money. If the at-the-money call delta is 0.50, the at-the-money put option must be -0.50. If a call option has a 0.80 delta, the same-strike put must have a delta of -0.20. In other words, if there's an 80% chance for the call option to be in-the-money, there's 20% chance for it to be out-of-the-money. And that means the same-strike put would be in-the-money. Forgetting about the negative sign on the put's delta, the call and put deltas must add up to one.

Delta's third interpretation is that it shows the option's share equivalence. If you have one call option with a delta of 0.50, even though the option controls 100 shares, right now it's behaving like 50% of that, or 50 shares. If you owned the call option and the stock rises one dollar, it will rise just 50%, or $50 – exactly the same as if you owned 50 shares.

Different interpretations are useful for different situations. The most important point to realize is that delta doesn't remain the same.

Just because an option has 0.50 delta today doesn't mean it always remains at that level. As the option gets deeper in-the-money, the market gains more confidence that it will remain in-the-money and will therefore pay more than the original delta. Conversely, if the option moves out-of-the-money, the market has less confidence it will expire in-the-money and will pay less for the next dollar move. The delta falls. Delta therefore changes as the stock's price changes.

You can see how it would be important to know how sensitive your option's price is in relation to changes in the stock's price. For equally good reasons, you'll need to know how delta will change. And for that, you'll need to know gamma.

Gamma measures the rate of change of delta and is sometimes called the "delta of the delta." If the $50 call has a delta of 0.50, the delta will change if the stock price rises. If the stock rises one dollar to $51, the delta may rise to 0.55. If it does, that means gamma was the .05 difference.

Right now, IBM is trading for $131.75 with the following deltas and gammas for the seven-day $130 call and put:

OPTION	PRICE	DELTA	GAMMA
$130 call	$2.60	0.68	.08
$130 put	0.80	-0.32	.09

With the stock at $131.75, the $130 call is slightly in-the-money, so the market has a little bit more confidence that it will expire in-the-money. That's why the delta is greater than 0.50 and showing 0.68. If the stock rises one dollar right now, the $130 call will gain 68 cents and trade for about $2.60 + 0.68, or $3.28.

But if the option moves further in-the-money, the market must be even more confident it will expire in-the-money, so the delta must change too. Delta will increase by the amount of gamma. If the stock rises one dollar right now, the new delta will be 0.68 + .08, or

0.76. In other words, if the stock rises one dollar, the new delta is the original delta + gamma. The option's delta is 0.68 now, but will become 0.76 if the stock rises one dollar.

Why such a big jump? Because there are only seven days until expiration. With so little time, it only takes a little bit of intrinsic value before the market believes that the option will remain in- the- money by expiration. The market's confidence is always a relationship between how far the option is in-the-money and the time remaining.

The put deltas work in a similar way. If the stock rises one dollar right now, the put's delta moves from -0.32 + .09 = -0.23. As the stock moves higher, the call deltas will increase while the put deltas will decrease. Keep in mind that when negative numbers get bigger, it really means they're getting "less small" so, ignoring the minus sign, the number will get smaller. For put options, moving from a -0.32 to -0.23 deltas is an increase. Any time the stock price rises, all deltas will increase by gamma. If the stock price falls, all deltas decrease by gamma.

Because the deltas must always add up to 1.0, the call and put deltas have the same gamma. In other words, if the call delta rises from 0.75 to 0.80, the put delta must have risen from -0.25 to -0.20 in order to keep the numbers adding up to 1.0.

Think of the delta and gamma relationship as you do when trying to figure out if your favorite sports team will win the current game. Two things will give you a lot of confidence. First, if your team has a large lead, you're fairly confident they'll win. High confidence is the same as a high delta. Delta shows the probability of expiring in-the-money. If your team has a big lead, you'd have a high degree of confidence they'll win.

Second, your team may only have a slight lead, but there may be seconds remaining on the clock. Even though it's a small lead, you're still fairly confident your team will win because, with no time left, a small lead is just as good as a big lead. Your confidence of you team winning is really the relationship between how big the lead may be – combined with the time remaining on the clock.

So even though this $130 call option is only $1.75 in-the-money, the next dollar move makes the market pretty sure it will remain in-the-money because there are only seven days until expiration. That's why there's such a big jump in delta.

At-the-money options have the highest gamma. In fact, all Greeks are maximized at-the-money with the exception of delta, which is maximized deep in-the-money.

In the previous section on delta, we said that if your stock moves by more than one dollar, delta will underestimate the move. Gamma is the reason. New traders may see their delta, for example, at 0.50 and believe that their option will increase $2 if the stock rises $4 right now. Because of gamma, however, that option will rise by more than two dollars. This is why you always have to remember that the Greeks are only accurate for small changes in the variable they're measuring. They constantly change, which is why they're important to know for today's markets. Things change quickly, and you have to understand how those changes will affect your positions.

If you buy an option, you have positive gamma, which is an interesting and beneficial property. That's one of the benefits of buying options. With positive gamma, call buyers automatically get increases in delta as the stock price moves. It's as if the call option is automatically buying more shares, but only if the stock's move is favorable. On the other hand, if the stock falls, call buyers will find their deltas are automatically reduced. The call option is automatically managing risk and reducing your exposure to the stock if it moves against you. Having this automatic hedging feature is a big benefit of positive gamma, and you only get it from buying options.

The same would be true for long puts, just in the opposite direction. If the stock price falls, your long put will automatically become shorter. If the stock price rises, the put automatically becomes longer, which means your position is acting like fewer short shares of stock. This shows that when you buy options, you need the underlying stock to move in your favor to generate profits which we also saw earlier by having to reach the breakeven point. Positive gamma means the trader needs price movement.

However, all Greeks can be reversed by taking the opposite side of the trade. If you sell calls or puts, you'll have negative gamma, and the effects are just reversed. If you sell a call option, you have negative gamma and will find that your call is making you shorter in a rising market. In other words, you're selling shares into a favorable market move. This is called "fading the market" and is a desirable property for some traders. For others it can pose a risk. The point to understand is that options give you many choices, and some are not so obvious. To really understand strategies, you have to speak Greek.

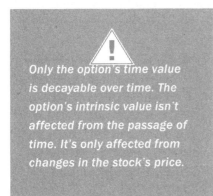

Only the option's time value is decayable over time. The option's intrinsic value isn't affected from the passage of time. It's only affected from changes in the stock's price.

Theta shows how much the option's price will change if one day passes. As you get closer to expiration, the option's time value decreases. That's because, at expiration, all time values must be zero. With no time remaining, there can be no time value. It's only the time value that's decayable over time.

The option's intrinsic value isn't affected from the passage of time. The only thing that changes the intrinsic value is changes in the stock's price. So as the option gets closer to expiration, some of its value must be eroding with each passing day. Theta shows that amount.

Theta was chosen because it's the Greek letter for "T" for time. In other words, theta shows how much your option's price will lose for the next trading day.

If you have the $50 call trading for $3 with theta of -0.02, then tomorrow's price is expected to fall by two cents, or to $2.98. Keep in mind that all Greeks are assuming all other factors will remain the same. Obviously, if the stock's price falls tomorrow, that will drag the option's price down by more than two cents. Theta just assumes that only the passage of time has occurred.

At-the-money options have the highest theta. Remember, all Greeks are maximized at-the-money, with the exception of delta. Theta increases as the expiration date approaches. If you buy an option, you have negative theta, which means your position will lose money over time. If you sell an option, you have positive theta, which means that position will increase a little bit each day. However, don't think this means it's a guaranteed asset and that your position just increases without bound every day. When you sell an option, the most you can make is the amount received, which is generally a small, fixed amount. Theta shows how much of that is being accrued to you with each passing day.

To succeed with options, don't think that negative theta is bad and positive theta is good. Many traders get hung up on theta and feel it's always best to have positive theta and therefore sell options. However, while positive theta is beneficial to option sellers, it also represents their compensation for the risk they accepted. Negative theta, on the other hand, is the price the buyer pays for having the right to walk away from the deal. It's the price of positive gamma.

The option buyer gets limited risk and unlimited gains. Those are big benefits, and yes, you'll pay for those through theta. Always approach options strategies with trading plans in mind. Select strategies that allow you to reach your goals safely. Sometimes it may be positive theta, and other times it may be negative. Don't get focused on a single Greek and think it always has to be the same. Options are tools, and if the tools change for the job, the Greeks will change too.

Vega is the rate of change of an option's price for a one percentage point increase in volatility, which is also called a one-tick change in volatility. A one percentage point increase means you're adding one to the volatility number and not increasing it by one percent. For example, if volatility is 20%, then a one percentage point increase, or one-tick increase, would make it 21%.

Vega is not actually a Greek letter, as the Greeks don't have a letter for "V" so the word vega was chosen to sound like a Greek letter to represent volatility.

Recall that volatility is the mathematical measure that shows the fluctuations around the stock's average price. As those fluctuations increase, call and put options become more valuable. Volatility is non-directional, so higher volatility means there's a better chance for the stock's price to rise, which is good for calls. There's also a better chance for the stock's price to fall, which is beneficial for puts. All options – calls and puts – increase in value as volatility rises. The question is by how much? Vega shows the answer.

Vega is maximized for at-the-money options. If you buy an option, you have positive vega. If you sell an option, you have negative vega. For a given strike price, vega will increase as time to expiration increases. That is, longer-term options are more sensitive to changes in volatility.

For instance, assume you have the $50 call trading for $3 with a vega of 0.15. It's currently priced at 20% volatility. If volatility rises to 21%, the option's price will rise to $3.15. If volatility falls to 19%, the call's price will fall by 15 cents to $2.85.

Volatility plays a crucial role in strategies. Vega shows how responsive your options are to changes in volatility.

Rho measures the change in an option's price for a one-percentage point, or one tick, change in the risk-free interest rate. The Greek letter "R" is used to represent changes in the interest "rate." For example, rho shows how much your option's price will change if interest rates rise from 1% to 2%, or from 5% to 6%, for example.

The risk-free rate is usually benchmarked to the Treasury bill with the same number of days to expiration. If you have a 30-day option, you'd look at the 30-day T-bill rate to find the current interest rate being used to price that option.

All financial assets have some sensitivity to interest rates because it's always the minimum opportunity cost for money. Whenever you spend money on an investment, you cannot also leave that money in the bank to earn interest. You miss out on that interest, so it has to get accounted for in the pricing. Call option prices increase from rising interest rates while put option prices will fall.

Call prices rise because you are technically borrowing money when you purchase a call. If you buy a one-year $100 call for $8, for example, you have the right to pay the $100 strike at expiration – you don't pay it today. Therefore, you're controlling the $100 stock for only $8 and can leave the remaining $92 in your money market to earn interest. Had you purchased the shares instead, you would have paid the full $100 today and would not be able to earn interest on that difference. Option buyers recognize they are benefiting from this additional interest, so that benefit gets factored into the call option's price.

Put options work in the opposite way; their prices fall as interest rates rise. As interest rates rise, investors become more inclined to delay the purchasing of shares so they can hang onto their money to earn interest. If they do wish to buy shares, they may actually turn to selling puts to delay their purchase – and to collect more cash on which to earn interest. Because of the increased selling, put prices fall as interest rates rise. If interest rates fall, the opposite happens: call prices fall while put prices rise.

If you buy options, don't be too excited if the Fed raises or lowers interest rates and think your call or put options are going to get a sudden boost or loss in value. Option prices are not very sensitive to changes in interest rates unless they are very long term options with high strike prices. Because of this, most option traders do not spend a lot of time worrying about rho. More importantly, the Fed usually changes interest rates in 25-basis point increments, or 0.25%. Whatever the rho value may be, your option's sensitivity is probably one-fourth of that.

For example, the current risk-free interest rate is about 0.23%. You buy the 30-day, $50 call for $1.15 with a rho of .05. If the interest rate rises one full point percentage point, your call's price will increase to $1.20.

However, look what happens when you buy an at-the-money call on an expensive stock with a lot of time to expiration. Let's make the stock price $200 with one year to expiration. Now the at-the-money call is priced about $16 with a rho near one dollar. As with any financial asset, the longer the time, and the bigger the potential payment, the bigger the interest charge.

Rho is always positive for calls and negative for puts, which means increasing interest rates will raise call prices and decrease put prices. Rho increases as call options move in-the-money and decreases as put options move in-the-money. Rho also increases for longer-term options.

All of the Greeks are "sensitivity" measures. Sensitivity measures show how responsive the option's price is based on a small change (whether increase or decrease) in a particular variable. It's difficult to generalize about each Greek since there are potentially six factors that influence the option's price – stock price, strike price, time to expiration, risk-free interest rate, dividends, and volatility. All must be considered. At any time, you're never going to see one variable change while all others sit exactly still. If interest rates change, stock prices change, and volatilities change. Still, it helps to manage risks if you know how sensitive your options are to key factors that affect an option's price. Fortunately, we can always find them by looking at the Greeks.

Visualizing the Option Advantage

The Greeks are more than just mathematical calculations to help you monitor risks. They can help you visualize the option advantage. Let's say you purchased 50 shares of stock for $100 per share. That position's profit and loss profile is a straight line, and you'll gain dollar-for-dollar if the stock price rises – but you'll lose dollar-for-dollar if the stock price falls. That's the big risk you'd like to avoid:

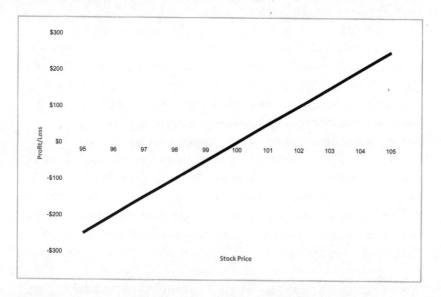

But now that you understand the Greeks, let's visualize the benefit you get by using options instead. Rather than buying 50 shares of stock, you buy the at-the-money $100 call for $2. Because this option is at-the-money, it has a delta of 0.50, and therefore behaves like 50 shares of stock. So even though the option controls 100 shares, right now it's behaving like 50 shares. At this point, the long 50 shares and long call option are behaving the same. As long as the stock's price stays close to its current $100 price, both positions – the stock and $50 call – will perform the same. By purchasing the call, though, at least you have a cost advantage by paying $2 rather than $50. However, because options have gamma, you're going to see an even bigger advantage appear.

If the stock price rises, the call option will gain delta. It begins with 0.50 delta now, but will eventually grow to 1.0 if the stock continues to rise. That increasing delta is due to gamma. It's as if you're getting free shares added to your account – but only if things go your way.

The advantage doesn't just work on the way up. Deltas will decrease if the stock price falls. If the stock price falls, the option will automatically continue to reduce the risk. Remember, positive gamma means that your position increases deltas if the stock price rises but decreases deltas if the stock price falls. It's as if you have a private trader managing the stock position for you. If the market rises, you'll automatically buy more shares in the rising market. But if the market falls, rather than taking the dollar-for-dollar loss, you'll end up with fewer shares. That's gamma in action, and it's one of the biggest, yet most misunderstood option benefits.

If we overlay the long stock position with the call option, it's easy to see the option advantage. Notice whether the stock price rises or falls, the option trader outperforms the stock trader. The profit and loss profile for the option is curved, and that means you make more money if the stock rises, but lose less if it falls. The curvature in the chart is because of gamma. There's no better edge for survival in today's markets.

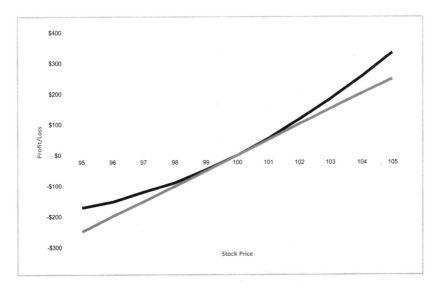

Once you master options strategies, you'll be able to manage
these Greeks in other interesting ways that ensure you can
outperform any stock strategies. Options are not risky. They're
just tools for adjusting risk, and the Greeks make these
adjustments easy to see. Risks can longer hide, because you now
have the tools to uncover them.

Investitute Takeaway

The Greeks are mathematical measures that show how sensitive
option prices are to various factors. Delta shows how sensitive
option prices are to changes in the stock's price. Gamma shows
how sensitive delta is to changes in the stock's price. Theta
shows how sensitive option prices are to changes in time.
Vega shows the sensitivity to volatility, and rho designates the
sensitivity to interest rates. Greeks are essential for managing
today's risks. Risks are only a threat if you can't see them.
Understanding the Greeks makes them visible.

RULE 13

Opportunity First, Strategy Second

American psychologist Abraham Maslow, famous for creating Maslow's hierarchy of needs, had insightful words about adaptability: "To the man who only has a hammer, everything he encounters begins to look like a nail."

Options traders also have a hierarchy of needs: We first find the opportunity – then apply the strategy. Unfortunately, most traders are just taught strategies. Without knowing how to apply them – or monitor, roll, or morph – they end up with positions that can be exactly opposite of what they're trying to accomplish.

If you're just taught strategies, every situation appears to be the perfect opportunity for that strategy. For example, when traders learn covered calls, every situation appears to be the perfect opportunity for a covered call. In reality, it's probably not. But if it's the only tool in the kit, they have nothing to compare it to. Once they learn about vertical spreads, every problem now looks like it can be solved by a vertical spread – even though they would have chosen a covered call last week. Don't expect success by guessing.

Options are tools, and are designed to solve different problems. You'd probably expect to get some pretty strange looks if you

walked into Home Depot and asked the salesperson to show you the
very best tool in the store. Their response would be, "It depends on
what you're trying to do."

Pete and I get the same question quite often from traders – what's
the best strategy? We can't answer it because we don't know
how they're applying it. It depends on what they're trying to do.
Sometimes we'll want to make use of the time value, other times the
intrinsic value. Other times we may focus on delta, gamma, or theta.
The strategy depends on the opportunity, not the other way around.

Today, however, it's not hard to find education companies that do
the opposite. They teach strategies, and according to their ads,
only the best strategies. That immediately tells you that they're
limiting choices. Traders will use them to apply to many situations.
Once traders complete the training, however, every problem looks
like it can be solved by those strategies.

The problem is that the computer doesn't know how you're
applying it. You can click on a specific strategy and send the order.
That doesn't mean it was a good choice. You have to identify the
opportunity first, then select the proper strategy.

One of the most egregious examples is the credit spread. Today,
you have web sites, books, blogs, and other financial sites that
do nothing but teach credit spreads. People get hypnotized by
the word credit and use the credit spread in all situations – rather
than applying it to certain opportunities for which it was designed.
Let's take a look at credit spreads and you'll see why it's so
important to select the opportunity first – then apply the strategy.
Your success depends on it.

Vertical Spreads

A popular strategy among traders is the vertical spread. It's not
our goal to teach you all the ins-and-outs of this strategy but,
instead, to show the importance of focusing on opportunity first,
then strategy.

A vertical spread is constructed with all calls or all puts. The trader buys one strike and sells a different strike with the same expiration month. In Rule #7 on morphing, we saw the Home Depot January 2016 120/125 vertical spread, which was constructed by buying the $120 call and selling the $125 call:

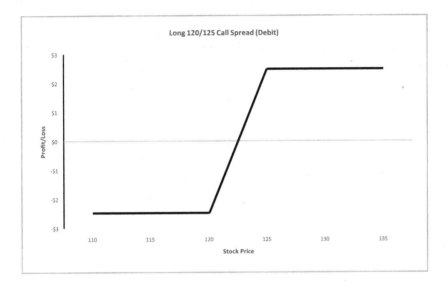

This was a debit spread, which just means you had to pay money for it. In the example, the spread cost $2.50, which is the most you could lose. You now know why it must be a debit: The $120 strike is lower than the $125, so it must cost more. You'll spend more money for the $120 call than you'll receive for the $125 call, so on a net basis, it costs money. Just because it's a debit, does that make it necessarily bad?

Not at all. You have the right to pay $120 per share, and the obligation to sell for $125, so you could *earn* the five-dollar difference. The spread is an asset. However, it's not guaranteed to produce the $5 gain, so the market will price it at something less than $5. The stock could close below $120 and the entire spread would be worthless. In trading terms, the market "discounts" the maximum $5 value since it's not guaranteed. In this example, the spread cost $2.50 but could grow to a $5 value. That leaves the trader with the potential to make $2.50 or lose $2.50, which is exactly what's shown in the above profit and loss diagram. The debit spread is one choice for traders, but they can also use another version called a credit spread. Are traders better off using credit spreads?

The Credit Spread

What would happen is we used the same strikes but used put options? What if we bought the January 2016 $120 put and sold the $125 put?

Surprisingly, the graph would have exactly the same shape:

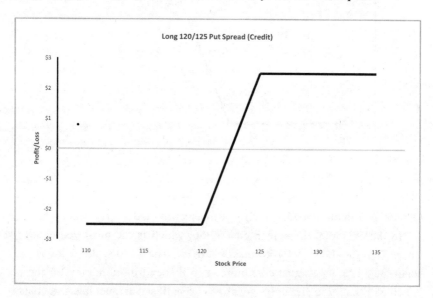

As long as you're buying the lower strike and selling the higher strike, it doesn't matter if you're using calls or puts: Both end up with bullish profiles. One way we teach students to remember this is to think Buy Low – Sell High, with the initials being BLSH, which looks like "bullish." Buying the call spread is identical to selling the put spread. (The reverse would be true too. Buying the put spread is identical to selling the call spread. Both would be bearish.)

However, if you use put options, you'll end up with a credit. Remember that higher strike puts are more expensive than lower strikes, so if you buy the low-strike put and sell a higher-strike put, it's a credit. It's the word "credit" that causes inexperienced traders to come to a screeching halt and choose this as a strategy – usually a permanent one. Why look further? How much better can it get than getting paid to place the order? This is exactly what happens to traders who focus on the strategy. Yes, credit spreads always produce credits, but let's dig a little deeper...

With the credit spread, you have the obligation to buy for $125 and the right to sell for $120. You could lose the $5 difference. The credit spread is a *liability* – not an asset like it is for the debit spread. In this case, you'd receive a $2.50 credit but are liable for the potential $5 risk. The credit spreader is acting more like an insurance company and taking in a one-time fixed premium in exchange for a potentially bigger liability. The maximum you could make is $2.50 and the most you could lose is $2.50 – exactly the same as the debit spread.

It may seem logical that credits are better than debits, which is why so many traders specialize in credit spreads, but once you break them down, they are mechanically identical.

The debate about vertical spreads comes down to this: The debit spread costs money, but it's also an asset. Its value can increase, which is why you're paying for it. The credit spread is a liability. You receive money for it, but it can cost you the difference in strikes. Anyone who argues that credit spreads are better than debit spreads is also saying the liabilities are better than assets. They're just arguing from one side of the balance sheet.

Still, if the debit and credit spread can both gain and lose $2.50, wouldn't it be better to take the $2.50 credit rather than paying for the spread? Again, that's another misperception about spreads. With the debit spread, the broker will debit your account for the maximums loss, or $2.50 in this example. For the credit spread, the brokerage firm isn't concerned about your maximum gain; it's concerned about your maximum loss.

Even though you have a $2.50 credit, you have the potential $5 loss, so the broker will debit the account for the $2.50 difference. The result: the debit spread and credit spread both create a $2.50 debit to your account. Who would have thought? The miraculous credit spread also ends up being a debit in the end. So much for miracles.

We can't emphasize it enough. The debit spread and credit spread are mechanically identical. There's no reason to single out credit spreads as the best strategy. Yet, most options traders do. That's the mistake that happens when you focus on they strategy.

Now, let's see how things change when you focus on the opportunity. Right now, there is a slight skew on the puts. That's an opportunity. A skew just means that traders are willing to pay a little more than what a pricing model would suggest, and we'd need to buy that to complete the credit spread. That would harm our profits.

It's easy to see the skews if you don't focus on the strategy. Look at both and find the opportunity. Here's how to do it:

The January 2016 120/125 spread was identical whether you chose the debit spread or the credit spread. That won't always be true. If we look at the December 120/125 call spread, it was trading for a $2 debit, so the maximum gain is $3. The 120/125 put spread was selling for a $2.94 credit. The most you could make is the $2.94 credit. The maximum loss is $2.06. Now compare the two spreads:

SPREAD	MAXIMUM LOSS	MAXIMUM GAIN
Buy 120/125 call (debit)	$2.00	$3.00
Sell 120/125 put (credit)	$2.06	$2.94

In this case, the debit spread wins. Granted, not by much – just six cents – but at least you didn't pay for a class that taught you how to minimize profits. But if you had been taught to use credit spreads – which many places do – you would have sold the put spread. You can't always say you're going to be better off on the credit side of the board. When you look for the opportunities, however, you'll see the best profits, and ultimately, that's what you're after. That's what you'll find when you use strategies to capitalize on opportunities.

The differences can get more pronounced. Priceline's 1300/1310 call spread costs $4.50. This is a $10 spread, so the maximum gain is the $10 difference in strikes. If you pay $4.50, the most you can make is the $5.50 difference. The put spread is selling for $5.25, so the most you can make is $5.25, and the most you can lose is the $4.75 difference. Now compare the two:

SPREAD	MAXIMUM LOSS	MAXIMUM GAIN
Buy 1300/1310 call (debit)	$4.50	$5.50
Sell 1300/1310 put (credit)	$4.75	$5.25

Once again, the debit spread produced bigger gains and smaller losses. Of course, this will not always be true; otherwise, we'd always teach to use the debit spread. You now see why that's not any better idea. Sometimes the opportunities will lie on the credit side; other times they'll be on the debit side. You'll only see them, however, if you're looking for opportunities. If you looked only at credit spreads, you missed both of these opportunities. To survive the new markets, the rule is opportunity first, strategy second.

The Covered Call

The covered call is another strategy that is often used – and abused – by investors. The strategy is often touted as an income-producing strategy. In some ways, that's true. However, what you're really doing is accepting cash today in exchange for giving up possible future rewards. Investors who sell calls against their entire portfolios often end up regretting it. The reason is, eventually, all of the top-performing stocks end up getting "called away" and the investor ends up holding all of the losers.

If an investor liked the portfolio for the long term, Pete and I would be more inclined to keep some of the upside open, perhaps selling put spreads underneath it, or possibly call spreads above it. We may also do a partial write, where we may own 1,000 shares of stock but sell fewer, say eight calls against it. That leaves 200 shares free if the price takes off. All of these choices still generate cash flow without limiting the upside.

However, if you're focused on strategies, the covered call looks like the perfect solution for every situation. It may actually end up being the worst thing you could do if you're trying to generate long-term cash flow against your entire portfolio. If you live by the mantra opportunity first, strategy second, you'll never fall into that trap.

As an investor, remember that you have a hierarchy of needs. First, focus on the opportunity. What is it about market prices that's setting up the opportunity? Opportunities do not just lie in the stock price moving up or down. Sometimes they're in the Greeks, skews, and volatility. This is why we focus so much on finding opportunities with our students. While they all master the strategies, they only count if you know how to apply them.

We've even built in scanners in the OptionsHouse platform that allow traders to search for countless opportunities based on technicals, fundamentals, volatility, and unusual activity. You can even create your own custom scans. No matter how you decide to invest, today's market require that you find the opportunity first, strategy second. You'll spend your time accomplishing financial goals rather than looking for nails to hammer.

Investitute Takeaway

Options are tools, and strategies are just ways of applying those tools. To make the most of your investing, look for the opportunities first – then apply the strategy. When you can identify an opportunity, the strategy becomes evident. You'll be able to clearly see if that strategy is capitalizing on the opportunity you've identified. It doesn't work the other way around. If you just learn strategies, you may be applying them to the wrong opportunity. Opportunity first, strategy second.

RULE 14

Think Twice Before Exercising Early

Few people like to exercise early, so you're probably thinking you can skip this rule. Who wants to get up at 5 a.m. to go jogging? We're talking about a different kind of exercise – one that most traders will do – even though it's usually a big mistake. When you're trading against computers, you can't afford to make senseless mistakes.

Option buyers have rights to buy or sell shares of stock by exercising their options. If you exercise a call option, you'll buy 100 shares of stock and pay the strike price. With a put, you'll sell 100 shares of stock and receive the strike price. Remember, only option buyers can exercise. The sellers, or short positions, have the obligation to take the opposite side of the trade if they get assigned.

While there are two types of options, calls and puts, there are two styles of options: *American* and *European*. American style options give buyers the right to exercise at any time during the option's life. European styles only allow the owner to exercise on expiration day. However, both styles can always be closed at any time prior to expiration. In other words, if you buy options on either of these styles, you can always sell them and take your profits, or reduce losses, prior to expiration. You never have to wait until expiration to get out of any contract. What separates the two styles is if you wish to exercise the option and physically buy or sell the shares.

Traders generally cannot choose which expiration style they want; the option is either American style or European style. All stock options are American style, while most index options are European style, although a few trade under both styles. The S&P 100 index (OEX) is American style but it also trades under XEO (letters reversed) which is European style.

But one thing is for sure: Equity options are always American style. If you buy equity options, you're allowed to exercise at any time to buy or sell the shares. If you exercise a $50 call, you'll buy 100 shares of the underlying stock and spend the strike price per share, or $5,000. If you exercise a $50 put, you'll sell 100 shares and receive $5,000. You're just using the options to buy or sell shares. It's easy to do with a couple of mouse clicks, which just confirms that you want the broker to submit instructions to the Options Clearing Corporation (OCC).

It may be easy to do, but it's usually the wrong thing to do – if you're exercising early. How can it be wrong if you've met your target and have a guaranteed profit? For instance, let's say you owned the $50 call for $3 and the stock price rises to $60. If you wanted the $7 profit, wouldn't it make sense to exercise the call, pay $50 for the shares, and immediately sell them for $60 to collect the guaranteed $10 difference? It sounds like a good idea, and with one small exception, there's absolutely no benefit in exercising a call early. What's worse, there are significant drawbacks – costly ones. Most of the time, you can only do harm, and never capture a single benefit by exercising a call early.

To make things even stranger, for put options, there can be times when it makes sense to exercise early, but even this is questionable. Put options are just the opposite of calls, so while it's usually bad for the call buyer to exercise early, it may be good for the put buyer. Most of the time, however, you're better off just closing calls and puts and not exercising early.

Even though option buyers have the right to exercise at any time, the minimum condition where it would even make sense is if the options are in-the-money. If you have the $100 call, you wouldn't exercise it if the current stock price was below $100. By exercising, you'd pay $100 for stock that's worth less than $100 – not a good deal. For put holders, you wouldn't exercise if the stock price was above the strike. If you did, you'd sell shares at a price below the current market. But the decision goes far beyond this. In most cases, you'll need the options to be trading in-the-money with little to no time value.

To survive the new markets, let's see why you don't want to exercise early. We'll start with call options and show you the strongest case first, then we'll move to the one exception.

No Dividends, No Early Exercise

It is never advantageous to exercise a call option early if the stock pays no dividends.

The decision to exercise a call option early can be fairly complex, so let's start with the easiest case first: If the underlying stock pays no dividend during the option's life, it's never advantageous to exercise a call option early. It's clear and simple – no dividends, no early exercise.

Currently, IBM is trading for $133.75. Let's say you bought the IBM January 2016 $130 call, with 60 days to expiration, for $6.75. You have the ability to make an unlimited amount if the stock price rises because there's no limit as to how high a stock's price can go. However, to your advantage, the most you can lose is $6.75.

Now let's say that IBM later rises to $140 per share, and your $130 call is trading for $10.80. If you exercise your call and pay $130 per share, and immediately sell the stock at the current $140 price, you'll make the $10 difference. But notice that you can do slightly better by closing the call in the open market for $10.80. If you exercise, you make $10; if you close, you make $10.80.

As long as time remains on the option, you'll be better off by closing
the option since there's a time premium (extrinsic value) that you'll
collect. If you exercised and immediately sold, you only collected
the $10 intrinsic value. However, if you closed the option, you also
collected the $10 intrinsic value – but you also captured the extra
80 cents of time value. Any time you exercise an option, you give
up the time premium. You can either close an option, or you can
exercise it, but you can't do both. If you exercise the call early, that
the time premium is gone, so that's the first reason you don't want
to exercise early. You're losing the time value. You're worse off, but
that's usually the least of your worries...

By exercising early, you take early physical possession of the
shares. You're now holding 100% of the downside risk. If you
kept the call instead, you can only lose the initial $6.75 you had
invested. Once you exercise it, you immediately give up that benefit.
With IBM at $140, there's a very good chance it could fall more
than $6.75, and holding the shares is too big of a risk in today's
market. Always remember that one of the biggest benefits you have
as the call buyer is the right to walk away. You paid for that right, so
use it as long as you can.

This asymmetrical property – unlimited gains but limited losses – is
one of the main reasons that traders buy calls in the first place.
In other words, traders buy call options to avoid holding the risky
stock. Traders are naturally drawn to this beneficial feature, so
don't give up the benefit early. Hold onto it as long as you can. If
you want to own the shares, that's fine. Just wait until expiration
before exercising.

But what if the stock continues higher? Won't I be better off
by owning the shares? It doesn't matter. You're locked into the
$130 purchase price. Time doesn't affect it. The stock's price
doesn't affect it. You're not getting a better price by exercising
early, so there's no benefit in exercising early. The stock could
rise to $300, $400, or more. It doesn't matter. Your purchase
price is guaranteed to be locked at $130, so there's no need
to rush. The risk is not the stock price rising, so let it run all

it wants. The risk is to the downside, so don't accept that risk sooner than necessary.

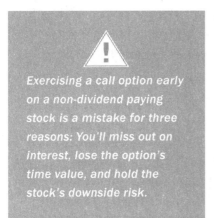

Exercising a call option early on a non-dividend paying stock is a mistake for three reasons: You'll miss out on interest, lose the option's time value, and hold the stock's downside risk.

So there's two big reasons to not exercise early: You give up the time value, and you end up holding all of the risk sooner than necessary. But there's a third reason...

By exercising early, you're giving up any interest that could be earned on that money. If you exercise today, you'll spend $130 per share, or $13,000 to own the 100 shares. If you wait until expiration, you'll spend the same $13,000. There's no difference. There's no benefit. By exercising early, however, you're just paying for the stock sooner and missing out on any interest that could be earned.

If your goal is to take delivery of the 100 shares of stock, there's no problem with that. The problem is taking deliver *early*. By exercising the call early, you're giving up your time premium, missing out on any interest to be earned, and – the biggest risk of all – you're now holding all of the downside stock risk. Exercising a call option early is a triple whammy. If there's no dividend that was paid, there's absolutely no benefit in exercising early.

The One Exception – Maybe

For every rule, there's usually an exception, and early exercise is, well, no exception. If the stock pays a dividend during the option's life, it *may* make financial sense to exercise early. However, just because a stock is about to pay a dividend, doesn't automatically make it a candidate for early exercise. Too many traders misinterpret this rule to mean that you always exercise to capture a dividend. That's definitely not true. We're just saying it may be beneficial to collect the dividend under some conditions.

Let's say IBM has risen to $140 and you own the $130 call, which is really close to expiration, so it's worth exactly the $10 intrinsic value, a condition called *parity*. When an option is trading at parity, it's all intrinsic value and no time value (or very little). When your long call is trading at parity, it may pay to exercise it early to capture a dividend.

Let's say the stock pays a one-dollar dividend tomorrow. You wish to own the 100 shares and are going to exercise at expiration in the next few days. In the meantime, the stock is about to pay a dividend, and there are some stock price adjustments that occur with a dividend. When a stock pays a dividend, the dividend amount is subtracted from the stock's price on the *ex-date*, which is the official date the stock trades without the dividend.

If IBM is $140 now but goes ex-dividend with a one dollar dividend tomorrow, it will open for trading one-dollar lower at $139. The stock's price is reduced because one dollar per share was just paid to all shareholders. If the stock was worth $140, it must be worth $139 after the dollar dividend is paid.

Let's say your $130 call is trading for $10 with the stock at $140. When IBM opens for trading tomorrow, it will open down one dollar at $139. That means your call option will fall from $10 to $9, so you instantly lose one dollar too.

But if you exercised the call prior to the ex-date, you'll own 100 shares at $130 with the stock at $140 – a $10 unrealized gain. When the stock opens at $139, your stock will lose one dollar, but you'll also collect the dollar dividend which means you have a total $10 again. So if you don't exercise, you lose one dollar. If you exercise early, you avoid that loss. The entire purpose of exercising early to collect a dividend is purely to keep from losing the value of the dividend. It's more to hedge the expected loss rather than for making a financial gain. If you choose to exercise, the same principle applies – you want to wait as long as possible before exercising. Exercise the call the day before the ex-date.

Here's the catch: If you exercise, don't forget that you're now holding the stock's downside risk early, and you must ask yourself if that's worth it for the relatively small dividend. For some traders it will be; for others it won't. This is why we say it's not cut and dry as to whether you're better off by exercising early to collect the dividend. It depends. Financially speaking, you're a little better off by collecting the dividend. From a risk perspective, you're probably not.

Yes, you're collecting the dividend, but always balance that with the risk you accepted to get it. If somebody walked up to you and offered to pay you one dollar to accept the full downside risk of IBM for one week, you'd probably say no. But phrase it as though investors will be "missing" the dividend, and all too often they jump on the offer. It's usually not a good deal. For today's markets, you have to consider if it's worth holding the shares for the small dividend. Think twice before exercising early.

Options Give You Better Choices

As professional traders, Pete and I like to show our clients a better way to exercise for dividends. Remember, opportunity first, strategy second. Most of the time, the market will price the same-strike put at a greater price than the dividend. In this example, if we could sell the $130 put for more than the one dollar dividend, we would choose to do that.

We'd be long the $130 call and short the $130 put, which creates what is called a *synthetic stock position*. Synthetics are a fascinating study within options, and one we cover in depth for our clients. But the basic idea is easy to understand: By holding a synthetic stock position we're mathematically holding long shares of stock. If the stock price is above $130 at expiration, we'll exercise the call for the shares. If it's below $130, we'll get assigned on the short put and be required to buy the shares. No matter what happens to the stock's price, we're guaranteed to be long the shares at expiration. Because of that, the market treats the long call, short put combination exactly like shares of stock.

However, by selling the put, we received a premium greater than the dividend, and we didn't have to part with our money early to get it. We're better off than traders who exercised early. This is why we said that even though early exercise may make sense to collect a dividend, in most cases it's still a mistake. Better strategies exist. You just need to know where to look.

In this example, we assumed the $130 call was trading for exactly the $10 intrinsic value with the stock at $140. For all other times, if the option is trading for more than intrinsic value, it's usually an automatic deal breaker for exercising early. Let's say that IBM rose to $135 and the $130 call is trading for $7.50. The call has $5 of intrinsic value and $2.50 time value. If you exercise early to collect the $1 dividend, you'll give up the $2.50 time premium, you'll miss out on any interest that could have been earned on the exercise price – and you'll hold all of the downside risk early. It's an instant losing deal.

The only time it may make sense to exercise a call option early is if it's trading close to parity (there's little to no time value), a dividend is being paid, and you're willing to hold the downside risk. Most dividends are usually small, but exercising early exposes you to big downside risk.

Unless a dividend is unusually large, it's usually a risky move to exercise a call option early.

Exercising Put Options Early

Two of the reasons why exercising call options early is a mistake is that you're accepting the full downside risk of the stock and parting with your cash early. However, put options work the opposite way, so they have a potential benefit. When you exercise a put option early, you're selling shares and sweeping cash into your account earlier than if you waited until expiration, and that allows you to earn a little more interest. That's the only benefit. You're not benefiting from getting the shares out of your account because they're protected by the put option anyway. In other words, if you don't exercise early, you're not at risk by holding the shares.

You have the long put to protect that value. The only reason for exercising a put option early is to gain a little more interest than you otherwise would have collected – that's it.

Even though receiving cash early in order to earn interest makes financial sense, you still have to consider if it's worth the effort for today's non-existent interest rates. The additional amount of money you're going to make is not worth talking about. You're better off holding the shares and hoping for a rebound. You can always exercise the put and sell shares for the strike price, so there's no additional downside risk. You would, however, be better off if the share price rebounded sharply above the strike and the put expired worthless. It's worth taking that chance, no matter how remote it may be. Of course, it's possible we may see rates rise to a level where it would be beneficial to exercise early. How does an investor figure out if it's worthwhile?

If you're thinking of exercising a put option early, there's a simple test you can do see if it's the right time. You can look at the put's delta, which we talked about in Rule #12 on the Greeks. If that delta is -1.0, or very close, it's probably worth exercising. That just means the put option is so deep in-the-money that the market feels there's nearly a 100% chance (-1.0 delta) that the put will remain in-the-money. If there's virtually no chance for the stock to rebound above the strike price, you might as well exercise it and grab the cash early.

New investors are tempted to exercise options early. It appears to make sense when you can exercise a call and pay less than the current market price. Once you understand how option prices work, you'll see that you're better off by closing the call in the open market to collect the time value on top of the cash value, or intrinsic value. Better yet, you won't be holding the risky shares early – and that's the biggest benefit for today's fast-moving markets. Options give buyers the right to walk away from the deal. They get the advantage to wait and see what happens with stock prices. Most of the time, it's not worth destroying that advantage for a small dividend.

Investitute Takeaway

Option buyers have rights to buy or sell shares of stock. You're not ever required to buy or sell the shares, but if you do, you must submit exercise instructions. However, with only one exception, exercising a call option early to buy shares of stock is a mistake: 1) you're giving up the option's time premium, 2) you're missing out on the interest you could have earned on your money by paying for the shares early, and 3) more importantly, you're holding all of the stock's downside risk.

Remember, you can always exercise at expiration and pay the strike price, so there's no reason to take delivery of the shares early. For put options, it may be beneficial to exercise early. The only thing you're going to gain is a little extra interest by getting the cash into your account sooner. Even with exercising puts, there's an optimal time. Only consider exercising early when the put's delta is near -1.0. If you exercise it sooner, you may miss out on the chance for the stock to rebound, which would be more advantageous. Exercising options early is an easy mistake to make, but one you can't afford to do in today's uncertain markets.

RULE 15

Don't Get Caught with Ex-by-Ex

Sometimes we're the beneficiaries of technology – and other times we're the victims. As author Mitch Ratliffe pointed out, "The computer lets you make more mistakes faster than any invention in human history – with the possible exceptions of handguns and tequila."

For options traders, the computer can also let you make a mistake. It only happens at expiration, and the problem will become more pronounced as trading speeds increase.

Option buyers have the right to exercise calls or puts. As we pointed out in the previous rule, under most conditions, it's a mistake to exercise early, but there could be times when you'd want to actually buy or sell the underlying shares. If you do, it's usually best to wait until expiration, and all you have to do is submit exercise instructions by clicking a button. But there's one exception where you may end up exercising an option automatically, and if it's not what you wanted, it can cause unexpected trouble – not as much as handguns, but certainly more than tequila.

As options trading grew in popularity, the administrative processes had to be streamlined as well. The Options Clearing Corporation

(OCC) created a rule to automatically exercise any long options –
calls or puts – if they were in-the-money.

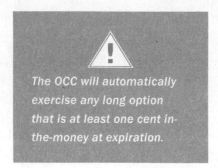

The OCC will automatically exercise any long option that is at least one cent in-the-money at expiration.

Through the years, there have been changes to threshold of what defined in-the-money, but now we're down to just one cent for equity and index options. Without this rule, brokers would have to submit individual instructions for all traders who wanted to exercise options, across all expirations and strikes. There's just no time.

This procedure is called *exercise by exception*, or ex-by-ex. You
may also hear it called automatic exercise. Whatever the name, it
can cause trouble for unsuspecting traders.

For example, let's say you bought a $50 call. On expiration Friday,
the underlying stock is trading at least one cent in-the-money
or more, so $50.01 or more. If you do not close that option by
selling it in the open market, you'll own 100 shares of stock on
Monday morning and will pay the $50 strike price, or $5,000 plus
commissions to do so. The OCC is going to assume you wanted it
exercised. Whether it's a good assumption or not doesn't matter. It's
the rule. With new markets and new speeds come new rules, and to
make the most of investing, you must understand how they work.

The Right to Exercise – And Refuse

As the buyer, you have the *right* to exercise, but you also have the
right to refuse the automatic exercise. Remember, as the option buyer,
you're not required to ever buy or sell the shares. The automatic
exercise process is a way to streamline the process for brokers.

If you see an expiring option is in-the-money, or looks like it may
end up in-the-money, you can certainly call the broker and place
instructions to not exercise the option. It's your right, but you must

communicate that to the broker. The default is to exercise. It's the exception to the rule.

This rule catches new traders off guard for a simple reason: If the stock is trading at $50.01 at expiration, the $50 call is trading for one cent. If you sell it to close, you'll receive one dollar – but probably pay more than that in commissions. Traders realize they're better off by not exercising, so they leave the option alone – and end up with 100 shares of stock on Monday.

As markets change, rules change, and we've had to change too. Pete and I have insisted on two changes for investor protection at OptionsHouse. First, you'll never be charged a commission greater than the proceeds from an option sale. If the $50 or call is trading for one cent, you'll receive one dollar from closing it, and the commission will also be one dollar. It's a wash. There's no cost to you, so there's no reason to not close it. We do that because it's in everybody's best interest to close any options that you don't want to be exercised. It's the simplest, most cost-effective way to give traders the incentive to close all expiring options.

Second, if you don't have the cash in the account (or margin buying power) to handle the exercise, the option won't be exercised. If that $50 call is in-the-money but you don't have at least $5,000 cash or margin buying power, we'll assume it was an oversight. We'll block it for you. However, we still like to see traders take the responsibility to close all expiring options, so if the broker has to constantly step in to prevent the automatic exercises, there may be a $25 fee. However, if you do have the equity, and you didn't call to decline the exercise, then automatic exercise will occur.

The main point to understand is that you're never required to exercise an option – even if it's in-the-money. You can always call the broker and place instructions to not exercise. Always be sure to check with your broker as most have different cutoff times. For OptionsHouse, those instructions must be place no later than 4:20pm ET on expiration day.

Automatic Exercise with Put Options

Put options work in a similar way, just the opposite direction. To trigger automatic exercise, put options also have to close at least one cent in-the-money. That means the stock price must close below the strike by at least one cent. If you bought a $50 put and the stock closes at $49.99 or lower on expiration Friday, you'll automatically exercise and sell 100 shares for $50 per share. Just as with call options, you have the right to call the broker on that day and say you don't want it exercised. But if you do nothing, you'll end up selling 100 shares and receiving the strike price, or $5,000 less commissions.

However – and this is important – if you don't own the shares, but you do have the cash or margin buying power, you'll end up with a short stock position – one of the riskiest positions of all. In other words, just because you don't have the shares in your account doesn't prevent the sale from going through. Shares are sold, and you owe 100 shares back to the broker. You've sold shares you don't own, and that's a *short stock* position. It's risky because there's no limit on how high a stock's price may rise, so there's no telling how much you'll have to pay to close it out on Monday.

If you don't have the cash or margin buying power to take a short stock position, OptionsHouse will block the exercise from going through. Just as with call options though, if it becomes an ongoing habit, you may get charged a $25 fee. It's still a small price to avoid holding short shares of stock.

New Markets, New Risks, New Rules

Automatic exercise creates a new risk in today's markets. As information flows faster, and people can place trades faster, prices can change faster. Out-of-the-money options can quickly become in-the-money. The auto-exercise process has created a new risk for today's markets. For example, let's say you bought the $50 call, and on expiration Friday, the stock is trading below the strike, say $49. You decide to do nothing since it appears the option will expire out-of-the-money and end up worthless. Might as well head to the beach.

However, the stock rallies to at least $50.01 going into the closing bell. Maybe the company is releasing earnings on Monday and speculators are banking on a positive report. Perhaps it's computerized trading feeding off of each other. Whatever the reason, if you stopped watching the stock late Friday afternoon, you're going to end up owning 100 shares on Monday. Yes, you could sell the shares on Monday, but there's no guarantee that Monday's price will be anywhere near Friday's close. That's the big risk of automatic exercise. If Friday's rally was because corporate earnings will be released before Monday's bell, you may not get the opportunity. If earnings are bad and the stock price plummets – you still own the shares. The key is to prevent the shares from landing in your account in the first place. You must understand automatic exercise.

Exercise by exception is a procedure the OCC uses to assist with the large amounts of exercises that brokers must submit. It's not intended to be a shortcut for investors who want to exercise options. If you want to exercise an in-the-money option, it's still a good idea to submit exercise instructions to fully communicate that intent to the broker.

Computerized trading created faster markets, and with that speed has come new rules. There's no risk of automatic exercise if you understand the rules. Risk comes from learning the hard way and finding just how quickly a computer can allow you to make mistakes at expiration. The new rule is simple: Close all expiring options, and you'll never have an unwanted surprise.

At OptionsHouse, it won't cost you anything to close, so there's no reason not to. But if you forget about how fast markets can change, you may find that your out-of-the-money is suddenly in-the-money. If you end up with automatic exercise, and it's not what you wanted, you may be the victim of technology rather than the beneficiary. And that may just leave you needing tequila.

Investitute Takeaway

Automatic exercise applies to long options only – those you
purchased. If any long option is at least one cent in-the-money at
expiration, it will automatically be exercised. For long calls, that
means you'll buy 100 shares of stock and pay the exercise price.
For puts, you'll sell 100 shares of stock and receive the exercise
price. Put options carry additional risk, because if you don't have
the shares to sell, you could end up with a short stock position – a
much bigger risk than a long stock position. The easiest way to
prevent any unwanted surprises is to simply close all long options
at expiration. Alternatively, you can contact the broker and say
you don't want the exercise to go through. The biggest risk with
unwanted automatic exercise, is it you're never sure what prices
will be on Monday when you try to close the position. That's too big
of our risk for today's markets. It's a new risk. Preventing surprise
exercises is a new rule of investing.

RULE 16

Don't Leave Your Portfolio to Chance

Long-term investing has benefits. The longer you invest, the more time prices have to run, which means more profits to you. The problem is not the math – it's the psychology. People don't respond well to fear. As soon as markets begin to fall, investors don't want to sell and lock in a guaranteed loss – so they do an even worse thing – they hang on and try to gamble their way out. Gambling and hoping should never be part of your trading plan. The problem is that markets will often continue to fall. Remember, trends last longer than people expect, and the downside is no exception. Eventually people reach a breaking point, the point where they can't take the pressure anymore, and prices go off a cliff.

With today's fast-paced electronic markets, these panic-driven declines will be more frequent – and larger. It's all part of having computerized trading as part of the process. While we do benefit from computers by having more liquid markets and faster executions, we can also be victimized. While investors join the panic, computers join the party. Computers see the orders lining up, so they join too. For them, it's free money. The problem is, computers don't have emotions. They'll continue to sell just as long as everyone continues to panic.

But think about what's happening. If everybody's selling,
there'll be no sellers tomorrow. You're probably at a bottom. Of
course, to continue holding is easier said than done, but most
investors throw in towel right at the worst possible time. There's
no question that buying high and selling low doesn't work.
But buying high and selling at the absolute low is worse. It's a
problem for today's markets, and that's why there are new rules.
Options can easily solve this problem with a technique called beta
weighting. It sounds complicated, but if you can work a mouse,
you can beta weight. It's super easy.

What is Beta?

Beta is a mathematical measure that shows the relationship between
a stock's performance and the overall market, or S&P 500 index. By
definition, the S&P 500 has a beta of 1.0. That's the benchmark, so
it never changes.

If you own a stock with a beta is 2.0, it just means your stock is
usually twice as volatile as the S&P 500. If the index rises 5%,
you'd expect your stock to rise twice that, or 10%. Conversely, if
the S&P falls 10%, you'd expect your stock to also fall by a factor
of two, or 20%. Beta just shows long-term relationships, so just
because the index may rise 5% for the year, for example, doesn't
mean that your stock definitely rose 10%. Beta just shows the
general correlation.

If your stock has a beta less than one, say 0.5, it means it's half as
responsive as the index. If the index rises or falls 10% for the year,
you'd expect your stock to only be up half that much, or up or
down 5%.

Beta and volatility are related, but they're different concepts.
Most high-volatility stocks also have high betas, but not always.
Volatility measures the fluctuations around the average stock
price. However, beta shows the relationship between the stock's
performance and the S&P 500. Because of this, you can get what
seems to be paradoxical results. For example, Apple Computer

(AAPL), which is considered a fairly high-volatility stock has a beta of 0.83. However, General Electric (GE), which is considered a low-volatility stock has a beta of 1.3.

If the S&P 500 rises 10% during the year, you'd expect Apple to be up only 8.3%, but GE to be up 13%. Just remember that the S&P 500 is the benchmark with a beta of 1.0. If any stock's beta is less than 1.0, it's expected to be less risky than the overall market. If it's greater than 1.0, it's expected to be more volatile than the overall market. You can easily find any stock's beta in the OptionsHouse platform.

Beta also helps investors figure out their stock-picking prowess by calculating risk-adjusted returns. If you bought one stock and earned 15% for the year, you may think you outperformed the market if the S&P 500 only rose 10%. However, if your stock had a beta of 1.5, you just matched the market. You took extra risk, but were adequately compensated for it. On a risk-adjusted level, your return is 15%/1.5 = 10%, so you just matched the market.

You can also use beta to see how risky your entire portfolio is relative to the S&P 500. For instance, let's say you had the following dollars invested in four stocks:

STOCK	DOLLAR VALUE	PORTFOLIO %	BETA	BETA* %
IBM	$10,000	10%	0.60	.06
Apple	$20,000	20%	0.83	0.17
GE	$30,000	30%	1.3	0.39
Priceline	$40,000	40%	1.50	0.6
Total	$100,000	100%		1.22

Ten percent of your portfolio is in IBM, which has 0.6 beta. If you multiply 10% by the stock's beta, you get that stock's contribution to your overall portfolio, or .06, which is shown in the final column. Twenty percent of your holdings are in Apple, which has a beta of 0.83. If you multiply 20% by 0.83, you get 0.17. If you do this calculation for each stock and add up the final column, the result is 1.22. That's the portfolio's beta weight. That means your entire portfolio is behaving like one stock that happens to have a beta of 1.22. The portfolio is 22% riskier than the S&P 500. Intuitively, this should make sense. Notice that the first two stocks make up 30% of your portfolio, and they have betas less than 1.0. However, 70% of your portfolio has betas larger than 1.0, so the average of all four should be greater than 1.0.

If the index rises 10%, you'd expect your portfolio to be up 1.22 times that, or 12.2%. The same would hold if the index fell 10%. If you've ever wondered just how much risk you're holding, betas can give you a very quick and accurate answer. Now that know the basics of betas, let's see how you can use this information to protect your portfolio when market conditions head south.

Portfolio Insurance

Knowledgeable investors often use put options as a form of insurance. It's a great idea, but tough to do in practice, especially if you have a large number of stocks. Each position needs to have a separate put option purchased. Each trade takes time, and each trade needs to be monitored. If you had 30 stocks in your portfolio and needed to get it insured quickly, it would be time consuming – and expensive. If markets are falling quickly, by the time you go through the entire portfolio, the majority of the damage may be done. Is there a better way? That's the problem beta weighting solves.

Beta Weighting

Professional traders know that being able to place quick insurance on a portfolio is critical for success. It may help you to ride through longer-term periods, such as through rough economic times like we had in 2008 and 2009. You could also use beta weighting for short-term insurance, such as getting through earnings season.

To beta weight, you have to select an index to weight it against, which is usually going to be the S&P 500 index. When a portfolio is beta weighted against the S&P 500, it just means you're taking a diverse portfolio of stocks and finding the mathematical equivalent number of S&P 500 shares that you're holding. It's easy to do in the OptionsHouse platform – just click a button. Here's the way you'd find the answer. In the example, you had $100,000 invested in the market. The first step is to find the equivalent number of shares you could have purchased in the S&P 500, which is currently 2087.30. Therefore, if you could buy shares of this index, your money could buy $100,000/2087.30, or 47.9 shares. However, if you bought 47.9 shares of the S&P 500, it wouldn't behave exactly like your portfolio because it has a beta weight of 1.22. We have to multiply those numbers together to get 47.9 * 1.22 = 58.45 shares. That means your entire portfolio is behaving as if you owned 58.45 shares of the index.

That's a lot of work, but look how easy it is to do in the OptionsHouse platform. We put the previous four stocks in the same proportions into the paper money account, which any account holder can use for simulations. Just click a button, and your entire portfolio is instantly analyzed:

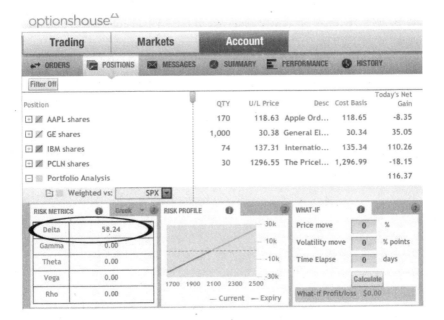

The platform shows a delta of 58.24, which is saying it's behaving like that many shares. The small difference is due to rounding and the index's value changing slightly. That means your portfolio is mathematically behaving as if you owned about 58 shares of the S&P 500. If you wanted to buy insurance for the entire portfolio, you'd just simply buy S&P 500 puts. That's much easier, faster – and cheaper – than buying puts on each individual stock.

Notice that the profit and loss diagram is also shown in the above diagram. It's a straight line since we're only holding shares of stock. It's telling us that even though we have four different stocks in this portfolio, they're collectively behaving like 58 shares of the S&P 500. If the index rises one point, you'd expect this portfolio to increase by $58. And because it's a straight line, you'd expect to lose $58 for each point fall in the index. The beta weight gives us a much better idea of the overall risk of the portfolio relative to the overall market.

Because each put contract controls 100 shares, you'd be over-hedged if you buy one put. In other words, you only need insurance on 58 shares, but you're buying insurance for 100 shares. However, you could also use the SPY, which is a 1/10th index of SPX. The SPY is an exchange traded fund (ETF), so it trades just like a stock. Because SPY represents 1/10th of SPX, your portfolio is behaving like 580 shares of SPY – exactly 10 times more.

If you're unsure of the math, just type "SPY" as the underlying for your weight, and OptionsHouse will do the calculations for you:

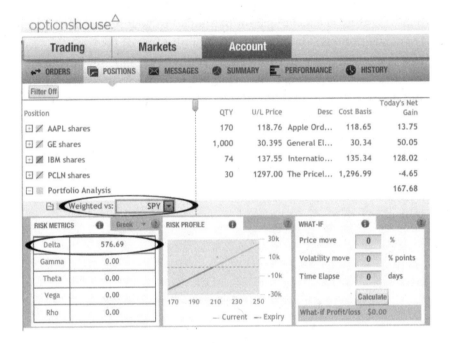

By using SPY as the weight, your portfolio is behaving like 580 shares of SPY. Now it becomes easier to hedge. You can buy five puts, and be a little under-hedged (since you effectively control 580 shares), or you can buy six puts and be a little over-hedged. But in less than a second, you can mathematically convert your portfolio into any index and make one easy put purchase. So if big news is around the corner, or earnings season coming up next month, you can insure your portfolio in under a minute – no matter how many different shares of stock or options you may own.

News travels fast in today's markets. There's no time to go through each stock and place protective put options to insure against possible declines. Who has time for that? Now that you understand beta weighing, you do. You can use the same methods used by professionals to quickly maneuver through bumpy times in the markets. To make the most of investing, beta weighting is not only a new tool, it's a new rule.

Investitute Takeaway

Beta weighting is a technique for putting all of your positions –
stocks and options – into one common unit. Most of the time,
investors weight their portfolios against the S&P 500 index,
but any ticker can be used. Beta weighting allows you to view
your entire portfolio in terms of the overall market to understand
how your profit or loss will be affected by market moves. Beta
weighting allows you to efficiently hedge your portfolio when
market conditions get shaky and you want to put on quick, effective
insurance on your entire portfolio.

RULE 17

Use Extended Sessions to Lock in Unexpected Profits

As comedian Steven Wright observed, "The early bird
gets the worm, but the second mouse gets the cheese."
Sometimes it pays to be late. To survive the new markets,
you have to know how to lock in options profits by using the
after-hours markets.

The stock market is normally open for six-and-a-half hours from
9:30am to 4:00pm ET, which is called the regular trading hours,
or RTH. But you're not just limited to those hours to buy or sell
shares of stock. You can trade shares prior to the open, or after
the market close.

These extended sessions used to be limited to institutions, such
as banks and pensions funds, along with high-net-worth investors.
But with the advent of electronic communication networks (ECNs),
nearly anyone with a brokerage account can access them. ECNs are
considered a separate class of SEC-permitted Alternative Trading
Systems (ATS).

For the Nasdaq, pre-market trading operates from 4:00am to
9:30am ET. For the New York Stock Exchange, it's from 8:00am
to 9:30am. For both, after-hours runs from 4:00pm to 6:30pm ET.

You can definitely see the prices at which trades are being executed during these times.

Most brokers only access ECN with times closer to the open or closing bell. For OptionsHouse, you can trade the pre-market from 8:00am – 9:30am ET and from 4:00pm – 5:00pm ET.

However, these ECNs do not operate like markets during regular hours. Instead, ECNs are computerized networks primarily set up by brokers to communicate their clients' orders to other brokers in an effort to get trades matched.

For example, one broker may have a customer order on its books to buy 100 shares of IBM at $130, which may get matched to another broker that has a customer order to sell 100 shares at the same price. Clients benefit from getting orders filled, and brokerage firms benefit from cutting out the Nasdaq or New York Stock Exchange's fees. All trades, however, do get reported to the exchanges. The important point to understand is that these are electronic communication networks; they are not regular markets.

Benefits of Extended Sessions

Even though ECNs are not traditional markets, you will see the highest bid and lowest offer, just like a regular market. Placing orders in these markets is just as easy as it is during regular trading sessions, and you can even trade odd lots – fewer than 100 shares.

The extended sessions show how traders are reacting to news. If IBM closes at $130 during the regular session and releases earnings after the bell, you may see it trading higher, say $133, in the after-hours market. Traders are just trying to buy and sell prior to the next day's opening in an effort to gain an edge. Perhaps the price will be $135 tomorrow morning after everyone digests the news and decides to buy. Or, maybe it will be trading back near $130 and sellers had a nice opportunity to capitalize on the enthusiastic buyers. Whether you're a buyer or seller, ECNs allow you to place orders and trade among the quotations being communicated between brokers.

Risks of Extended Sessions

While ECNs do provide benefits, there are risks to consider. First, there's low volume, and that means the bid-ask spreads can be wide. Extended sessions usually account for less than 5% of total trading volume. Because of the lower liquidity (fewer traders) and lack of information, the bid-ask spreads will usually be wider than during regular trading hours.

In the IBM example, you may see traders bidding $133 and asking $134.50. Another problem is that most ECNs limit your view of other ECNs, so the prices you're viewing may only be those transmitted through the one network you're viewing. Depending on the networks your broker is connected to, prices may be quite different from other ECNs.

Institutions also account for a large part of the volume. Because the sessions are thinly traded, prices are usually more volatile than during regular hours. It's easy to get whipsawed during these markets.

Although some ECNs do allow market orders – orders guaranteed to fill – most brokers do not allow them. Because these are not traditional markets, market orders can get filled at prices far different from what you expected, mostly due to the low volume and volatility. As a result, most brokers require that you use limit orders. A buy limit order can only execute at your limit price or lower. Sell limits can be executed for your limit price or higher. Because you'll most likely have to use limits, you're not guaranteed to get orders filled during extended sessions.

Using Extended Sessions to Lock in Call Option Gains

Extended sessions are nothing new. Instinet was the first in 1969. But as our markets have grown, conditions have changed, risks increased, and the way we use these systems has changed too.

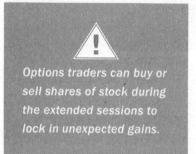

Options traders can buy or sell shares of stock during the extended sessions to lock in unexpected gains.

How do options traders benefit from extended sessions? You can't trade options on ECNs, but you can use them to lock in options profits, and it's a necessary tool for today's volatile markets. Traders overlook it, and it could be costly.

For example, let's say you decide to take a speculative position in a $50 stock that's about to release earnings. You buy five $50 calls for $2, or $1,000 total. After the bell, the company posts great earnings, and in response, the stock soars to $60 in the after-hours markets. If that's the stock's price on the opening bell of the regular session, your $50 call would trade for at least the $10 intrinsic value – quite a jump from your $2 purchase price.

By seeing it trading that high in the after-hours, you're thinking you'll be ready to pounce on the opening bell and sell your calls. There's just one problem: Who's to say the price will still be that high? It's not uncommon to see some stocks trading at big premiums during the after-hours markets – but then down on the opening bell. Your opportunity is now. Don't forget – opportunity first, strategy second. The opportunity seems to be there, but how can you capture that gain if the options market isn't open?

If you want to take your profits, you can place an order to sell 500 shares of the stock in the after-hours market, provided you have the appropriate margin buying power to do so. The next day, just submit exercise instructions and that will cover your short position. It's a self-financing strategy because the proceeds from the sale of stock more than covers the exercise price. That is, you received $30,000 from selling 500 shares at $60, but the exercise price cost 500 * $50, or $25,000. The $5,000 difference is your profit.

Notice that would have been the same result if the stock opened tomorrow at $60. With the stock at $60, the $50 call would be worth at least the $10 intrinsic value. Because it's deep in-the-money and almost no time until expiration, there won't be any time value to speak of, so it's basically worth exactly the $10 intrinsic value. By selling your five calls at $10, you'd collect $5,000 – exactly the same outcome as selling the shares at $60 after-hours and exercising your $50 call.

The risk is that you don't know if the stock will be worth $60 on tomorrow's opening bell. It may be worth less. That's the risk, and exactly how selling shares in the after-hours market can allow you to lock in gains.

Naturally, the big news may hit the market prior to the opening bell. It's the same difference. Just sell the shares in the pre-market and exercise your call that day.

Even though profits are nice, there's always the potential for big missed opportunities by closing your entire position. In this example, our big fear was falling stock prices, but it's also possible the price continues higher tomorrow. This is where Pete and I teach traders how to hedge positions. Usually, the better idea for any situation is to at least lock in some gains. If you can recover all of your initial investment, that's even better. That way you can let the profits run if there are more to come.

If you feel the stock price will continue higher, consider selling 200 shares of stock during after-hours and exercising two contracts the next day. That way, you know for sure you've captured $2,000 – double your initial $1,000 investment. You can't lose. However, if the stock continues higher, you'll make more. It's a great hedge against loss, while still leaving the upside free and clear to run.

There's a risk with that decision too: If the stock drops, you would have been better off selling 500 shares. But that's the benefit of 20-20 hindsight. Those are things nobody knows. By closing two calls, the one thing you know is that you have a for-sure $1,000 gain – a 100% profit – that cannot be taken away no matter what happens.

You could, of course, sell any number of shares to get more cash and bigger profits, at the expense of fewer additional gains. It's all about tradeoffs. If you were less confident about the stock price rising higher, you may decide to sell 400 shares. That locks in a for-sure $3,000 gain, and leaves one call option free and clear for you to profit more. The one thing that should be consistent, though, is to learn how to hedge so you can lock in guaranteed gains when possible.

Options allow traders to lock in gains and manage risk better than any other asset. No matter how confident you are that the stock may continue trading higher on tomorrow's opening bell, there are always unknown unknowns. If those earnings had been released on September 1, 2001, there's a good chance those gains would have all been gone on the opening bell – and your contract is about to expire. Just because the earnings are super strong, don't think that other news can't drive all prices lower. Hedging your positions allows you to act on current prices, and using the after-hours can play an important role in hedging today's fast markets.

Locking in Gains Using Puts

You can use the extended sessions to lock in gains with put options too. With puts, however, you'll *buy* the shares rather than sell them. Just as with call options, you'll need the proper margin buying power to do so.

For example, let's say you have five $50 put options. After an earning's report or other big news event, the stock's price dramatically drops to $40 in the after-hours. If the regular session was open, the put would be worth the at least the $10 intrinsic value. You could take your chances and wait for the opening bell and hope the stock's price is still $40. But you know how we feel about hope as a strategy. What else can you do?

Just go into the after-hours market and buy 500 shares at $40. The next day, just exercise your $50 put, which means you'll sell your shares and receive the $50 strike. The result is that you purchased shares for $40 and sold them for $50 – a guaranteed $10 gain. As with call option, it's a self-financing strategy. You don't need to use any cash to buy the shares since the exercise will more than take care of the purchase price.

To make the most of investing, you have to walk a fine line between fear and greed. That means you must understand how to lock in gains when possible, but also maintain the room for continued profits. Trends last longer than people expect, and those long-term trends are the source of your biggest profits. But you must be in the position to profit from it, and to do that, you must manage the unknown risks.

By trading in the extended sessions, you have a way to lock in gains when unexpected – and exceptional – profits appear. It's better than relying on hope, and finding out that on tomorrow's opening bell, those gains are gone. Sometimes profits show up late, and if you understand the extended sessions, it can pay to be the second mouse.

Investitute Takeaway

The extended sessions allow traders to buy and sell shares of stock prior to the opening bell, or after the closing bell. For OptionsHouse, traders can trade one-and-a-half hours prior to the opening bell, and for one hour after the close. By using these pre-market and after-hours markets, traders can lock in gains on calls and puts if breaking news occurs outside of the regular trading hours. If you have a call option and want to collect the intrinsic value, just sell shares in the extended sessions, and exercise the call the following day. For put options, buy shares in the extended sessions and exercise the put the following day. The exercises offset the purchase or sales, and you're just left with the profit. Speculating during the extended sessions can be risky, but using them to lock in options gains can be one of your best defenses against today's uncertain markets.

RULE 18

Beware of the 90% Myth

From Sasquatch to the Loch Ness Monster, it's incredible how myths can exist in a world where information flows so freely. For options traders, there's a myth that has also been passed on since the beginning of time – at least since 1973 – when options were first publicly traded.

We're sure you've heard that 90% of all options expire worthless. If you haven't, you will. It's one of the mostly widely spread "facts" to new options traders. Not only is it wrong, it's dangerous. It causes traders to overstep their risk boundaries thinking they have a trading edge. Unfortunately, for these traders, the only edge they find is the cliff – and the wrong side of it. To succeed in today's fast markets, you don't need to be trading that close to the cliff.

A Little Options History

If so many traders believe 90% of options expire worthless, what are the facts? The Options Clearing Corporation (OCC) is the largest equity derivatives clearing firm in the world. As you can imagine, they keep lots of data on what happens each year, which is published on its web site at optionsclearing.com. Since its 1973 inception, about 60% of all options are closed in the open market every year. That just means if you bought an option you sold it to get out of it (or if you sold it, you bought it back). About 30% of the contracts expire worthless, and about 10% are exercised. For any given year, there may be a spread of about 5% on either side of these percentages. So for worthless options, about 25% in a low year and 35% in a high year. But never 90% – not once.

Not only does the 90% myth not hold up with historical facts, it never had a chance to, nor will it ever. If you look at any options quote board, you'll see calls on the left side and puts on the right. Pick a stock price such that 90% of the calls would expire out-of-the-money. That same stock price, however, makes 90% of the puts in-the-money. Every out-of-the-money call must be matched with an in-the-money put. You can't pick a stock price where 90% of the options would expire worthless. It's a mathematical impossibility.

Still, people want to hang on to myths. You'll hear this one spread on Internet sites, books, and seminars. If you are ever able to ask anyone where this number came from, the best you'll get is that it's a "known options fact." If traders want to believe in Bigfoot or other mythical creatures, it doesn't pose a big problem to profits. Believing that 90% of all options expire worthless creates a unicorn of a different color.

The problem is that with today's technology and market speeds, traders are searching for any edge they can find. So when they're introduced to this little 90% gem, they immediately think they have an advantage by selling options. After all, if you sell a bunch of options and 90% expire worthless, what more could you ask for? It's obviously a winning strategy. It's obvious – and wrong. That's the Bigfoot of options trading. It's just a big myth that has held on for decades. The myth is even more dangerous, however. Even if it was true that 90% of all options expired worthless, it doesn't follow that you'd be better off selling options. Understanding the math is important for surviving today's markets.

The Math Behind the 90% Myth

Even if you did win on 90% of your trades, it doesn't mean you keep 90% of the proceeds you collected and just pay back 10%. Instead, if you sell naked calls or puts, you actually keep 100% of the premiums collected, just like an insurance company.

But the amount you owe depends on your potential obligations on the remaining 10% of the contracts. That's not a fixed amount. If you receive $1,000 in option premiums – and keep 100% of them – but pay out $10,000 in damages, it's not a winning strategy. It's so simple, even a Sasquatch could do it. But still, people insist that selling options is a winning strategy because they think they're winning 90% of the time.

Selling options is no different than writing insurance policies. Insurance companies may collect premiums year after year without any big payouts. That doesn't mean it's safe. Just ask many of the insurance companies who had to make good on Florida policies when hurricanes Charley, Frances, Ivan, and Jeanne pummeled the coasts in 2004. Actually, you can't ask them – they went bankrupt. The few who did survive packed up and left and won't write in Florida anymore. The point is that if the risks are too big, the premiums appear too small – even though they get to keep 100% of the premiums most of the time.

Whenever you're in the business of collecting a single payment in exchange for a potentially much larger payoff, forget about the attractive 90% figures that may be tossed around. They're not painting the full picture.

Price is the Equalizer – Part II

In Rule #4, we said price is the equalizer. Because of price, all investments must be equally attractive in terms of risk. All benefits are priced into the option. Once you realize that price equalizes all market, you'll see another reason why sellers cannot have a consistent edge – especially 90% of the time.

For instance, right now Priceline (PCLN) is trading for $1,225, and the December $1200 put (18 days) is trading for $20. This put is $25 dollars out-of-the-money, so it seems like easy money to sell one of these puts and collect $2,000 cash. Even better, if you're right, you don't even have to buy the option back, as it will just expire worthless. If you believe you have a 90% edge, it seems like money in the bank.

However, think about price. Just like a point spread, there has to be a point where you start losing the perceived edge. For a football game, it's the point spread. For this put option, it's the $20 price. If traders felt the $20 price was too high, they'd continue to sell, and price would fall. If it was always true that sellers had the advantage, you'd see that put option's price continue to fall to $19, $18, $17... and so on all the way down. Even if it hit one dollar, if you believe you have an edge by selling, push the price even lower.

At some price, you'll have to recognize the absurdity of the argument. You can say that sellers have the advantage, so let's go sell a bunch of Priceline puts – even if we only get 10 cents over the next 18 days. The reality is that if there's a selling edge, traders will continue to sell *until the edge disappears*. And you know where that point is? The market price.

If the price has stabilized at $20 right now, buyers and sellers can't quite figure out which side is better to be on – just like a point spread on a football bet. Instead, the better way to view price is that it's the price where buyers and sellers see the option as fairly priced. If it's fairly priced, you can't say that sellers have the edge. Once you understand the role of price, it's easy to see why you can never say that sellers should expect to sustain some type of long-term winning edge.

Sure, it's true that in some cases sellers will end up winning. But it's also true for buyers. The point is that when you're looking at today's options prices, it's a dangerous thing to assume that if you sell at that price, you must have an automatic edge. You'll definitely know at expiration, but you don't know today. At expiration, however, it may be too late. The hurricane may have already hit shore. While you may still be unsure about the legend of Bigfoot, you will be sure that option sellers don't win 90% of the time. It's a better rule to learn now rather than in the new world of high volatility.

Investitute Takeaway

It's widely believed that 90% of options expire worthless. It's not true historically. It's not true mathematically. Traders further compound the problem by misinterpreting the myth and believing it means they'll win 90% of the time by selling options. Once you understand the role of price, you'll see it can't be true either. The best path to success is to stick with your trading plan. For the right person, selling options may be a perfect solution to a problem. But notice we're using opportunity first, strategy second. Don't focus on strategies first, especially when founded on myths.

RULE 19

Don't Let PDT Control Your Account

Professional traders have long known the advantages of letting winners run and cutting losses short. Inexperienced traders, however, believe it's safer to "get in and get out." Shoot for the quick profits. Do unto the market before it does unto you.

Doing that, however, guarantees you're only going to have small gains – if you have any at all. If you don't allow yourself to have any gains, you're not going to end up with any. It's a mathematical fact that if you add up a bunch of zeros you still end up with, well, you get the idea.

Still, some people love to get in and get out, which is called *day-trading*. It's a style where traders go long or short during the day, but close all positions by the end of the day to avoid the risk of carrying positions overnight. The problem is, just as many risks can occur during the day, and day-trading creates a style of trading where you accept small gains in exchange for potentially big losses.

As the speed of markets has increased, so have the risks of day-trading. In response, Finra (Financial Industry Regulatory Authority) has implemented a rule to mitigate the risks of day-trading. Unfortunately, many new traders aren't aware of how these rules or how they're calculated, and you may end up getting locked out of your account –

even if you're not a day-trader. It's called the pattern day-trader rule (PDT), and it catches traders off guard. If you don't understand how it works, it can prevent you entering any orders – except closing trades – for 90 days.

A day-trade is exactly what it sounds like. It's defined as any position that you've opened during the day and closed by the end of the same day. If you buy 100 shares of IBM in the morning and close them – or any portion – at any time during that same day, it's a day-trade. The number of shares doesn't matter. You could have purchased one share of IBM and it's still a day-trade.

The reason for the sale doesn't matter. You could buy 100 shares of stock and place a stop order, which is an automated order to sell the shares if the price falls at or below a certain level. If you buy 100 shares of IBM at \$130, you may decide to place a stop order at \$128. If IBM falls to \$128 or below, it triggers the sale. Stop orders are designed as a risk management tool. If the price falls and you're not there to place an order, the computer will execute it for you. Even though your intention may have been to hold the shares for years, if a stop order executes on the same day you bought the shares, it also counts as a day-trade.

Short sales carry the same rules. If you short 100 shares of IBM during the day and buy them back during the same day, it's also a day-trade. For any trade, if you hold to the next trading day, it'll never be considered a day-trade. You could buy shares of stock one minute before the closing bell and sell them on the next day's opening bell. That's not a day trade since it was held overnight. Day-trades only occur if you open and close a position in the same trading date.

If you execute four or more day-trades within any five-business day period, you will be labeled a pattern day-trader.

The pattern day-trader rule says that if a trader makes four or more day-trades in a rolling five-business-day period, provided the number of day trades does not exceed 6% of the customer's total number of trades for that same five-day period, the trader is labeled a pattern day trader. *Options are included in the calculation.* That's Finra's definition to gauge whether traders appear to be engaged in day-trading, or if there's just an occasional day-trade.

For example, let's say you entered 20 trades during the past five business days. If one was a day trade, you're okay since that's only 5% of the total trades, and you're allowed up to 6%. But if two of those trades were day-trades, now they total 10% of your total trading activity for that five-business day period. You're now over the 5% mark – and you're now labeled. The moment that second trade gets executed, your account is immediately flagged as a day-trading account.

It's not necessary to engage in day-trading to be labeled as a pattern-day trader. If the brokerage firm knows, or has good reason to believe that you'll be engaged in day trading, it can immediately label your account as a day-trading account. If you walk into a broker and ask to open an account because your friend is teaching you how to day-trade, it'll be immediately labeled as a day-trading account. Regardless of how your account gets the designation, what happens next?

You must bring your account up to at least $25,000 equity, which means you must deposit cash, stocks, bonds, or other assets that bring your total equity to that minimum level. If your total account value already exceeds $25,000, there's no need to worry about the pattern day-trader rule. Your account gets labeled as a day-trading account, but you can go on trading as if nothing ever happened.

But for those who do not have $25,000 equity, the rule poses problems, as no new trades are allowed until that minimum equity is met. If you don't bring the equity to $25,000, your account is restricted for 90 days. The only thing you can do is close existing orders. Alternatively, you can pay off any margin balances, close any short positions, and trade as a cash account. A cash account has no margin ability, and you must have a margin account to trade options. So if your account gets labeled as a pattern-day trader account, and you do not bring the equity up to $25,000, you'll be restricted from all options trading for 90 days. After 90 days have passed, the restriction is removed, and the clock starts over. Enter four or more day-trades over a rolling five-business-day period, and you'll get restricted again.

The Risks of Being Labeled a PDT

With the speed of today's markets, the patter day-trader rule plays a more significant role. You may have every intention of not being a day-trader, but you can still end up being labeled as one – and being locked out of your account for 90 days. A typical scenario is that you may buy several stocks or options and place stop orders on them. The market gets turbulent during the day, and the stop orders are triggered the same day. From your perspective, you were just practicing good risk-management skills. In the eyes of Finra, you're day-trading. Even though it may not have been your intention to day-trade, market volatility can cause you to be labeled as one.

The risks stretch much further than that. For traders who do understand the pattern-day trader rule, they may end up with some stop orders triggering the same day. In an effort to avoid the label, they end up holding other positions – perhaps riskier – through the next day in order to avoid the restriction. So it has been argued that the PDT rule causes some traders to engage in riskier activities. Whether it's a good rule or not, is certainly up for debate. But it is the rule, and it comes with the new markets. Instead, traders have to understand the new rules in order to manage the new risks.

Changing Markets, Changing Rules

As we mentioned in the preface, the New York Stock Exchange (NYSE) and Nasdaq are going to eliminate stop orders and good-til-canceled orders (GTC) beginning February 2016. In their opinion, a lot of the market volatility is caused from triggered stop orders, which causes prices to fall further, which causes more stop orders to trigger, and on it goes. It becomes a cascading series of sales, where each stop order ends up triggering yet another.

These exchanges are also concerned that traders end up with regrets if stock prices bounce back. During high periods of volatility, stop orders can be executed very far away from the current stock price. In most cases, the stock price recovers, and investors are left regretting that they ever placed a stop order in the first place.

While the exchanges' intentions to do away with stops may have been good, remember that people will always respond to incentives, and we may end up with more volatility. If traders are not allowed to use stop orders, they're not going to stop trading. Instead, they'll look for other ways to manage risk, and that changes their actions. Rather than placing stop orders and forgetting about it, we may find traders now standing by their computers, watching every twist and turn in the market. With more traders watching, it may accelerate the number of trades being placed – exactly the opposite of what was intended.

Without stop orders, we may end up with greater price swings – more volatility. Falling stock prices, for example, may take longer to find a bottom. During rapid market declines, prices will eventually reach a level where speculators will take the risk and buy shares. However, they may only be willing to do that if they can place stop orders. If stops are no longer permitted, speculators may not be as willing to step in and slow down the selling pressure. If there are fewer speculators to put buying pressure on falling stocks, we may see prices fall further.

Even though stop orders may be eliminated, the greater price swings may cause traders to manually place sell orders. Those will count toward the PDT label as well. Whether you sell or not, don't be surprised if we end up with more market volatility.

Of course, there's no reason the brokerage firms can't create stop orders from their platforms and simply trigger market orders once a certain price level is reached. If that happens, traders will still run the risk of being labeled a PDT by using stop orders. The debate on whether the elimination of these orders is good for market will probably be settled a short time after the rule goes into effect.

There's a better approach for risk management. Understand that markets change, and you must understand the new rules. This is exactly why options are becoming essential. The exchanges and stock investors are debating over the risks and benefits of stop orders. Options traders, however, have a better weapon.

Options Are Stops

If you buy a call option, you automatically have a type of stop order in place. The most you can lose with a call option is the amount that you paid. If you're speculating with IBM, why use stops? IBM is currently trading for $138.50, and the April 2016 $135 put (30 days to expiration) is trading for $1.25. By purchasing this put, your stock's cost basis increases to $139.75. However, you know for sure that you can always exercise and receive the $135 strike. The most you can lose is the $4.75 difference, or 3.4%. You still retain all of the stock's upside potential, but you have a guaranteed stop of 3.4%.

You can even use an interesting risk calculation we call Ron's Risk Calculation, which our lead trainer used as a specialist on the trading floor. Rather than just buying calls instead of stock, base your risk in terms of dollars. For example, let's say you're willing to buy 100 shares of IBM at $138.50. That's $13,850 to invest.

If you're willing to accept a 10% loss, that's $1,385. Take $1,385 and buy call options instead. The IBM April 2015 $135 call (30 days to expiration) was trading for $4.75. If you buy one call, it will cost $475, and you're still controlling 100 shares of IBM, but you're also guaranteed to not lose more than the $475. That's even better than the $1,385 you were willing to lose, but couldn't guarantee by using the actual shares and stops. You could also choose to buy two calls for $950. Now you're controlling 200 shares and still have a known maximum loss that's well below $1,385. Even though you may be trying to limit your losses to 10%, you cannot guarantee that by using shares and stops. You can with options.

There's no reason to gamble in today's markets. Make sure your risks are known. And that means you must know your options.

Stop Orders Are Not Guaranteed

Traders like to use stops, but many erroneously believe they're guaranteed to limit losses. Stop orders are not guaranteed. In fact, stops used to be called "stop loss" orders because traders believed they stopped, or prevented, losses. After many losses and complaints, the SEC ruled that market professionals cannot use the term "stop loss" any more, which is why they're now just called stops.

If you placed a stop at $135, the stock could close near $135 – and gap down the next day by $20 and be worth $115. Remember, stop orders trigger at or below the stop price, so if your stop was set at $135, it's triggered and sold. The problem is that you sold for $115 even though you were expecting $135. The $135 put will never do that. Put options always work. The stock could open the next day down $20, $30, or more – it doesn't matter to you. You can always exercise and receive the $135 strike.

In trading terms, stop orders are *path-dependent* tools while options are *time-dependent* tools. They behave differently. A path dependent tool just means that its effectiveness depends on the path that the stock price takes. For example, if you placed a stop at $135 on IBM and you get stopped out near that price before the shares fall sharply, then the stop worked beautifully. It got you out just in the nick of time before the crash. However, if the price moves slowly to a price just under $135 and triggers your stop – and then rockets to $150 – it was a big disappointment. The stop triggered you out just before the big run. The stock's path determines the effectiveness of the stop. That's a path-dependent tool.

However, in both of those scenarios, had you been holding the $135 put, you would have come out exactly where you wanted. In the first scenario where the stock continues falling, all you have to do is exercise the put and you'll get your $135. In the second scenario, if the stock falls to just below $135 and then rockets to $150, just let the put expire worthless and you'll capture 100% of those gains. Options traders get to wait to see what happens to the stock's price first – and then decide what to do. They have the right to walk away from the deal. That's what makes them a superior tool. In today's volatile markets, when even the exchanges are trying to decide what to do, you need time-dependent hedges. You need options.

Change Your Approach

With all the expected market volatility, you need a new approach. If you don't have $25,000 to invest, you have to be careful about opening and closing positions during the same day – including options. If you execute four or more day-trades within a five-business day period, you'll be labeled a pattern day-trader.
Using stops can cause accidental labeling too, but they're just as permanent. Even if you can hold the position for just one day, you'll avoid an accidental trigger of the PDT label. Using options, however, creates an automatic stop order – a time dependent one – that will never cause you to worry.

Investitute Takeaway

The pattern day-trader rule was created to require higher equity requirements for traders engaged in day-trading. If you place four or more day-trades within a rolling five-day period, you'll be labeled as a pattern day trader, provided the day trades exceed 6% of the total trades during the same time. If you use stops, it's easy to inadvertently be labeled as a day-trader, which means you'd have to deposit at least $25,000 equity, or be limited to closing transactions only. With today's market volatility, you're better off using options and let their limited downside quality manage your risk.

RULE 20

Learn to Reduce Risk – And Let Profits Run

Markets have changed, and investors must change too. The one thing that hasn't changed is that you must reduce errors. That's the golden rule of investing. But as markets become more computerized, large price swings are more likely, and that means stock investors are more likely to shaken out of positions early – and at losses.

We've talked about many different new rules of investing, so let's close with a couple of strategies to show how you can definitely become a better investor by using options.

Let's say you want to invest in the markets. As part of your trading plan, you'd like to continually invest, and buy more shares on dips. But you're also fearful of losing money, so you'd like to manage the risk. What can you do?

If you're like most investors, you'd buy shares of stock, ETFs, or mutual funds. The big problem with those choices is that your profit and loss diagrams is a straight line. You can make 100% of the gains in exchange for 100% of the losses:

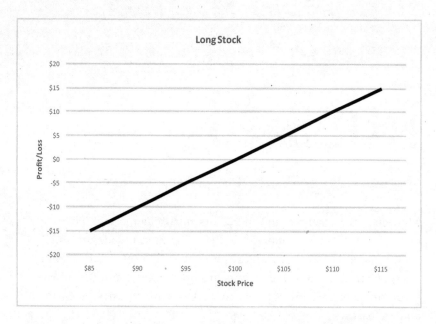

Those are extreme outcomes, and exactly what you want to avoid in today's markets. There's no reason to accept unlimited losses in exchange for making an unlimited amount of money. Risk is never defined as missing out on rewards, so let's see if we can use options to give up some of the upside in exchange for sharply guarding the downside.

If you're not sure which stock to buy, it's never a bad idea to use the broad-based market, such as the S&P 500 index. Remember, the majority of professional money managers can't beat that index. In fact, going into the close of 2015, the S&P 500 is down about 2% and Warren Buffet's Berkshire Hathaway is down about 13%. By using this index, you'll own 500 of the largest, most highly capitalized companies in the world by purchasing one investment.

The S&P 500 "spiders" or SPY is currently trading for $209.35. It's a good choice, but it's also expensive. If you want to buy 100 shares, it'll cost nearly $21,000. What if you're trading in an IRA and don't have that much in the account – and can't make any contributions until next year? Now you'll resort to choosing less expensive – and riskier – choices. Already, you're seeing one of the big risks that investors face. It's difficult to invest in the markets without having to put a lot of money into an investment. Of course, you're not required to buy in 100-share lots. You could choose to buy fewer shares, but then your sensitivity to changes in the index is also reduced. If you buy 20 shares, for example, you're gaining $20 for each dollar move in the index. It will be a slow climb to reach your goals. Is there a way you can reduce the cost – and gain some leverage?

Options as a Strategic Alternative

One simple way to limit the downside and gain leverage is to simply buy an at-the-money call option. This is the first choice of most novice investors who have some options knowledge. However, at-the-money options have a delta near 0.50, so your sensitivity to the shares is cut in half. Shares of stock have 100 delta since your profits and losses always rise and fall dollar-for-dollar with changes in the stock. But if you buy an at-the-money call, your deltas will be reduced to about 50%. Even though you may buy one contract and control 100 shares, right now it's behaving like half that, or 50 shares. But there's a bigger problem with at-the-money options that's usually overlooked.

Your breakeven point is pushed far forward. The S&P 500 index is currently $209.35, and the January 2017 $210 call (424 days) is $16.45. With this option, your breakeven is $209.35 + $16.45 = $225.80. That means you'd need the index to climb nearly 8% – just to get your money back. Historically, the index usually returns 7% to 10% in a year, so giving up 8% before you're going to make the first dime isn't a good choice. You're giving up nearly *all* of your expected gains, but could still lose $16.45. We're looking to create a position where you give up some of the gains but also manage the downside risk.

The at-the-money option would be an okay strategy if you felt the index was going to make an explosive move. But the new rule says opportunity first, strategy second. Your opportunity is to simply invest. It was never stated that you were expecting an explosive move. Buying the at-the-money call is a mismatch in risk and reward. It's not part of your trading plan. What else can you do? This is where understanding strategies, and how to alter risk-reward profiles will help you survive the new markets.

The Stock Replacement Strategy

There's a necessary strategy for today's stock investors. It's one we teach our traders who want to control shares of stock, but greatly alter the risk-reward profile in their favor. It's called the *stock replacement* strategy. It's one that Pete and I use when we want to effectively take ownership of the stock, gain leverage, and greatly limit the downside risk. Let's take a look at how the strategy works, and we'll let you be the judge if options are risky.

Traders who are familiar with options hear the name of this strategy and think it just means to buy a call option as a substitute for the shares. That's definitely not true. As we just found with the at-the-money call, it's hardly a substitute for shares when your breakeven point is pushed far forward. Using higher strikes only makes things worse. The $220 call, for example, is trading for $10.84, which makes the breakeven point $230.84, or a 10.3% increase. All option strikes are not created equally. They're different tools for different opportunities.

While the $220 call is cheaper, it doesn't mean it's better, or less risky. Price is not risk. However, many traders would choose an out-of-the-money strike like this, lose money, and then think all options are risky. Without question, the $220 strike is risky, but it's not the only choice we have. We have many other strikes, and each one creates a different set of risks and rewards.

To master today's markets, it's not enough to understand options. Instead, you have to understand option mechanics, so you can make them work for you. It's a process, and it requires a little time. But the stock replacement strategy is one of the most powerful, yet simple to understand. What makes it work?

Time Value Defines an Option

To understand how the stock replacement strategy works, remember that it's the time value that makes an option an option. It's what defines an option. The only reason for paying any time premium is for the right to walk away from the deal. If there's no time value on an option, it's not really an option.

At-the-money options will always contain the highest amount of time premium. The reason is simple. At-the-money options have about a 50-50 chance of expiring in-the-money. If you had thousands of at-the-money options, about half would expire in-the-money and half would expire out-of-the-money. It's not any different from a coin flip. The market recognizes there's a tremendous amount of uncertainty whether this option will ever be exercised. Consequently, traders are willing to pay the highest insurance premium – the most time value. There could be a big advantage in walking away from the deal and just letting the call expire worthless, so traders are willing to pay the price.

However, as you move away from at-the-money options, the time premiums shrink. In other words, as you move more in-the-money or out-of-the-money, time premiums get smaller. If all strikes have the same expiration, shouldn't they all carry the same time value? Not at all. Each has a different probability for expiring in-the-money, so the market will change its willingness to pay for the insurance.

Take a look at a few of the SPY January 2017 strikes with 424 days to expiration:

CALL STRIKES	PREMIUM	INTRINSIC VALUE	TIME VALUE
198	21.64	11.35	10.29
199	20.95	10.35	10.60
200	20.28	9.35	10.93
205	19.63	4.35	15.28
210	16.45	0	16.45
215	13.52	0	13.52
220	10.84	0	10.84
225	8.45	0	8.45
230	6.35	0	6.35

The $210 strike is at-the-money, and it has the greatest time value of all the strikes at $16.45. As you move to higher or lower strikes, you'll notice the time values *decrease*. This is because traders are becoming more certain of the outcome at expiration. For the higher strikes, traders have good reason to believe those strikes will probably expire worthless, so they're not willing to pay a lot of time value for the right to walk away. They have a feeling that buyers will probably not be exercising those strikes, so why pay a lot of time premium for the right to not exercise?

A similar idea holds as you move to the lower strikes. Those strikes are getting more and more in-the-money, which is why they have lots of intrinsic value. The further in-the-money you go, the more confident traders will be that the option will remain that way. As an extreme example, assume there was a $10 strike. If you bought that call, you'd obviously have to pay the $199.35 difference; that's the intrinsic value, or the cash value.

You could always exercise right now and pull $199.35 from the option, so it must be worth at least that much. But how much extra would you pay for the right to walk away and let the option expire worthless? With it this deep in-the-money, you should see that it's virtually impossible for it to expire worthless, so there's no value in trying to insure an event that has no chance of occurring. You shouldn't be willing to pay one penny for the right to walk away. The chances for those deep-in-the-money options to expire worthless are decreasing, so the time values are decreasing as well.

You also saw this principle at work in Rule #5 on pricing boundaries. As a call option's strike gets closer to zero, it's becoming closer to shares of stock. Stock does not have a time value. Therefore, as the call options get closer and closer to shares of stock, that time values must get closer to zero. If you look deep enough, you may find a call trading for purely intrinsic value and no time value, which means it's trading at parity. At that point, it's no longer an option. It's stock.

The Magic of Parity

If a call option is trading at parity, new traders believe it's an extremely expensive option. But the word parity means equivalence; in other words, it's equivalent to stock.

For example, let's say the stock is trading for $100 and you find the $80 call is trading for exactly $20. That's all intrinsic value and no time value. Because there's no time value, it's trading at parity. If you check the breakeven point, you'll find it's the $80 strike + $20 premium = $100 stock price. In other words, if you paid $20 for this call and exercised it by paying $80, you would spend $100 – exactly what you would have spent to buy the shares. There's absolutely no additional risk in this option compared to just buying the stock.

However, there is a downside benefit. If you purchased this call, the most you could lose is $20. That's not true if you bought the shares for $100 – even if you used a stop order. Remember, stop orders cannot guarantee you're going to get $80 for your shares. When options are trading at parity, they're actually better than stock. The stock trader cannot outperform the options trader, but could do much worse. That's the magic of options trading at parity.

You'll generally only find options trading at parity if they're close to expiration – or if they're extremely deep in-the-money. At this point, we just like to show that call options trading at parity are not expensive options at all, nor are they risky compared to the stock. They're stock with a built-in stop order that's guaranteed to work. How will that help you as an investor?

If there's any time remaining, it's difficult to find a call option trading exactly a parity. However, we can get close. And if we get close, you'll find that we can find an asset that behaves about like shares of stock – but pay a whole lot less.

For example, take a look at some other SPY call options that are much deeper in-the-money:

JANUARY 2017 (424 DAYS)				
SPY = $209.35				
CALL STRIKES	PREMIUM	INTRINSIC VALUE	TIME VALUE	DELTA
135	74.47	74.35	0.12	93.7
140	69.64	69.35	0.29	93.1
145	64.86	64.35	0.51	92.5
150	60.20	59.35	0.85	91.3
155	55.62	54.35	1.27	89.7
160	51.12	49.35	1.77	87.7
165	46.74	44.35	2.39	85.4
170	42.45	39.35	3.10	82.7
175	38.28	34.35	3.93	79.7

If you focus on just the premiums, they do appear to be very expensive options. However, focus on the part that makes them an option – focus on the time premiums. You'll see that the time premiums are fairly small, which means these deep in-the-money calls are behaving much more like shares of stock rather than options.

Even though there's more than one year to expiration, the $135 strike is trading for $74.47 and only contains 12 cents worth of time value. The breakeven point is $135 + $74.47, or $209.47 – just 12 cents higher than the current stock price. Twelve cents also happens to be the time value. It's no coincidence: For any in-the-money call, the breakeven point is always going to be greater than the current stock price by the amount of the time value. The time value represents the amount of the "insurance policy" for having the right to walk away and have a maximum $74.47 loss.

This option is trading for just 12 cents above parity, so it's basically stock. There's very little "option" in this deal. With the stock at $209.35, if you buy the $135 call, you have an immediate benefit equal to the difference, or $74.35 – that's the intrinsic value. That's just the cash value, so it doesn't represent any additional risk compared to the stock buyer.

For example, let's assume that another trader buys the shares for $209.35. You decide to buy the $135 strike for $74.47 instead. Now assume the stock price falls all the way down to the $135 strike at expiration, which is more than one year away. How did both of you fare?

The stock trader lost $74.35, which is the intrinsic value. You, on the other hand lost $74.47. You're just 12 cents worse off than the stock trader. That's because the intrinsic value doesn't count as a unique risk in the option. It's a risk that's common to both the stock buyer and the option buyer. With the stock at $209.35, by purchasing the $135 strike, you had an immediate advantage of the $74.47 difference – and you must pay for that advantage. Buying this option doesn't put you into a risky asset compared to buying the shares. Instead, it amounts to nothing more than a $74.35 down payment on the stock, along with a cheap 12-cent insurance policy – the time value – attached. That insurance policy allows you to decide if it's ever worth paying the $135 strike in one year. Until then, just leave the $74.47 at risk, which is much less than the $209.35 you'd have at risk by buying the shares.

Once you see that an option trading at or near parity is a better solution than buying shares of stock, we can do even better.

The Stock Replacement Strategy

A lot of benefits are found by purchasing call options trading near parity. They behave almost identically to shares of stock. Well, as with any strategy, we'd always like to get a blend of certain qualities. Do we really need to go that far in-the-money so that the option is nearly a perfect replica of stock? After all, it's possible that the stock price falls, and while we have a lot less money invested compared to the stock investor, we still have over $74 into the position. Maybe it would be better to pay a tiny bit more time premium in exchange for getting an option that's a whole lot cheaper.

Take a closer look at the time values in the previous table. Rather than buying the $135 call, wouldn't it make more sense to buy the $140 strike and pay $69.64? You're only paying 29 cents in time value – not big deal – and still pretty close to parity. But you've lowered your cost by 6.5% from $74.47 to $69.64. As long as we can keep getting big decreases in price, but only small increases in time values, it makes sense to continue using higher strikes.

Professional traders usually find that around the 80 to 85 delta range is where they find the best deals. It's the sweet spot. It's a small range of strike prices that represent a really good approximation of the stock – but at drastically lower prices. Other calculations can be used to fine-tune the analysis, but to make things easy, let's just say the stock replacement strategy requires that you buy a call option with an 80 to 85 delta. It's that simple to find.

For the January 2017 expiration, that would be the $160 strike trading for $51.12. That's a whole lot less than $74.47, but it comes at the cost of accepting $1.77 in time value. Still, the breakeven point is $160 + $51.12, or $211.12, or less than one percent above the current index price.

Now that you've learned how to locate the stock replacement call, what are the benefits?

Benefit #1: Cheaper Cost

The most obvious benefit is that you can control shares of the S&P 500 for only $51.12 rather than $209.35 – a 75% reduction. By using the stock replacement strategy, you have more opportunities to invest since you can now buy shares that you may otherwise have not been able to afford. It would cost nearly $21,000 to buy 100 shares of SPY. By purchasing the $160 call instead, you've laid out $5,100 to control 100 shares. You're more cash efficient. Further, if you're investing for your retirement in an IRA, you may not have that much in the account, and may not be able to contribute more money until next year. The stock replacement strategy allows you to invest in your best selections since you're now able to afford a wider range of stocks.

Okay, so there are benefits, but is the $160 call riskier than the shares? If the index falls to the $160 strike, you'll lose the entire $51.12 premium. However, had you purchased the shares instead, you'd lose $49.35. By using the call, you stand to lose an additional $1.77 – exactly the time value. However, in exchange for that additional loss, you have a wider range of investments from which to choose. The stock replacement strategy just made everything cheaper, but that's only the first of many benefits.

Benefit #2: Better ROI

Because you're paying less for the same shares, you're going to have a better return on your investment, or ROI. In this example, you're paying roughly $51 rather than $209, which is about 25%, or about one-fourth the cost. Depending on the time to expiration and the stock's volatility, you'll find that the stock replacement strategy usually creates anywhere from 3:1 to 8:1 leverage.

In this case, you're paying one-fourth the price, so for any given increase in the index, your performance will be four times as good. That's because you're controlling 100 shares and will capture dollar-for-dollar of any index increases at expiration, but you're only investing one-fourth of the money.

If the S&P 500 rises 5% next year, your returns will be four times better, or 20%. If the index rises 10%, you'll make 40%. These increased returns are a reflection of the mathematical leverage you're gaining from this option.

The stock trader, on the other hand, must pay the full $209 price. By using the stock replacement strategy, you're paying $51 – and have the right to decide if you want to pay the $160 balance in the future. In effect, you're borrowing the $160 strike – but without actually borrowing money. It's a mathematical leverage since you don't pay the full share price – nor are you ever required to.

Isn't the leverage a double-edged sword? If your performance if four-times better if prices rise, won't it be four-times worse if prices fall? For most investments, if you have leverage on the way up, you have it equally on the way down too. That's not true for options. By purchasing the call, the most you can lose is the amount paid, or about $51, but there's no limit on how much you can make, so there's an asymmetrical payoff that's adding another benefit.

If you are a stock investor looking for leverage, however, you'd have to do that by borrowing money from the broker, which is called margin trading. To engage in *margin trading*, you have to deposit 50% of the shares' total price and would borrow the remainder from the broker. By borrowing 50%, you'll get 2:1 leverage, not 4:1 like you got by using the stock replacement strategy.

In this example, the shares cost $209, so you'd deposit half of that, or about $104.50. That's still $10,450 – more than twice the amount needed to buy the option. However, unlike the stock replacement strategy, you'll pay margin interest to the broker on the $10,450 balance. That interest will more than exceed the $1.77 you spent on the option's time value. But there's even more danger with margin trading.

If your equity falls below a certain level, usually 30% for most brokerage firms, you'll have to send in more money which is called a margin call, or maintenance call. In other words, you must maintain at least 30% equity at all times. Here's how it works:

Market Value Long	$20,900
– Debit	$10,450
= Equity	$10,450

When you purchased 100 shares for $20,900, that's the market value that you own, also called the market value long. The amount borrowed is the debit, which is $10,450. Your equity is the remaining $10,450. If you take your equity and divide it by the market value long, it's exactly 50%. That's the required starting point.

For any given increase in the market value long, you'll find your equity increases by double. Again, that's because you have 2:1 leverage by only paying 50% of the stock's value. If the index rises 5%, your equity rises 10%.

However, if the market falls, you'll also lose at the rate of 2:1 – all the way down to a stock price of zero. That's not true for stock replacement. It stops all losses at the $51 paid. With margin trading, you can lose far more than your initial investment.

If the market falls and pushes your equity below 30%, you've got a maintenance call. For instance, if your market value falls to $14,800, your equity is $4,350:

Market Value Long	$14,800
– Debit	$10,450
= Equity	$4,350

If you divide your equity by the market value long, your equity is 29%, so you've fallen below 30% and would have to send in $90. That would bring your equity to $4,440 and your equity to 30%. If you're unable to meet the maintenance call, the broker will close the position for you. If that happens, it also means you were probably forced to close when the market was at an absolute bottom – the worst time to sell.

The stock replacement strategy will never allow that to happen. In fact, if you're a pattern day trader, you're allowed to take your equity down to 25%, but only for the trading day. You have to have it above that level by close of business. But compare that to the stock replacement strategy: You'll never have a margin call, you'll never pay margin interest, you'll never be forced to sell, you'll never lose more than you have into the position – and yet you're at 25% equity for the entire life of the contract.

If you're used to trading stocks, especially on margin, the first two benefits of stock replacement win hands down against stock. There is simply not one benefit that the margin stock trader has over stock replacement – and all at a cost of $1.77. If that's impressive, bigger benefits are yet to come.

Benefit #3: Limited Risk & Gamma

The third benefit of stock replacement is that you'll have a known, limited risk. The most you can lose is the amount paid. In this example, it's $51. You can't make that same claim by purchasing the shares at $209. And you definitely can't make that claim by using margin.

Because this option is so deep in-the-money, it's unlikely you could ever lose the entire investment. But that's part of the point: It's so deep in-the-money that few people think it will ever fall out-of-the-money. That's why it's behaving like shares of stock. You're just paying the extra $1.77 time value as an insurance policy in the unlikely even the stock does fall below the $160 strike. It's a relatively cheap insurance policy, because few traders think it's ever going to be used. Traders are reasonably certain this option will become shares of stock in the future, so they're willing to treat it like shares of stock today. Somebody will most likely be exercising this call at expiration. The $1.77 time premium is just a small insurance policy in case you're wrong. It's a small price to pay for sound risk management in today's uncertain world.

However, if the stock price does drop, you're not going to lose dollar-for-dollar like you would with shares of stock. That's because long options have gamma, which we covered in Rule #12 on the Greeks. Gamma is the characteristic where a call option decelerates its losses if the stock falls, but accelerates the gains if the stock rises.

In the following chart, you can see the bold line represents stock replacement while the gray line represents 100 shares of stock:

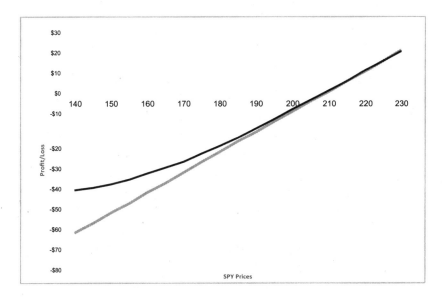

If the SPY falls, the $160 call will decelerate losses for you. That's what's causing the separation of the two lines on the left side of the chart. Both traders are losing money, but the stock replacement trader loses less. For each dollar the index falls, the call option automatically sheds some of its deltas. That's gamma working for you to manage risk. The stock trader, on the other hand, continues to lose dollar for dollar all the way down. That's too big of a risk for today's markets, especially when we hedged it for $1.77.

On the other hand, if the SPY rises, the call option will accelerate its gains and eventually match the 1.0 delta of the shares. That's why you can't really tell a difference between the two strategies on the right hand side of the chart. Both profit and loss curves are nearly identical and overlap. If you were able to zoom in really close, you'd see that the stock profit and loss diagram beats the stock replacement on that end of the chart by $1.77. That's the time value we spent to get gamma. Once you understand the stock replacement strategy, you'll see that by spending the time value, you give up a small amount of gains if you're right. But in exchange, you get tremendous benefits – far bigger – if you're wrong. That's exactly the type of risk-management skills you need to survive today's markets.

The wonderful thing about gamma is that it could your very first options trade, and gamma doesn't require any skill or risk management knowledge. The option decelerates the losses all by itself. That's gamma coming to your rescue.

Stock traders may think they have the ability to manage that risk. However, when the markets are falling, it's easy to get lured into the psychology of holding and hoping. The stock replacement strategy will never let that happen to you. And once again, you have to ask if it's worth the $1.77 to pay for that benefit. It's a wonderful property to have – just in case you're wrong. For today's markets you absolutely must have those risks defined at the time of the trade, and there's no better way to accomplish that goal than by using options. Investing success depends on reducing errors, and you cannot buy a more perfect risk-management tool.

Benefit #4: Diversification

The fourth benefit we get from using stop replacement is a diversification effect. Because you're able to control the same shares for less money, you're more cash efficient. That means you can spread the same number of dollars across more investments. In this example, if you have about $21,000 to put into SPY, everything's in that index. But by using the stock replacement strategy, you've only spent 25% of that, so you have more cash to put into other investments.

By diversifying your holdings, you're not putting all of your eggs in one basket. If one stock takes a nose dive, you'll have others that can prop you up. If you're just holding a few stocks, that's too risky in today's markets. If those shares are in similar industries, all can fall even though the bad news my only be related to one company.

Of course, the S&P 500 is already well diversified, so you don't necessarily need to use the cash to diversify. Instead, you could use it to buy more on dips, or to beta weight if times get rough. When all of your money is tied up, however, there's not much you can do. You're at the mercy of the markets – and the machines.

It doesn't matter how much money you have, you're always better off when you can spread those dollars across more investments. Even if you choose to hold only a few companies, you'll still be better off since you'll have extra cash to buy when prices fall. If you dump all your money into the shares, there's not much you can do. When you're cash efficient, you have opportunities. The stock replacement strategy allows you be more cash efficient compared to any other strategy.

Benefit #5: Roll, Roll, Roll!

In Rule #6, we showed you the benefits of rolling options. When you use stock replacement rather than shares, you can roll that option multiple times through the year. Each time you do, you're sweeping cash into your account and reducing the overall risk in the position. By reducing the risk – and the fear – you're in a better position to manage the market volatility that normally would shake you out of the position. There's no fear in hanging on. Go ahead, let your profits run.

Stock traders cannot do that. Instead, they watch their unrealized gains pile up, get nervous, and sell way before the real money is made. Options traders don't have that fear. When you're using stock replacement, each time the market rallies, you can sell your current call and buy a higher strike, which always produces a credit to your account. That's superior risk management – managing the downside risk while holding out for bigger gains.

Time for the Jury

Okay, now that you've seen the stock replacement strategy, let's review the benefits so you can judge the results. The stock replacement strategy costs less, limits your risk, produces a greater ROI, never creates a maintenance call, never charges you margin interest, automatically hedges downside risk if the stock falls, diversifies your portfolio, and allows you to roll for greater profits.

At expiration, the long stock position will outperform the stock replacement strategy by the amount of the time value for all stock prices above the strike price. In our example, the shares will outperform by $1.77 for all stock prices above the $160 strike.

Below the $160 strike, however, the stock replacement strategy outperforms the long stock. It's a classic financial hedge: Give up a tiny bit of profits if things go well, and exchange that for a bunch of benefits that have far greater value. And here's the best part of all: If you don't feel it was worth the $1.77 time value, drop down to the $155 strike and reduce it to $1.27. But you'll have to ask if it's worth increasing your cost from $51.12 to $55.62 to shave of 50 cents of time value. But we'll let you be the judge.

Even if you decide to go all the way down to the $135 strike and pay $74.47, you're still better off than buying shares of stock. At some strike, you'll have to agree that it's far better than using shares of stock. When you find a strike price where you agree, you'll see why options are not risky. They're just tools for altering risks and rewards and it's up to the trader – you – to decide what's best.

If you like the stock replacement strategy, we're just getting started. Imagine what will happen when you learn vertical spreads, diagonal spreads, butterfly spreads, backspreads, condors, collars, and covered calls. It's an entirely new world that's perfectly adapted for managing the new risks of today's changing markets. If you want to reduce errors, you must change too. Start by using the stock replacement strategy, and you'll see it's a strategy that's hard to replace.

Investitute Takeaway

The stock replacement strategy is simple to use, as it just requires you to locate an 80 to 85 delta as a substitute for the shares. By locating an option that deep in-the-money, it's behaving far more like shares of stock, but at a greatly reduced cost. The lower cost creates limited risk, leverage, better ROI, and diversification. More importantly, the strategy allows you to acquire gamma, which automatically manages the downside risk for you. Most of all, by using options, you're able to roll with the position indefinitely. That allows for greater profits for less risk.

RULE 21

Teach New Tricks to Old Strategies

It's often said that the best defense is a good offense. We can turn
that around: The best offense is a good defense. That's how it works
with options strategies. By knowing different ways to construct
them, you can turn an offensive strategy into a defensive one, or go
from defensive to offensive.

For most investors, the covered call strategy is used more offensively to
shoot for large capital gains. For today's markets, an interesting tactic is
to use them defensively. Construct them in ways to greatly lower your
downside risk, but still allow for enough profit to match your goals. To
invest in the new markets, sometimes it means teaching new tricks to
old strategies.

The *covered call* is a stock friendly strategy, which means it requires
the investor to own shares of the underlying stock. And since most
investors get their start by investing in shares of stock, the covered
call is most investors' initiation into options. Consequently, the strategy
is often talked about like an entry-level strategy, designed for the sole
purpose of giving investors a harmless introduction to options.

Mastering options begins by understanding that each strategy
should be treated with respect. Just like entry-level skydiving, small

misunderstandings can be dangerous. The reason is that stock investors have one dimension to worry about – the stock price rising or falling. But when you throw options into the mix, you now have many factors to contend with. Not understanding them doesn't make them go away. It just means it's a matter of time before you find out the hard way.

When you uncover the covered call risks, you'll find this strategy is not so basic after all. And with a slight twist, it's capable of taming some of the toughest risks in today's market.

Covered Call Strategy – the Basics

When you enter a covered call, you buy the stock and then sell (or write) a call option against those shares. The shares of stock can be purchased at the same time the call is sold, which is called a buy-write because you're buying the shares and selling or "writing" the calls as one transaction. On the other hand, the shares could have also been sitting in your account for months or years. It doesn't matter how you got the shares or how long you've held them, as long as they're in your account, you can write calls against them.

Probably the most important point about using covered calls is to make sure you're holding shares of stock you'd be willing to hold anyway – even if it wasn't optionable. If you're buying the shares just so you can use the covered call strategy, you're focusing on strategy first. Remember, opportunity first, strategy second. Don't ever buy shares of stock that you're not comfortable holding, no matter how tempting the strategy may be.

Once you have shares, all you have to do is sell calls in a 1:1 ratio against your shares. For example, if you own 100 shares, you'd write one call. If you own 200 shares, you'd write two calls, and so on. What did you do by selling the calls?

Think back to the rights and obligations that options convey. Call buyers have right to buy 100 shares of stock. Call sellers, on the other hand, have the potential obligation to sell shares. By selling calls, you receive cash in your account, but in exchange, have the potential obligation to sell your 100 shares. It's a *potential* obligation because it's up to the call buyer to decide if it's worth exercising. It's the buyer's choice, or option to choose. As the call seller, it's your obligation to fulfill the obligation if the call is exercised. If the call buyer decides to use (exercise) his call option and buy your shares, you have no choice in the matter. The shares will be swept from your account and you'll be credited with the strike price in cash, less commissions.

If you have shares that, for some reason, you don't want to ever be taken away, don't write covered calls, period. It's a bad idea. Sometimes investors are concerned about triggering a tax consequence. Or maybe they own shares given to them by their uncle 10 years ago, and they'd be embarrassed to say they sold them. Whatever the reason, if you sell calls against shares you don't really want to sell, you're acting like a naked call writer – who just happens to own 100 shares of stock. It's a dangerous mismatch is opportunity and strategy.

The important point to understand now is that selling calls creates the potential obligation to sell your shares for the strike price. For example, if you buy 100 shares of stock for $50 and then write a $55 call against them for $3, you have the potential obligation to sell those shares for $55 no matter how high that stock may be trading. That is, you'll miss out on all possible profits above $55. Your profit and loss diagram looks like the following:

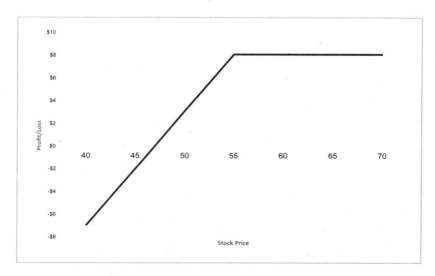

Notice that the first point of maximum gain occurs at the strike of that $55 short call. Whenever you sell options, your maximum gain always occurs at the strike of the short call. You can see how the chart flattens for all stock prices above the $55 strike. Again, that's because you've sold off your rights above $55. Somebody else is going to own those shares if the stock reaches $55 or above. New traders often think the covered call's risk is that you may miss out on some of the future gains. But remember, risk is never defined as missing out on rewards.

The covered call's risk is if the stock falls, which can be seen by looking at the left side of the chart. As the covered call writer, you have unlimited losses. That's because you're holding the shares, less the small premium received. This why you have to be certain you're comfortable holding the shares. Don't ever buy shares just because the call premiums appear high and you want to collect that apparently free money. They're high for a reason. When you see high option premiums, it's because the stock is volatile and traders don't want to hold the shares. They're willing to pay others to hold the shares. Instead, always focus on the shares first. If you'd be willing to hold the shares whether options existed or not then that makes a better candidate for covered calls.

By selling the call, you received the $3 premium, which lowers your cost basis. Because you originally purchased the shares for $50, after selling the call, your cost basis is reduced to $47. Active covered call writers will generally sell calls month after month against their shares and continue to reduce their cost basis. That's a big benefit of the covered call. Investors can make receive consistent premiums with each one reducing the stock's cost basis.

Option sellers play the role of an insurance company. If an insurance company sells a policy, its accepting cash today based on nothing more than a promise to fulfill the terms of the contract. If you sell a call, you're accepting cash in exchange for a promise to sell 100 shares of stock for a fixed price – if the option buyer decides to buy the shares. At some point, however, it's every investor's goal to sell the shares, so this potential obligation is not a risk in the strategy.

While it's true that you may end up selling your shares far below the current market value, it's not a risk of the strategy since it still represents a profit.

Why is it called a *covered* call? If you sell a call option without owning the shares of stock, it's called a naked call since you don't have the shares in your account to deliver. If you're assigned on a naked call and forced to sell 100 shares of stock, you must go into the open market and buy those shares – and there's no telling what that price might be. Because of this, naked call writing is considered to be among the riskiest of all option strategies since there's no limit as to how high a stock's price can rise.

This is why you should never write contracts that represent a greater number of shares than what you own (such as writing five contracts against 400 shares). By always writing in a 1:1 ratio (or less), you're never exposed to the unlimited upside risk. In other words, the upside risk of naked call writing is "covered" because you'll always be able to deliver the shares at a known cost. You've already paid for those shares and that cost will never change. However, it doesn't mean the strategy is without risk just because it has the word "covered" in its name. It's only the upside risk of a naked call that's being covered. When you use covered calls, you're still holding 100% of the downside risk, less the premium received.

As long as you remain in the covered call position, you have limited upside potential since the most you will ever receive for your shares is the strike price. By capping your upside potential profit, the covered call strategy is designed for those investors who have a *neutral* to *slightly bullish* outlook on the stock. You should not write calls on stocks you feel will make explosive upward moves nor should you write calls on shares you think will fall considerably in price.

This is another mistake made by new investors. When they learn that call buying is bullish and call selling is bearish, that's true – assuming there are no other assets in the mix. When they hear about the covered call and find it entails selling calls, they jump to the conclusion that it must be a bearish strategy since they're selling calls. It's not. You own the shares, and that changes things – dramatically. As we found in Rule #5 on pricing principles, the shares will always be worth more than any call, so you'll always have a large downside risk with the covered call. This is why Pete and I always recommend that new traders are comfortable with the shares they're holding.

Before entering into a covered call, you should be reasonably confident that the stock price will fluctuate sideways through the life of the option (neutral outlook) or you should feel it may climb somewhat higher (slightly bullish). Don't ever use a covered call because you're bearish. That's one of the mistakes that new investors often find out the hard way about the strategy. Always make sure you're looking at the opportunity first – the one that meets your goals – and then find the strategy that solves that problem.

Covered Call Philosophy

The goal of the covered call writer is to collect many option premiums over a long period of time. Every time you write a call option against your shares, you are lowering your cost basis on those shares. This reduces your risk since you're reducing the amount of cash you have invested. Covered call writers are not attempting to profit from sharply rising stock prices; remember the strategy is neutral to slightly bullish.

It's okay if the stock price rises, as that's not a true risk in the strategy. Rising stock prices still produce the maximum gain for the strategy. It's just not the main goal of the strategy. If you are truly bullish on the stock, you should just buy the call and hang on. Covered call writers, on the other hand, have limited upside potential because they're obligated to sell their shares for a fixed price. So the strategy is not designed as an optimal way to make money from rising stock prices. Instead, the goal is to generate your profits by writing calls over and over – collecting premiums – against those shares.

The benefit is that the option premiums are known at the time of the sale. The future possible stock gains aren't. In the earlier example, if you buy shares of stock for $50, you don't know what the future gains will be, if any. But once you sold the $55 call for $3, that's instant cash. You know you've received that. Just like the insurance company, you keep the premium regardless of what happens. That's your compensation for accepting the risk of holding the shares. Covered call writers are accepting a fixed, known amount of cash today in exchange for selling off the unknown future gains in the shares.

To see if covered call writing works for you, it helps to know several profitability calculations. You should never use the covered call strategy "just because" you've heard about it or heard it's good. It's just a tool, and you need to make sure it carries the right risks and rewards to help you accomplish your goals.

Return If Exercised

One calculation you'll want to check is called the *return if exercised*. To calculate it, you simply find the percentage increase between the cost basis and the strike price. In this example, you paid $50 for the shares and sold the $55 call for $3. You spent $50, but received $3 back, so your effective cost basis is $47.

If the long position exercises, you'll end up selling for $55, for a 17% return. Most of the time, option sellers will write fairly short-term options because longer-term options are financially better deals for buyers, as shown by the square-root pricing relationship in Rule #5.. If this option was only for 30 days, your annualized return is 12 times higher. So even though $3 may not seem like a terribly big number, you have to realize that it was earned over a short time. It's not the $3 you want to focus on. It's the $3 relative to $50 over 30 days that matters.

However, one misperception that usually plagues covered call writers is when they write out-of-the-money options, such as in this example. Because of that, the returns are magnified and not as good as they appear. In this example, most of that gain is strictly from the stock price moving from the current $50 price to the $55 strike. It had nothing to do with the proceeds from the call. Whether you sold the call for $3 or three cents made no difference. The five-point move from $50 to $55 was strictly due to stock price movement. Because of this, another calculation to check is the static return.

Static Return

Another helpful calculation is called the *static return*, which calculates the return if the stock's price is unchanged or "static" at expiration. In the "return if exercised" calculation, we allowed for the stock's price to rise from the current $50 price to the $55 strike. Again, that gives us a possible bigger return – but only if the stock price rises. How will you fare if the stock price remains at $50? In other words, what's the true contribution of the option premium on your returns?

Your cost basis is $47, so if the stock price remains at $50 at expiration, your return is the $3 difference divided by your $47 cost, or 6.3%. As before, if this call was written over a 30-day period, the annualized return is 12 times bigger, or over 76%. This clearly shows that covered call writers can make money on stocks without any movement in the stock's price, and is definitely another tactic that cannot be done with stock alone.

The static return doesn't assume the stock's price will remain unchanged throughout the life of the option. Instead, it assumes that it will *finish* at the same price. Whether this is a realistic assumption or not, it's simply meant to give us an idea about the rate of return from the option time premium alone and does not consider movements in the stock's price. This is why it pays to compare the return if exercised to the static return.

In these examples, the static return is 6.3% while the return if exercised was 17%. These two figures show that, if the call is exercised, the majority of that return is due to the stock price movement from $50 to $55. Even though the return if exercised looks impressive, you have to realize that the majority of that is from the stock price moving, which you would have collected anyway had you not written the call.

Another mistake made by new traders who write out-of-the-money calls is to ignore the static return and just focus on the return if exercised. As an extreme example, what if you bought shares for $50, but sold the $70 call for five cents. If you just looked at the return if exercised, it's over 40% and looks impressive. But by comparing it to the static return, you see it's a small fraction of one percent. In other words, your cost basis is $49.95 and you could sell for $50 if the stock price remains the same. That's the true contribution of the call to that strategy in that instance. Always be sure to blend risk and reward. When writing calls, don't get too hung up on the return if exercised calculation if the static return isn't meeting your financial objectives.

Breakeven Return

Another calculation Pete and I like to check is the *breakeven return*, and it's becoming more important in today's markets. Remember, when you sell a call, you're receiving cash, which reduces your stock's cost. Therefore, you can afford to have the stock price fall by the amount of the premium collected – and just break even. The breakeven calculation gives you the size of the downside hedge in the strategy. To survive the new risks, you always want to pay special attention to the risks that are being hedged. The maximum gains count, but don't overlook the ways in which the strategy is offering protection against adverse price moves.

In this example, the stock could fall by the amount of premium received from selling the call, which is $3. The $3 cash collected acts as a downside hedge in the event the stock falls. If the stock falls $3, that represents a drop of $3/$50, or 6%. In other words, you can afford to have the shares fall 6% from the current $50 price down to $47 and just break even. If you just owned the shares and they fell to $47, you'd be down 6%, so the sale of the call gives you a cushion, or a hedge against adverse price moves. The breakeven calculation shows the size of that hedge.

If we overlay the long stock position with the covered call, you can see the benefit of the downside hedge. The sale of the call lowers the stock's cost basis from $50 to $47, so it shifts the breakeven point lower than it otherwise would be. Notice that the covered call graph shown in bold, is shifted more to the left side of the chart. That's the $3 hedge. The covered call writer enjoys a small downside hedge in case prices fall, but can also make substantial gains if the stock price rises:

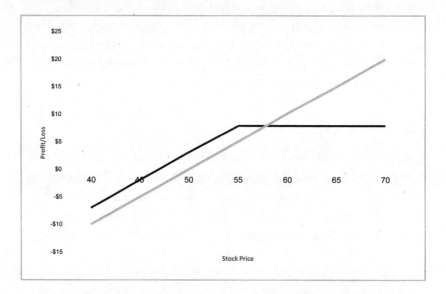

Again, it's a classic hedging strategy. As a covered call writer, you're accepting a known cash payment today, which lowers your cost basis and breakeven point. It also creates a known cash payment that's obviously better than nothing if the stock price goes nowhere. If the sale of the calls can accomplish your goals, it's hard to ignore the covered call strategy.

Max Gains and Losses

The maximum you can ever make from a covered call position is the amount of time premium received from the sale of the call plus any potential capital gains that may be available as shown by the "return if exercised" calculation. Another way of looking at the maximum gain is that it's the difference between the cost basis of the stock and the exercise price. In this example, you wrote the $55 call for

$3, so your cost basis was lowered from $50 to $47. Your maximum gain occurs if the stock reaches $55, so the most you could make is the $8 difference.

If you had, instead, written a $50 call for $3, your cost basis is still $47, but you'd be capped at the $50 strike, so your maximum gain is the $3 difference. Your entire profit came strictly from the call's premium.

The maximum loss is the amount of the cost basis. In the original example, you sold the call for $3, which lowered your cost basis from $50 to $47. That's the most you could lose. It's highly unlikely that you'll ever see that happen because it requires the stock price to fall to zero. The better way to view the maximum loss is that you're on the hook for all falling stock prices, less the premium received. You own the shares, so no matter how far they fall, that value is coming from your account and just being offset by the relatively small premium collected. The risk is always to the downside with the covered call, and that's why you have to be sure you're confident in the stock's reliability before buying shares to use for the covered call.

You Can Exit at Any Time

There's nothing that says you must remain in the covered call position over the life of the call. In fact, most investors don't. The reason is that as time decay begins to work on the short call, it loses value. If you sold the call for $3 a month ago, it may fall to only 30 cents with a few days to go until expiration. It doesn't make much sense to continue holding the short call to squeeze out an extra 30 cents. Instead, most investors would buy back the call.

The effect is that they sold for $3 and paid 30 cents to buy it back, which nets then the $2.70 difference. Yes, they did slightly reduce their gains from $3 to $2.70, but they also are no longer under the obligation to sell the shares for $55. It's always important to balance risk and reward. If there's not much profit remaining in the short call, it doesn't make a lot of sense to continue sealing off your gains at $55 – no matter how remote that chance may seem. Once the call's price falls to a small fraction of what you sold it for, it's not a bad idea to close it out.

Will I Get Assigned Early?

If you write a covered call, don't expect to get assigned or "called out" early even if the stock's price is well above the strike price. In Rule #14, we showed that it's never a good idea to exercise a call option early with the possible exception of collecting a dividend. With a covered call, you have a short call position, and that means another trader somewhere has the long side of that trade. If your stock doesn't pay a dividend over the life of the option, don't expect to get assigned early.

However, if you do get assigned early, it's actually to your advantage. Rather than being upset, you should send the call buyer a thank-you card. That's because that trader who exercised early effectively made today the expiration. As the call seller, you were paid a premium to hold the shares for some time, say 30 days. But if you get assigned early, you effectively got paid the same premium for a shorter-dated call. As the covered call writer, the very best you can do is collect the $3 premium. You did. You got it early, and you got rid of the risky stock to boot.

That's another way of showing why it's not advantageous to exercise early. The buyer pays the call premium so that another investor will hold the shares for a given time. If you've paid the premium to buy a call, use the full time before exercising. The reverse holds when you sell the call. Don't expect the buyer to exercise early.

However, if your stock pays a dividend, then early exercise is a possibility. Remember, however, that it's only advantageous to exercise a call early if the dividend is greater than the time value given up by exercising. If there's a lot of time value remaining, there's a good chance you're not going to get assigned. If, for some reason, you don't want to see your shares called away prior to a dividend being paid, and it looks like it may be a candidate for early exercise, the only way to ensure that is to buy back the call.

Which Strike Should I Write?

One of the first questions new traders have is which strike they should write. There really is no correct answer although, upon reflection, some strikes will certainly sound better to you than others. If you remember the covered call is a premium collection strategy, it makes sense to sell an option that is rich in time premium; hopefully, you remember that is the at-the-money strike. It would also make sense to sell a relatively short-term option, say 30 days to expiration or so, since these options are hit hardest by time decay. By selling a short-term, at-the-money option, you have a mathematical advantage by bringing in a relatively large premium that will quickly lose its value, which is good for you as the covered call writer.

However, different investors have different objectives and every strategy comes with a unique set of risks and rewards. So we can't really say that selling the at-the-money option is the best. It certainly has a lot of nice characteristics, but there are always tradeoffs.

Which strike to write boils down to different philosophies of why you're writing the calls in the first place. Because options are classified as out-of-the-money, at-the-money, and in-the-money, then those are the different scenarios we can create with covered calls. Each comes with its own philosophy and its own set of risks and rewards.

Writing Out-of-the-Money Calls

One of the most common approaches is to write calls against your long stock position but with the intent of never losing the shares. These investors usually write short-term, out-of-the-money (higher strike) calls. Investors who write out-of-the-money calls are really hoping the stock will rise to the strike price (or very close) but still leave the call out-of-the-money at expiration. In our example, if you buy shares at $50 and write the $55 call, you're doing so to put the odds on your side that the stock's price will not reach that strike price by expiration. If the stock rises, however, you're capturing the gains. Selling the $55 call just added a little extra premium to your returns. Avid covered call writers with this philosophy hope this situation happens time after time, so they can write new calls when the current call expires while continuing to hang on to the shares. The sale of many call options can greatly enhance the returns that you may otherwise receive from holding the shares alone. In fact, if you successfully write calls month after month, it's possible to write your shares into a negative cost basis. That is, you may pay $50 for the shares, but end up collecting more than $50 in option premiums.

The biggest problem with writing out-of-the-money calls is that, unless it's a volatile stock, the premiums won't be that big. You're right back to the problem of selling options for small premiums but limiting your upside gains. This is why the static return is important, as it shows the true return just from the option's premium. Be sure to account for it in your decisions.

Writing At-the-Money Calls

If there were such a thing as a textbook definition of a covered call, it would probably be defined as one where the investor writes the front month (current month), at-the-money call. Remember, the idea behind the covered call is to collect a relatively large premium from an option that will quickly decay in value. The strike that carries the most time value and sharpest time decay is the at-the-money strike. Investors who write at-the-money calls collect the highest amount of time premium and also create a lower cost basis on the stock, which provides a little bigger downside hedge.

Investors who write at-the-money calls will not have the room for capital appreciation like out-of-the-money call writers. However, at-the-money calls provide a little more downside protection, so they are less risky. At-the-money call writers are seeking returns solely from option time values and none from stock price movement.

Writing In-the-Money Calls: A New Twist

Remember that covered calls provide a blend of sizable returns along with a downside hedge. It's up to the investor to find the right blend between the two. With today's volatile markets, option premiums can run high. An overlooked strategy for new investors is to write in-the-money calls. They usually never think of this because, on the surface, it doesn't make sense to buy shares at $50 but sell a $45 call, for example. It appears to be a guaranteed five-dollar loss. What they're not taking into account is that all options must trade for at least their intrinsic value – but there's also time value on top of that. If you sell the $45 call, it must be worth at least five dollars, so there's no automatic loss. It's just the time value that's providing the returns. But again, with today's volatile markets, the strategy can be impressive.

Let's say part of your trading plan is to shoot for 20% per year. That's higher than the markets typically return, so you're going to have to take some risk – or are you? Maybe the options markets can be used in a different way.

Amazon is currently $675.72 and the December 2015 calls have 31 days to expiration. Most covered call writers would immediately think to sell the $675 – or higher – strike. They're always focused on maximum time values, or maximum price appreciation. But if you focus on your goals, you'll see new opportunities.

The $655 call is trading for $32.72. That's $20.72 of intrinsic value, but $12 of time value. If that time value meets your goals, why not consider writing this call and give yourself a large breakeven percent?

If you buy shares for $675.72 and write the $655 call, you'll receive $32.72, which lowers your cost basis to $643. Even though you wrote an in-the-money call, notice that your effective cost is $643 but the stock is $675.72 – exactly $32.72 below the current stock price. Your cost basis is lowered by the total premium received.

By writing a deep in-the-money call, you have greatly increased
your breakeven percent, which is important for today's markets.
Now you can afford to have the stock fall from $675.72 to $643, or
5%. At the same time, you're putting the odds on your side that the
shares will get called away, which leaves you with a 1.8% gain for
31 days, or about 21% annualized. By using in-the-money calls, you
can often create profit and loss structures that have the rewards
your seeking, but at greatly reduced risks.

Why does this happen? Because there are speculators in the market
who are willing to pay large premiums for others to hold the shares.
If you were willing to hold the shares anyway, why not consider
using in-the-money calls as a way to collect that premium – and
accomplish your goals with less downside risk?

Incidentally, you're probably thinking that this is a very expensive
position. After all 100 shares is going to cost over $67,000. The
options market is currently solving that problem too as there are
"mini" contracts available on Amazon right now. A mini contract is
exactly like a regular call option, but it just controls 10 shares of
stock instead of 100. If you wanted, you could buy 10-share lots
of Amazon and still get this risk-reward profile. Once again, our
emphasis is that these are choices simply not available to stock
traders. How could a stock trader get a 22% gain, but have a 5%
downside hedge? If you're a stock trader, the only way you can
do that is to buy the shares and hope the price rises sufficiently to
meet your goals. The options trader has a much higher probability
for success – and a larger safety net if wrong. The tradeoff is that
the in-the-money call writer can't make additional profits other
than the time value. But if that's not part of the plan, it just doesn't
matter. Stay focused on the opportunity. Let the strategy gains and
losses fall where they may.

Regardless of which month or strike you choose to write, most
covered call writers wait for the time value to get near zero, which
will be close to expiration, and then write another call at that time.
The idea is to continually collect premiums over time. The covered
call strategy is usually not used as a "one-time" strategy, although it

certainly could be used in that way or for shorter-term applications. For the most part, the strategy is designed to be a long-term, systematic way to continually collect premiums and reduce the cost basis of your shares and enhance returns.

As you get more advanced, you'll find there are so many ways to construct strategies. For instance, rather than buying the actual shares of Amazon, why not use the stock replacement call as a proxy – and then write calls against that? That's actually a strategy called a diagonal spread. And if you like that, maybe you can write vertical spreads against the shares for income, but without giving up all of the upside returns. Or maybe you can write calls against the shares, but use the cash to buy protective puts and provide a bigger downside hedge -- a strategy called a collar. It's an easy way to finance the insurance by selling of some of the gains. The idea to understand now is that if you like the strategy ideas presented so far, that's barely scratching the surface. We just want to give you a small sample of the possibilities that await investors who have never experienced options. Options are not risky; they're just tools for adjusting risk levels to suit your needs. They're essential for investing – and survival – in today's risky markets.

Investitute Takeaway

The covered call strategy is a classic starting strategy for new investors. However, most are unaware of the downside risk and, instead, focus on the possible gains. That makes investors lean toward using out-of-the-money calls to increase the gains. With today's new markets, you must focus more on the risk. Always ask what happens if you're wrong. By using in-the-money calls, the covered call takes on a whole new look. You can still capture adequate returns – buy at a greatly reduced risk. Today's markets don't necessarily mean you have to learn complex strategies. Sometimes, mastering the market just means taking a fresh look at an old strategy.

RULE 22

You Must Take Action

In 1896, investors had to wait seven minutes. That's how long it took Charles Dow to calculate his Dow Jones Industrial Averages after the closing bell. Dow would manually sort through ticker tape to find the closing prices of just 12 stocks in the index at that time – not 30 like today – and scratch out his calculations by pencil and paper. These weren't big numbers either. The first closing price was about 41.

Today, the 30 Dow stocks are calculated instantaneously at every moment of the day. Ditto for the S&P 500, Russell 3000, and Wilshire 5000 indexes. That's 8,530 stocks analyzed effortlessly. In addition to the real-time quotes, we also get volume, charts, moving averages, and Greeks for every single option expiration and strike during that same second. It's impressive, until you find out the computerized robots – the algobots – are faster. Before the quotes are even calculated, the algobots can figure out where the trades are lining up and flash 30,000 quotes inside that second.

Whether you desire to invest, trade, speculate, or gamble, you have to have a way to defend against the instantaneous flow of information. Before you can take profits, you must take action.

The markets have changed. The rules have changed. You must change too.

Football legend Vince Lombardi said, "People who work together will win, whether it be against complex football defenses, or the problems of modern society."

Financial markets are a benefit to modern society. High-speed trading is a problem. The only defense you have is to use options to permanently alter risk-reward profiles to meet your needs. No matter what happens, you'll never have surprises you can't handle. Options always hedge. They never fail. They're required for today's risks.

But no option strategy can work until you put it into action. You must take the steps to learn how to combine them into strategies the algobots can't beat. Pete and I have done this successfully for decades and would like to extend the opportunity to help you solve the complex problems of today's investing.

The new rules of investing begin with options, but end with you. You must take action, and if we work together, you will win.

WOULD YOU LIKE OUR EXPERT HELP WITH OPTIONS INVESTING?

Glad you asked! As long-time owners of a top Chicago market-making business, we trained hundreds and hundreds of would-be professionals before we ever let them go down to the trading floor. Now we've refined our experience into a uniquely effective learn-at-home system.

Call 1-888-982-8342 to learn more about our range of customized education programs.

Investitute's Education combines:

1. The fundamental options concepts that every investor must know

2. Interactive lessons that deliver practical help and how-tos

3. One-on-one mentoring in the trading style that best fits your financial goals

Designed and Taught by the Pros

We've trained countless floor traders and now you can benefit from our professionally designed curriculum.

Profit In Any Market

The pros can successfully trade any market—up, down or sideways—and you can too!

Beyond the Basics—Way Beyond

The Investitute Education program goes deep. You'll learn all facets of options trading through your personalized curriculum designed by the very traders who learned from us. There's simply no better options education program on the market.

Many options traders learn the hard way, through expensive trial and error. Others plateau when market conditions change.

Investitute Education is a cost-effective way for independent investors to master the powerful, yet complex, craft of trading options. No one cares about your money more than you. Our purpose is to help you protect it, and do more with it.

To get started now, call 1-877-548-5582 for a FREE consultation with one of our education specialists.

We'll explore your personal goals, interests, strengths, weaknesses, and your trading experience. We'll decide together whether or not Investitute Education is the right fit for you.

NOTES

NOTES

NOTES

NOTES

NOTES

NOTES

NOTES

NOTES

NOTES

NOTES